Rupert Gray

Adrian Camps-Campins, *The St Vincent Jetty, Port of Spain*

Rupert Gray

A Tale in Black and White

by Stephen N. Cobham

Edited by Lise Winer

With annotations and an introduction by

Bridget Brereton, Rhonda Cobham,
Mary Rimmer and Lise Winer

Caribbean Heritage Series, Volume III

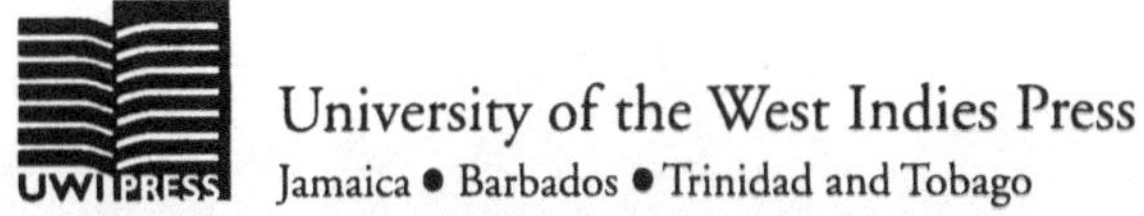

University of the West Indies Press

Jamaica • Barbados • Trinidad and Tobago

University of the West Indies Press
1A Aqueduct Flats   Mona
Kingston 7   Jamaica
www.uwipress.com

10 09 08 07 06   5 4 3 2 1

CATALOGUING IN PUBLICATION DATA

Cobham, Stephen Nathaniel.
Rupert Gray: a tale in black and white / by Stephen
Nathaniel Cobham; edited by Lise Winer with annotations
and an introduction by Bridget Brereton . . . [et al.].
p. cm. – (Caribbean heritage series; v.3)
Previously published: Port of Spain, Trinidad: Mirror Printing, 1907.

ISBN: 976-640-182-9

1. Trinidadian and Tobagonian fiction. 2. Interracial dating – Trinidad and
Tobago – Fiction. I. Winer, Lise. II. Brereton, Bridget. III. Title.

PR9272.9.C63 R87 2006   823.914

Cover illustration: Adrian Camps-Campins, *The St Vincent Jetty, Port of Spain.*

Book and cover design by Robert Harris.
roberth@cwjamaica.com

Set in Sabon 10.5/14.5 x 24

Printed in Canada.

CONTENTS

Acknowledgements

We acknowledge with pleasure the patience, generosity, scholarship and acumen of many people who assisted in explanation, translation and identification. Any errors of commission or omission are, of course, the editor's responsibility.

H.A. Collinson
Yasmin Baksh Comeau
Hans E.A. Boos
Adrian Camps-Campins
Stephen Cobham
Michel Degraff
Andrea Doukas
Gareth Griffiths (University of Western Australia)
John Hobbins (Nahum Gelber Law Library, McGill University)
Beverly Lemire (University of Alberta)
Ronald Noel
Leah Rosenberg
Edith Snook (University of New Brunswick)
Adrian Tronson (University of New Brunswick)

The editor is grateful to the National Endowment for the Humanities (United States) for a Summer Stipend grant in 1994 to work on this project.

We would also like to express our appreciation to Pansy Benn (Arawak Press, Jamaica) and to the staff at the University of the West Indies Press.

CONTRIBUTORS

Lise Winer is Associate Professor in the Faculty of Education, McGill University, Montreal, Canada. She is the author of *Trinidad and Tobago: Varieties of English Around the World* and articles on Caribbean language, literature and culture in *Dictionaries, English World-Wide, Journal of Pidgin and Creole Languages, Language in Society, Language Problems and Language Planning, New West Indian Guide,* and various anthologies.

Bridget Brereton is Professor of History at the University of the West Indies, St Augustine, Trinidad and Tobago. Her major books include *A History of Modern Trinidad, Race Relations in Colonial Trinidad,* and *Law, Justice and Empire,* as well as articles on gender and history in the Caribbean.

Rhonda Cobham is Professor of English and Black Studies at Amherst College, Amherst, Massachusetts. She has edited special issues of *Research in African Literatures* and the *Massachusetts Review,* as well as *Watchers and Seekers: An Anthology of Writing by Black Women in Britain.* Her essays on Caribbean and African authors and postcolonial theory have appeared in *Callaloo, Transition, RAL* and critical anthologies.

Mary Rimmer is Professor of English at the University of New Brunswick, Fredericton, Canada. Her publications include an edition of Thomas Hardy's *Desperate Remedies* and articles on Thomas Hardy, Margaret Laurence and Nino Ricci.

INTRODUCTION

The "Caribbean Heritage" Corpus in Trinidad

In his pioneering study of "the West Indian novel",[1] Kenneth Ramchand accepts Lamming's definition: "the novel written by the West Indian about the West Indian reality". That is, he considers for inclusion all literary works which

> have a West Indian setting and contain fictional characters and situations whose social correlates are immediately recognisable as West Indian. The books have all been written in the twentieth century; and their native West Indian authors include descendants of Europeans, descendants of African slaves, descendants of indentured labourers from India, and various mixtures from these. (1983, 3)

However, stipulating that the books must all have been "written in the twentieth century" by "native West Indian authors" arbitrarily cuts off novels that fulfil the other requirements, and which can prove crucial to understanding the development of later works.

The present series of historic re-publications comprises four Trinidadian novels published between 1838 and 1907. (Several addi-

---

1. "West Indies" and "West Indian" are the terms most often used traditionally to refer to both the anglophone Caribbean, that is, former British colonies whose official (and therefore literary) language is English, and also to the entire region, that is, both the islands of the Caribbean Sea and many of the countries on the bordering mainland, such as Guyana. Recently, the term "Caribbean" has been used more frequently in this manner. Both terms are used in these senses throughout the introduction and notes to this series.

tional works were "rediscovered" but excluded from this series; see details in the introduction to volume 1 in this series, E.L. Joseph's *Warner Arundell.*) These virtually unknown works constitute the roots of a much longer and deeper local literary tradition and foundation in Trinidad – and the anglophone Caribbean – than hitherto realized.

- E.L. Joseph's *Warner Arundell, the Adventures of a Creole* (London: Saunders and Otley, 1838) is the first novel set at least partly in Trinidad, and is a good candidate for the first Caribbean novel in English. Joseph came to Trinidad from England as a young man; he is well known for his *History of Trinidad,* which appeared the same year as the novel, and which demonstrates an intimate knowledge of the island. The novel takes place in a number of Caribbean settings, primarily Grenada, Trinidad, Antigua and St Kitts, as well as the Spanish Main (Venezuela and Colombia). In the story, Warner Arundell, a white creole of British descent, is born in Grenada and brought up in Antigua and Trinidad. He is defrauded by lawyers, studies law in Venezuela and medicine in England, then goes to seek his fortune. After many adventures, he is reunited with the coloured branch of his family, and with his Spanish lady love. (Reprinted in volume 1, 2001.)

- *Adolphus, a Tale,* by "Anonymous", was serialized in the *Trinidadian* newspaper, from 1 January to 20 April 1853. Given its viewpoints, it was probably written by a Trinidadian of mixed race, thus making it the first Trinidadian – and possibly Caribbean – novel by a presumably non-white writer born and raised in Trinidad (but see discussion below), and the first novel set almost totally in Trinidad. In the story, Adolphus, the son of an enslaved black woman raped by a white man, is raised by a kind Spanish-Trinidadian padre. Adolphus grows into a handsome, well-educated, noble character. He falls in love with Antonia Romelia, a beautiful mixed-race woman. She is kidnapped by the villain DeGuerinon, a cruel slave owner who appears to be white. Helped by Cudjoe, one of DeGuerinon's slaves, Adolphus and his friend Ernest rescue Antonia, wounding her captor. As Antonia is restored to her family, her mother dies in her arms. Adolphus and Ernest flee to Venezuela until it is safe to return, and Adolphus and Antonia are free to marry. (Reprinted in volume 2, 2003.)

- Mrs [Marcella Fanny] William Noy Wilkins, author of *The Slave Son* (London: Chapman and Hall, 1854), was a white woman of Irish birth, but who evidently spent some years living in Trinidad. *The Slave Son* was explicitly written to support the abolitionist movement in the United States. The heroine of the novel, Laurine, is a mixed-race freed slave who is working to earn enough money to buy the freedom of her mother, Madelaine, an enslaved black woman owned by St Hilaire Cardon. Laurine loves Belfond, a mixed-race slave, who has escaped from (his father) Cardon's estate, but she refuses to run away with him or to use stolen money to buy her mother's freedom. Belfond becomes involved in a conspiracy with his uncle, the African obeahman Daddy Fanty, to poison Cardon and his family. There are extensive scenes of brutal estate life under slavery; Mr Dorset, a white owner of a neighbouring estate, tries to treat his slaves more humanely. Belfond is recaptured by Cardon; Mrs Dorset and Laurine plead for him. A slave uprising leaves Cardon dead. Belfond and Laurine escape to freedom in Venezuela. (Reprinted in volume 2, 2003.)

- In Stephen N. Cobham's *Rupert Gray: A Tale in Black and White* (Port of Spain: Mirror Printing, 1907), the hero, Rupert Gray, is a highly educated black accountant, of noble character, who works for Mr Serle, a white businessman who thinks highly of him. When Serle's daughter, Gwendoline, returns from England, she and Rupert fall in love. Gwendoline's friend, Dr Florence Badenock, comes to visit. An ungrateful jealous black co-worker, Jacob Clarke, starts a poison-pen campaign against Rupert and alerts Serle to the affair. When Serle finds out, he attacks Rupert and refuses to forgive his daughter. Rupert goes to England under the patronage of a white English lady. Gwendoline falls into a decline, her father drinks himself to death, and Gwendoline finally dies also. When Rupert returns, as a lawyer, to Trinidad, he is contacted by Florence, and a court trial over the Serle estate ensues. In a dramatic courtroom scene, it is revealed that Gwendoline is still alive. Helped by her faithful maid,

Edith, she had fled to recuperate in Scotland with Florence. Rupert and Gwendoline marry and have children, and live happily – though shunned by "society" – ever after. (Reprinted in volume 3, 2006.)

Social context is a particularly important aspect of Caribbean literature (McWatt 1985). The novels in this series have a strong political and social impetus. Several speak out against slavery at a time when it was already abolished in Trinidad but still legal in the United States; Wilkins cites this explicitly as a reason for writing *The Slave Son* in 1854. All of the novels support more rights for the disenfranchised mixed-race (and sometimes for the black) segments of the population.

The novels also share an underlying thematic continuity with the non-class-based "social consciousness" of later Caribbean literature. As Ramchand explains:

> West Indian novelists apply themselves with unusual urgency and unanimity to an analysis and interpretation of their society's ills, including the social and economic deprivation of the majority; the pervasive consciousness of race and colour . . . the lack of a history to be proud of; and the absence of traditional or settled values . . . this social consciousness is not class-consciousness. This is one point at which the West Indian writer naturally departs from the nineteenth-century English novel with which he is most familiar. . . . Most West Indian novelists write about the whole society . . . the chaos . . . the open possibilities of their society . . . along with an interest in the previously neglected person. (1983, 4)

When did a literary tradition "begin" in Trinidad? Ramchand does not mention Trinidadian literature earlier than the 1934 publication of Alfred Mendes's *Pitch Lake*. In a more recent work exploring the origins of the "literary awakening" that occurred in Trinidad during the 1930s, Reinhard Sander (1988, 7) states that "until the late 1920s the literary scene in Trinidad, by contrast [with Jamaica], seems to have produced nothing very remarkable". He quotes Anson Gonzalez (1972), that there was "the occasional work of fiction"; however, Gonzalez himself had seen almost none of these (Gonzalez, personal communication, 1990). Similarly, J.R. Hooker notes that

Introduction

Until the 1950s, when Trinidad's literary talent began to astonish the English public, the island produced very little literature. Between Cobham and Naipaul there is only C.L.R. James. There was a small body of fiction preceding the 1907 appearance of *Rupert Gray.* All had grave weaknesses, mostly involving the melodramatic use of two-dimensional characters, but generally they used local settings and hung their plots on actual issues. (1975, 127–28)

(For another view on Trinidad's literary heritage in the nineteenth century, see Selwyn Cudjoe's *Beyond Boundaries: The Intellectual Tradition of Trinidad and Tobago in the Nineteenth Century* [2003].)

The "Trinidad Awakening" is now considered to have begun in 1927, with the publication of C.L.R. James's short story "La Divina Pastora". Writers such as C.L.R. James, Alfred H. Mendes, C.A. Thomasos, Percival Maynard and Katherine Archibald, who published short fiction in magazines such as *Trinidad* and its successor, the *Beacon,* experimented with various language registers in their narratives and dialogue, and the *Beacon*'s editorials campaigned for the use of more realistic themes, settings and language in local stories. In his introduction to *From Trinidad,* an anthology of writing culled from these journals, Sander points out that "what distinguishes the writers and intellectuals who were involved in the publication of *Trinidad* and *The Beacon* from [other earlier West Indian writers] is primarily their appearance as a group, which fostered the exchange of views and theoretical discussions and prevented creative loneliness and frustration" (1988, 2).

However, it would be a mistake to read this absence of a record of earlier group activity as a sign of complete literary stagnation. It now appears that literature in Trinidad was not totally asleep throughout the nineteenth and early twentieth centuries. The earliest novel in the present series predates James's story by eighty-nine years and Mendes's *Pitch Lake* by ninety-six years; the last of the novels was published only twenty years before the former and twenty-seven before the latter. That the novels were published over a span of time – 1838, 1853, 1854, 1907 – rather than during only one short time period supports a picture of a longer and deeper literary tradition than has been posited previously.

There is at present no way of knowing how much direct influence these novels had on writers, at the time or later. Certainly *Warner*

Arundell was publicly reviewed at the time of its first appearance, and *Adolphus* was serialized in a well-known newspaper. Though some copies of the published books were doubtless available, there were probably never many around, given the scarcity of known surviving copies today. Nevertheless, these novels manifest the same social, cultural and literary impulses, orientations and concerns that have been considered archetypally West Indian, both historically and currently, and are an integral part of Trinidadian and Caribbean literary tradition. Recognition of the deeper literary roots of this tradition should strengthen, rather than weaken, this view of thematic and stylistic continuity. The awakening did not arise without warning; indeed, the same impetus that drove the first works of literature had only lain "sleeping" until conditions arose in the 1930s that *re*awakened it.

Stephen Nathaniel Cobham, Author of *Rupert Gray*

We know little about the life of Stephen Nathaniel Cobham. What we do know (or can conjecture with some confidence) can be quickly summarized. He was born – probably in Trinidad – in the 1860s or possibly in the 1870s; he was almost certainly African-Trinidadian, or of mixed descent. He became a teacher, probably after education at a government primary school (a "ward school") or a state-assisted denominational school, and then a period as a student at the Normal (teacher-training) School in Port of Spain. On receiving his teachers' certificate, he probably taught at one or more government or assisted primary schools, including (for a time) Woodbrook E.C. (Anglican) School, situated in a suburb of Port of Spain. In 1901 or 1902, he left teaching to become a lawyer's clerk, with the aim of qualifying eventually as a solicitor. According to the anonymous reviewer of *Rupert Gray* in the *Mirror* of 18 July 1907, Cobham was "a gentleman who is aspiring, we believe, to legal fame, having abandoned the ingenuous sphere of the elementary school teacher for the ingenious one of the solicitor. He is not yet a full-fledged practitioner, but he has served his five years with an officer of the Supreme Court." In 1908, the year after the publication of his novel, Cobham went to British Guiana, and, according to J.R. Hooker, the biographer of Henry Sylvester Williams, "for personal reasons never returned to his family on the island" (1975, 134n95).[2] We have no further knowledge of Cobham's life, except the recollection of a surviving grandnephew, Stephen Cobham, that he went to become a newspaper editor in the Virgin Islands.[3]

We can, however, develop a fair sense of Cobham's ideas and aspirations in the early 1900s, partly from *Rupert Gray* itself, and partly from our knowledge of his political and civic activities. First, we know he was "race conscious", a member of a small but active group of educated black and mixed-race Trinidadians who were seeking to "uplift the race" and to combat the virulent racism of the day. He took an active part in the visit by Henry Sylvester Williams to Trinidad (though actually born in Barbados, Williams grew up in Trinidad) in 1901, when local branches of the Pan-African Association were founded. When Williams spoke at the hall of the Mutual Friendly Society in Port of Spain early in June 1901, Cobham also gave an "address" in which he "spoke at some length and was also cheered". Cobham was present when elementary school teachers gave a farewell dinner to Williams (who had begun his career as a Trinidad teacher) in the following month, and he proposed the toast to the Pan-African Association; he was described as "the principal person to bring about the function". (It may well be that Cobham was still teaching in 1901, leaving the service perhaps soon after.) And he was one of a group of members of a Roman Catholic friendly society who held a farewell reception for Williams on the evening before he left: "The speaker of the evening was Mr. Stephen Cobham, who, in the course of an eloquent address, referred to the enthusiastic manner in which Mr. Williams had undertaken the promulgation of the great and good work of the society" (the Pan-African Association).[4] Of course, we

---

2. Hooker gives no evidence for his assertion. For Cobham in British Guiana, see the *Mirror*, 3 March 1908. (This and all subsequent citations of the *Mirror* refer to the newspaper of that title published in Port of Spain between 1898 and 1916.) According to Selwyn Cudjoe, Cobham was born in Arouca, a village in north-east Trinidad where H.S. Williams lived as a child; he does not cite any reference for this statement (2003, 369).

3. Interview with Stephen Cobham, by Lise Winer and Hans Boos, 1995.

4. See the *Mirror*, 6 June 1901; 6, 8, 13 July 1901. See also Hooker (1975, 39–51); Mathurin (1976, 93–98); and Cudjoe (2003, 362–66).

can also infer from his novel that Cobham had a strong sense of race pride and a conviction that the educated person of African descent was obliged to work for the "upliftment" of the whole pan-African community.

It is also clear that Cobham opposed Crown Colony government as it operated in Trinidad in the early 1900s, and advocated the restoration of the elected Borough Council of Port of Spain (abolished in 1898–99) and the inclusion of elected members in the Legislative Council. This was a typical position of the black or mixed-race intelligentsia in Trinidad at this time, and was often combined with a race-conscious stand. When he praised Williams at one of the 1901 functions, Cobham said that "he hoped one of these days [Williams] would return with a charter of liberty that would make a man of every man – a charter not from the Secretary of State, but from the foot of the throne of Edward VII – a charter calling upon Ethiopia to stretch out her hands to Heaven and advance" (see note to p. 101). This statement neatly combines advocacy of elected and representative institutions for Trinidad with a pan-African consciousness (not to mention a naïve faith in the British monarchy). A few years later, lecturing on "Trinidad and the Trinidadians" to an audience in Georgetown, Cobham expressed the hope that his countrymen would one day "recover their full municipal rights and privileges and attain to the position of British Guiana in its representative form of Government". He was a great admirer of Edgar Maresse-Smith, who was a strong opponent of crown colony government in Trinidad between the 1880s and the early 1900s, and wrote a touching poem to commemorate the latter's death in 1905 (see below).[5]

Cobham was probably a Roman Catholic, like the majority of black and mixed-race Trinidadians in the early twentieth century. He was an active member of a Port of Spain Catholic friendly society, the Faithful Brothers of Souls in Purgatory; it was this body, probably comprising mainly lower-middle-class black or brown city men, that organized a farewell function for Williams in July 1901. Around the same time, the Brothers celebrated the eleventh anniversary of their society with a

---

5. See the *Mirror*, 13 July 1901; 31 January 1905; 11 March 1908.

Solemn High Mass at the Rosary Church, a procession with banners, and a luncheon at their hall on Upper Prince Street.[6]

By the time Cobham published his novel, he had been a lawyer's clerk for around five years, aspiring to qualify as a solicitor. It is clear from *Rupert Gray* that he greatly admired some of the black or mixed-race lawyers who practised in the colony's courts or were remembered after their deaths for their stellar courtroom performances. It is especially the non-white lawyers, who competed with white creole and British colleagues in their profession, who are singled out for mention in the novel; they were generally men active in public and political life as well as in the courts. Among Cobham's heroes were Sir Conrad Reeves, mixed-race chief justice of Barbados; Michael (Michel) Maxwell Philip, brilliant lawyer and solicitor-general of Trinidad in the 1870s and 1880s (see note to p. 39); Vincent Brown, the first non-white Trinidadian to be appointed the colony's attorney-general (see note to p. 39); and Maresse-Smith, a fiery opponent of Crown Colony government and a radical, race-conscious lawyer (see note to p. 58). These men were all deceased by 1907. Among the practising lawyers singled out (lightly disguised) in the novel's courtroom scene are several men, black or mixed race, active in anti-Crown Colony politics: H.A. Alcazar and C.P. David, both Unofficial Members of the Legislative Council in 1907; Emmanuel Scipio-Pollard; and Emmanuel M'zumbo Lazare (see notes to p. 79). No doubt Cobham aspired eventually to emulate their examples as politically active, race- conscious lawyers, though it is not clear whether he ever fulfilled that aspiration.

Finally – and Cobham himself might have put this first – we know that he was a poet and a writer who was a member of the small but ambitious literary circle of Port of Spain in the early 1900s.[7] The *Mirror* reviewer of *Rupert Gray* described him as "a poet with some pretensions to the name, some of his verses which have appeared in our columns possessing merit above the ordinary". Perhaps the poem he wrote on the death of Maresse-Smith in 1905 is representative:

---

6. See the *Mirror*, 5, 6, 13, 17, 18 July 1901.

7. There is a notice in the front pages prior to the novel itself, announcing: "Will appear soon, a second story, by the same author, entitled *Gertrude and Honora, or, The Two Cousins*"; no trace of this book – or notice of actual publication – has been found.

O patriot, leader, friend – what cruel loss
Comes heralding the year!
When will thy country cease to cherish thee?
When cease to shed a tear?

Behold besides thy grave she stands bereaved
In widow's weeds bow'd low;
Deep silence speak regret from heart to heart
Alike of friend and foe.

"This was a man" – whose teeming short life mov'd
On highest types of love
For all his kind – whose prayer was ceaseless work
Now ratified above.

Who reck'd not of the cost, nor shirk'd nor flinched
But held his cause the while,
And boldly dealt and took loud, lusty blows
And suffered with a smile.

And never for himself. Great Maresse-Smith
Where lies thy "dreamless head"
That spot we consecrate with grateful tears
Great Trinidadian dead!

And hast thou wrought in vain? Hast thou not sown
Where out in future-time
Thy country reaps proud harvest – known to thee
There in thy higher clime?

Where freely soaring on from strength to strength:
Beneath a higher plain
Thou'rt known as loyal to the noblest creed
The brotherhood of man.[8]

Cobham must have taken seriously his avocation as a writer. Soon after his novel was published, he lectured on "The Mission of the Poet" to a "large and appreciative audience" in Port of Spain:

---

8. See the *Mirror,* 31 January 1905; 18 July 1907 (in a review of *Rupert Gray*).

The lecturer dealt with the subject with grasp of principle and mastery of detail, and brought forcibly home to his hearers the fact that "The Mission of the Poet" is the highest calling, inasmuch as the poet is the teacher of all men of action, and they execute what he dreams. The lecture lasted for about an hour and the speaker discoursed from notes only.

Perhaps Cobham had lectured on such topics before, for the advance notice of the lecture signalled that "his ability is well known and he ought to secure a large attendance". Others, some certainly known to Cobham, were trying to write and publish their work in the city around this time. George Hubert Wilson, who died in 1901 at the age of forty-two, was a "playwright, novelist and poet", a friend of Cobham's, who appears in *Rupert Gray* as the author of the play performed in the Serle home (see notes to p. 58). In 1905, James Douglas Cameron published *Richard Malmort, or Trinidad and Trinidadians,* a poorly written, thinly fictionalized political tract against Crown Colony government. Soon after *Rupert Gray* appeared, the *Mirror* announced that William Howard Bishop, then principal of a private school and later, after World War I, a prominent labour leader (and a friend of Cobham's), was about to publish a novel called *Ex Post Facto, or After the Deed Was Done,* featuring a character based on "a gentleman well known in Trinidad Society". And in 1908 a local author, H.R. Macfarlane, published a "sensational novel" called *Mrs. Fairbain,* apparently an exciting read filled with "desperate developments".[9] Clearly, several people were writing in the colony at the beginning of the last century, even if the quality of their products might not always have been high; Cobham was part of a literary circle which seems to have taken him seriously, and he must have derived some support and encouragement from that.

---

9. For Cobham's lecture, see the *Mirror,* 14 and 19 October 1907; for Wilson, 13, 15, 16, 19 July 1901, and 3 August 1901; for Bishop, 7 October 1907; for Macfarlane, 5 February 1908. Of these works mentioned, we have been able to locate only *Richard Malmort,* which is too lacking in literary or historical merit to warrant republishing.

The Historical Context of *Rupert Gray*: Trinidad at the Start of the Twentieth Century

The census of 1901 recorded the population of Trinidad and Tobago at 255,148, of whom fewer than 19,000 lived in Tobago, but just over 54,000 lived in the capital city, Port of Spain – about 20 per cent of the total population (Anthony 1997, 445–46). Despite the small size of the colony's population, its political life was lively, its newspaper press was vibrant, and in the capital and a few other towns, many associations of different kinds ensured that citizens could participate in organized and collective endeavours. Port of Spain in particular was the base of a growing black and mixed-race intelligentsia to which Stephen Cobham belonged, which was active in political and associational life.

The most important political issues which agitated the members of this intelligentsia in the late nineteenth and early twentieth centuries had to do with reform of the Crown Colony constitution and the fate of the elected Borough Council of Port of Spain.[10] The colony's legislature, established in 1831, had no elected members and it was the goal of successive reform movements to secure a "mixed" Legislative Council that would include officials, nominated Unofficial Members and members elected by voters who could meet stipulated franchise qualifications. A spirited campaign for this goal was mounted in 1892–95, when Cobham was probably in his twenties or thirties. Among the leaders were several men who appear or are mentioned in *Rupert Gray*: H.A. Alcazar, C.P. David, Vincent Brown, Edgar Maresse-Smith and E.M. Lazare. Indeed, this movement – unlike its predecessor in 1885–88 – was dominated by fairly young, well-educated black or mixed-race lawyers; few white Trinidadians occupied leadership roles. These men organized an able campaign, which was on the point of persuading the Colonial Office to grant elected members when, in the middle of 1895, the British government changed and Joseph Chamberlain became secretary of state for the colonies. With his strong opposition to elected or representative institu-

---

10. The account of political developments in Trinidad between 1890 and 1914 which follows is based on the summary in Brereton (1981, 142–53). Fuller accounts are in Magid (1988, chapters 5–9); Will (1970, 189–226); and Samaroo (1969, 66–127).

tions for colonies with non-white majorities, and his unusually assertive style as secretary of state, he vetoed any change in Trinidad's constitution and shifted attention instead to the municipal arena, especially Port of Spain, ushering in an era that Magid calls one of "urban nationalism" (1988, 222–23 and *passim*).

It was a period of urban nationalism (1895–1914) in the sense that political agitation and opposition to Crown Colony government centred on Port of Spain issues rather than on the wider goal of constitutional change which came to the fore again in the period after World War I. After a protracted struggle with the Borough Council, which he accused of irresponsibility and mismanagement, Chamberlain issued an ultimatum at the end of 1898: accept humiliating terms which would virtually end the council's independence, limited as it was in any case, or face abolition. Alcazar, who was the mayor of Port of Spain during the crisis, struggled in vain for a compromise solution; Maresse-Smith, Cobham's hero, was a leader of the "no surrender" faction. In the outcome, Chamberlain decreed the abolition of the elected Borough Council and its replacement by a wholly nominated Board. This high-handed action outraged the black and mixed-race city lawyers, teachers and others for whom municipal politics had offered an important arena for self-assertion and leadership, and helped to radicalize opposition politics in the period after 1898.

Radical organizations and organs appeared in the city during these years. The Trinidad Workingmen's Association was founded in 1896 or 1897, and revived in 1906 by Alfred Richards, whom Cobham knew. (Richards was a trustee of the Catholic friendly society to which he belonged.)[11] The *Mirror* began publication in 1898 as a reformist daily newspaper sympathetic to the political radicals. Owned and edited by an English journalist and naturalist who had lived in the colony since 1886, Richard Richardson Mole, it positively reported the activities of the black and mixed-race radicals and intellectuals, throughout the colony but especially in the capital. (Mole also ran a commercial printing business, the Mirror Printing Works, which published *Rupert Gray.*)[12] A branch of

---

11. See the *Mirror,* 18 July 1901.

12. Advertisements for the following were included in the front pages prior to the novel itself: Muir, Marshall & Co. (stationers); Joseph Gonzales, Agar's Public Supply Depot,

the Pan-African Association was established in Trinidad in 1901 when its founder, Henry Sylvester Williams, visited that year; Cobham, we have seen, was one of those who organized Williams's visit and worked to found the local branch. Lazare, who appears, thinly disguised, in *Rupert Gray,* was the president of the local Pan-African Association branch. The *Mirror* gave extensive and supportive coverage to Pan-African Association affairs. Later in 1901, a group of politically minded city men founded the Ratepayers Association, ostensibly to safeguard the interests of Port of Spain ratepayers in the absence of an elected municipal body, but actually to agitate generally against Crown Colony government. It offered a natural home for former members of the Borough Council "no surrender" party, such as Maresse-Smith, and Lazare brought his middle-class and artisan followers from the Pan-African Association over to the Ratepayers Association early in 1902. The stage was thus set for the radicalization of the colony's politics which culminated in the Water Riots of March 1903, a serious affray that resulted in the destruction by fire of the main government buildings in Port of Spain and the killing of at least sixteen persons by police or troops (Brereton 1981, 149–51; Magid 1988, chapters 7–8; Samaroo 1969, 74–95).

It is entirely possible that Cobham was an eyewitness to, even a participant in, this event. Certainly he would have been sympathetic to the general positions taken by the more radical wing of the Ratepayers Association, led by his idol Maresse-Smith. Almost certainly, he followed the subsequent trial (for incitement to riot) of Maresse-Smith, Lazare

---

12. (*continued*) De Silva & Co., Cunningham Tomson & Co., Sail Loft, Waterman the Hatter, and Louis John & Co. (merchants); Rust, Trowbridge & Co., Singineau Bros., R.A. MacIntosh, Patisserie Swiss and The Brunswick Grocery (provisioners); Henry S. Adams, The City Drug Store, Medical Hall, Alfred Richards, Central Dispensary, Edgar T. Michell, Ramsey's Pharmacy, The Royal Pharmacy and South End Drug Store (pharmacies); Thompson's Livery Stable, J. Haynes-Clark Port-of-Spain Stables, De Silva's Livery Stables; A.G. De Silva (undertakers); Trinidad Dye Works; The Bee Hive (boots and shoes); R.W. Woodings (boots); Central Star Saloon; Crescent Photo Studio; Patriotic Assurance Co.; Fred O. Wilkes, St Clair Williams, Norman Lord, G. Donawa and Julian Roberts (collection, commission and house agents); William Kirton, Christopher Sandiford and G.F. Dewsbury (builders and contractors); Gittens' Carriage & Shoeing Works; J.M. Gaines (machinist); J.N. Cross (blacksmith); Franklin's Electric Printery; *The Star* newspaper; J.A. Cardinal (optician); and F.A. Skeete & Co. (La Basse Saw Mill).

and H.N. Hall, another English journalist who edited a radical magazine, the *Pioneer*; all three were acquitted by a local jury which needed only a few minutes to reach its decision. After the drama of the riots and the tragic killings, political agitation was considerably muted in the years between 1904 and the outbreak of World War I. In an attempt to placate the middle-class black professionals (and to undercut Maresse-Smith, probably the most radical politician of the period), the African-Trinidadian barrister C.P. David was made an Unofficial Member of the Legislative Council; after many setbacks and delays, it was finally decided in 1913 to restore the wholly elected Borough Council in stages between 1914 and 1917.

At the time that *Rupert Gray* was published, therefore, the colony's capital city had a wholly nominated municipal body; its legislature had no elected members; and memories were still fresh of the brutal events of March 1903. Cobham, we have seen, was a strong advocate for the restoration of the elected Borough Council and for the inclusion of elected members in the legislature (not achieved until 1924–25). He no doubt admired the men, mostly lawyers, who had led the anti-Crown Colony struggles of the years since 1892, many of whom appear in *Rupert Gray*: Maresse-Smith, Alcazar, Brown, David, Lazare and Scipio-Pollard. He was, in fact, a participant (admittedly not a leader) along with these men in Trinidad's "urban nationalism", dominated as it was by the non-white middle class to which he belonged.

Like so many members of Trinidad's black and mixed-race middle stratum in this period, as mentioned above, Cobham began his career as an elementary school teacher. By the time he was born, the colony possessed a network of government primary schools (ward schools), and after 1870 denominational schools run by the Christian churches could qualify for state assistance if they met certain standards. By the 1890s, these schools offered an elementary education to most creole children (that is, excluding Indian immigrants and their offspring). A promising boy or girl could be trained in the Normal School for a teacher's certificate, which opened up positions in the government and assisted primary schools. This was a crucial means of mobility that did not require a secondary education in one of the boys' colleges, which were fee-paying; almost certainly, this was Cobham's route into school teaching. Though teachers were badly paid, their status as members of the middle stratum was secure; indeed, they formed the nucleus of this stratum in nineteenth-century Trinidad. Many teachers, then as now, used the profession as a stepping-stone to other, more lucrative occupations. We can speculate that Cobham was motivated to leave teaching not only by a desire for a higher salary, but also by a positive ambition to enter the legal profession, probably stimulated by his admiration for the black and mixed-race lawyers who, as we have seen, led the opposition to Crown Colony government in the 1890s and early 1900s (Brereton 1981, 122–28; 1979, chapter 4).

Just as teaching was a primary route to social mobility, so was entry to the "lower branch" of the legal profession, or qualification as a solicitor. It was one of three professions (other than teaching) for which training could be accessed locally (the others were surveying, and practice as a druggist or pharmacist); and, unlike an elementary school teacher, a solicitor could earn a decent living. In 1871, it became possible in Trinidad to qualify as a solicitor by serving a period of apprenticeship as an articled clerk to a practising lawyer, then passing examinations set by the Law Society of England, but written locally. A person who had served as an ordinary lawyer's clerk for ten years could, after passing a preliminary examination, be articled for only two years before sitting the Law Society examinations; or one could come in directly as an articled clerk for five years (the "ten-year" and the "five-year" men). This newly opened opportunity attracted many men unable to afford a period of study in Britain, without which one could not qualify as a barrister, or a doctor (among other professions). Among them were Maresse-Smith and Lazare; Cobham hoped to follow in their footsteps.

So many men were attracted to this route that eventually efforts were made to close it. In 1894, a petition to the governor claimed that the legal profession was seriously overcrowded: there were then twenty-seven practising barristers, thirty-eight practising solicitors and eighteen articled clerks, who all, presumably, hoped to qualify for one or the other branch. As a result, an ordinance enacted in that year provided that only persons admitted to practise as solicitors in England could be admitted in the colony. But this illiberal measure, closing off an important means of upward mobility for lower-middle-class men, was itself reversed in

1896, when the system of locally administered examinations was reinstated. However, the 1896 ordinance did not restore the "ten-year" system by which a lawyer's clerk, who might not have attended a secondary school, could work for ten years, then (if he passed an examination) be articled for another two years, and thus be eligible for the final examinations. Instead, everyone had to serve five years as an articled clerk; a young man might leave one of the boys' secondary schools, pass the preliminary examination, and be admitted for a five-year term as an articled clerk. The ten-year-man system had been cut off. If Cobham left teaching and became an articled clerk around 1902, he would have been required to serve five years before being eligible to sit the final examinations around 1907, though we have no evidence that he did so.

Interestingly enough, the whole issue was raised yet again in 1907, when Cobham should have been close to completing his five years. By then, the profession was, naturally enough, even more "crowded" than it had been in 1894. In 1907, there were forty-four barristers and forty-seven solicitors, though a few of each were probably retired from practice, with a large number of articled clerks like Cobham aspiring to qualify as solicitors. When a group of lawyers' clerks petitioned for the restoration of the ten-year-man system (in operation between 1871 and 1894), some solicitors sent in a counter-petition, ostensibly on the grounds that the ten-year men were often incompetent, as well as because of the alleged overcrowding. No doubt they were afraid of losing the services of experienced, long-serving clerks, as well as fearing increased competition (perhaps from their own former clerks). The clerks, for their part, pointed out that many solicitors had retired, and that the growth in the population and trade of the colony made the increase in the number of new practitioners supportable. The debate occupied considerable newspaper space in 1907; but since Cobham apparently left Trinidad in 1908, perhaps for good, it seems he did not achieve his goal of becoming a solicitor in his native island.[13]

We have already noted Cobham's involvement in the visit by H.S. Williams to found a local branch of the Pan-African Association in 1901,

---

13. For this and the preceding two paragraphs, see Mathurin (1976, 22); Brereton (1979, 92–93); Will (1970, 206–7); Collens (1908, 128–30); *Mirror,* 17 July 1907; 8, 18, 24 December 1907; 7 January 1908.

and we have inferred from this, and from other evidence, including his novel, that he was race conscious. In no way did this make him untypical of his social group in the Trinidad of the early 1900s. Many educated black and mixed-race Trinidadians had participated – since the early 1870s, if not before – in a collective effort to counter the racism of the European world and to develop a race-conscious, at times pan-African, identity. Like Williams himself, Cobham grew up in a milieu where public debate on race issues was possible. Crown Colony though it was, the island had a free press, and there was always at least one paper whose columns were open to expressions of race pride and self-assertion. There were articulate black or mixed-race lawyers, journalists, doctors, teachers and artisans. People clearly felt confident enough to complain about discrimination and racism and to grope towards a counter-ideology.

Perhaps the first major figure (since emancipation) to embark on this project of racial "vindication" was J.J. Thomas, the African-Trinidadian educator, scholar of languages and writer. His achievements were a source of great pride to the non-white middle stratum in the 1870s and 1880s (he died in 1889), and his views – expressed in many letters to the local press as well as in his important book *Froudacity* – were strongly race conscious and pan-Africanist. He had read and been influenced by Edward Blyden, another icon of black consciousness mentioned in *Rupert Gray*. Another important leader was Cobham's hero, Maresse-Smith; he led the campaign for a high-profile celebration of the 1888 jubilee of emancipation in Trinidad. The debate on this issue, fought over many months in all the colony's newspapers, as well as in speeches and poems, galvanized race consciousness and helped locals to work out an ideology with which to counter racism. As we have seen, the Pan-African Association was founded (in London) by a Trinidadian, H.S. Williams, and many men and women, including Cobham, rallied to his banner when he came home to found a local branch. It is true that the Pan-African Association in Trinidad became moribund when its leader, Lazare, shifted his interest to the Ratepayers Association and the agitation against Crown Colony government in general, but other race-conscious groups emerged. In 1907, a Port of Spain Coloured Association was founded, led by a young Trinidadian, F.E.M. Hercules, and including several younger teachers who had not taken part in the local Pan-African Association in 1901. At its first meeting, a teacher, J.D. Regis, read a paper on "The Progress of the Negro Race since Emancipation" (*Mirror*, 10 May 1907, 6 July 1907; Hooker 1975, 108–11). Hercules himself became an important "race leader" in Britain and the United States after World War I. By the early 1900s, in fact, Trinidad had an educated middle stratum whose members were, in general, race conscious; Cobham would have been somewhat unusual if he had lacked such an ideological orientation.

In an excellent discussion of the world view of the Port of Spain black and mixed-race intelligentsia of the period, William Smith points out several reasons for their willingness to stand up against the withering racism of their times: they had received a relatively good education in the urban elementary schools, government and assisted, and in some cases, in the boys' secondary colleges; they had almost certainly been taught, at the elementary level, by black or mixed-race teachers who enjoyed considerable prestige in their communities; they saw around them successful non-white professional men; they enjoyed formal legal equality with whites as subjects of the British Empire, unlike the situation of most African Americans at the time; and they belonged to, and often led, a network of clubs and associations such as friendly societies, masonic lodges, debating and literary societies, and theatrical clubs. For those who were lawyers, the law provided training for public life, whether at home (as solicitors) or in Britain (as barristers). For such men (and just a handful of women), a race-conscious world view, and the self-confidence to articulate it publicly, could become quite general (Smith 2000, 336–52).[14]

Of course, as Smith explains, ambivalence about "white" values and culture was typical of the members of this group. They were opponents of racism, but they were not generally advocates of a "black identity" nor supporters of Afro-Creole culture; that would come later in the century. For them, upliftment of the race required them to demonstrate their achievements in the context, and by the standards, of Western civiliza-

---

14. This thesis focuses on the careers of Maresse-Smith, David, Alcazar and Lazare – all men who are the "originals" of characters in *Rupert Gray*.

tion and Christianity, seen as *self-evidently* superior. They knew they would have to prove their fitness to enjoy equality with the "master race", and such fitness included adopting the symbols of respectability and mastering Western culture. Unlike their descendants in the era of decolonization, they could not afford to be cultural relativists. With a few exceptions, they did not accept the legitimacy of non-Western (including African) religious or cultural practices; they accepted British values as benchmarks of civilization, and celebrated the achievements of black and mixed-race West Indians who were recognized for their mastery of British culture, above all in the metropole. Their theatre, music and literature were thoroughly European, and few of them valued Afro-Creole cultural forms. (J.J. Thomas's recognition of the French Creole language in *The Theory and Practice of Creole Grammar*, published in 1869, was an exceptional and ground-breaking analysis, and remained at the vanguard of positive linguistic attitude well into the late twentieth century.) At the same time, it would be a mistake to dismiss them as "Afro-Saxons" interested only in their own advancement; for they saw their struggle to "vindicate the race" as being fought on behalf of the whole ethnic community, not simply themselves, and they were faced with a dominant ideology of racism of extraordinary virulence and spread (Smith 2000, 336–52). Much of this ideological complex of race consciousness combined with an acceptance of European civilization as self-evidently superior can be seen in *Rupert Gray* (see also discussion below). Cobham shared a basic world view with the Trinidadian lawyers studied by Smith, his contemporaries and probably his role models.

Rupert Gray was first advertised in the *Mirror* (whose printing shop had published it) on 7 July 1907. Interestingly enough, the first few times the advertisement ran its wording was: "A New Local Novel. Read *Rupert Gray* The Lover of the Hour, by Stephen Cobham". Soon this was changed to "The *Book* of the Hour" (emphasis added), possibly reflecting some apprehensions about highlighting the black-white love story which forms the centre of the plot. An anonymous reviewer assessed Cobham's novel in the *Mirror* on 18 July 1907. After a concise, wittily written summary of the plot, the reviewer concluded:

He has made a daring attempt to illustrate in story the prejudices and diffi-culties that beset the path of an honest, ambitious negro in the West Indies, and Mr Cobham has certainly achieved a large measure of success in his essay. The literary style is however, sadly deficient, even for a first published effort at fiction. Short, jerky, spasmodically sounding sentences are of far too fre-quent occurrence, while there are several instances of defective syntactical construction. Mr Cobham's prudence in laying bare, in the manner that he has, the greatest social problem in the West Indies may be questioned by some. There can be no doubt, on the other hand, as to the accuracy of his portrayal of the inner feelings and sentiments that are entertained in connection with the matter. These social problems are perhaps far better left alone to work them-selves out, as they are bound to do in time either *vi et armis* ['by force of arms'], or by the final operation of the law of the survival of the fittest, or (bet-ter than either of these methods) by the complete strengthening of the bonds of a common humanity. The world is yet in a state approximating troglodytism with respect to this very vexed question and Mr Cobham's work is not likely to improve that primitive attitude towards ethnological ques-tions. The book is well worth reading, however. It is interesting as a true pen picture of certain conditions to be found in every British West Indian colony and with respect to his maiden effort, Mr Cobham is to be congratulated on the fact that its virtues are far more numerous than its defects.[15]

The reviewer chose not to speculate on whether the "honest, ambi-tious negro" who is the novel's hero was based on any actual local per-sonage. We think that Cobham may have modelled his hero on Henry Sylvester Williams, and perhaps also on C.P. David: both were African-Trinidadians of "pure" ancestry, both were barristers, both were known to Cobham. The choice of the name "Gray" may, perhaps, be significant; Williams and David had both studied at Gray's Inn in London, one of the four Inns of Court (see note to p. 99). When Cobham was a young man, there was a "Gray's Inn Literary Association" in Port of Spain, led by

---

15. See the *Mirror*, 18 July 1907. A search through the *Port-of-Spain Gazette* (the other local daily newspaper) for July, August and September 1907 revealed no review, or other notice, of *Rupert Gray*. Perhaps the theme of interracial marriage made it too sensitive for this paper, which generally spoke for the white creole community, to deal with. Moreover, there was considerable rivalry between the two papers, and this may have also made the *Gazette* reluctant to notice in any way a novel published by its rival.

Maresse-Smith, whom he admired (Mathurin 1976, 10, 14n28). Both Williams and David were race-conscious, outspoken men who were much admired by the Trinidad middle class; both opposed Crown Colony government, though Williams was more focused on pan-African and empire-wide issues than on local issues. We have seen that Cobham was one of the group of Trinidadians who welcomed Williams when he returned home in 1901 to launch the local branch of the Pan-African Association, and he must have felt pride when David became, in 1904, the first black (as opposed to mixed-race) man to sit on the Legislative Council.[16]

A striking similarity between Rupert Gray and Williams is that they both married white women. Gwendoline Serle is a creole of "pure" English ancestry; Williams married Agnes Powell, an Englishwoman whom he met through their mutual work in the temperance movement in London. Though the Powell family did not approve of the match, it was clearly a happy (though rather brief) union, resulting in several children, like that of Rupert and Gwendoline at the end of the novel. When Williams came home in 1908 to live and practise in Trinidad, he was probably the only black professional with an English, or a white, wife, and no doubt their social position was quite isolated. We know she had great difficulties when Williams died suddenly in 1911 and she was left a poor widow with several children (one posthumous).[17] Williams – like Rupert Gray – believed in the equality of the races and was no advocate for racial exclusivity; his marriage to a white woman, therefore, was not inconsistent with his pan-African views any more than Rupert's was with his anxiety to uplift his people. But whatever might be tolerated in the great liberal metropolis of London, black-white marriage was dynamite in the West Indies in the early 1900s, as the *Mirror*'s reviewer hinted; and Mr Serle's bitter denunciation of such unions was no doubt representative of the general views of the local white community. Even more than

---

16. For Williams, see Hooker (1975) and Mathurin (1976); for David, see Smith (2000, chapter 3) and Samaroo (1971, 73–89). For Henry Sylvester Williams's legal training, see Noel (2004, 3–11).

17. Interview with Henry Sylvester Williams's granddaughter, Jennifer Sylvestre-Williams, by Bridget Brereton and Lise Winer, 2002. For more on Agnes Williams, see Noel (2003).

Agnes Powell, who was an Englishwoman, Gwendoline as a white creole had betrayed her caste and could only be condemned to social isolation and contempt.[18]

The theme of black-white sex – albeit within marriage – gives Cobham's novel its "sensational" element. In other respects, there is much in the book which faithfully reflects the world view of the Port of Spain black and mixed-race intelligentsia to which its author belonged. The action – apart from Rupert's stay in London and his briefly summarized travels – takes place in and around the capital city of Port of Spain; we have few glimpses of the island as a whole or of the countryside. There is a scene in the city's Botanic Gardens, but little attempt to describe the beauties of the rural scenery. It is in this context that we can notice the general invisibility of the Indo-Trinidadian population. Large numbers of indentured labourers from India had been arriving in the island since 1845, and by 1907 at least a third of the total population comprised the immigrants and their descendants. But few lived in or around Port of Spain in the early 1900s, except for the suburb of Peru Village (now St James) to the west of the city, which Cobham hardly mentions. Most lived on or near the sugar and cocoa estates in the rural areas, or in peasant villages and settlements in the central and southern districts of the island. Port of Spain was a "creole" world, to which Indians, even ex-indentured or locally born ones, rarely ventured; and those Indians who did frequent the city tended to be poor and uneducated. The more vicious and prejudiced of the stereotypes – dirty, disease-ridden and prone to violence – are deployed by Jacob Clarke in his "Junius of the West" epistle about Trinidad. This is somewhat balanced by the novel's descriptions of this population as hard working: "industrious Indian matrons" and "coolies" who "staggered under heavy burdens".

---

18. Even in England, interracial marriage was still problematic. In a celebrated case of 1899, for instance, Kitty Jewell and Peter Lobengula (reputedly a son of King Lobengula of Matabeleland) caused a media sensation with their several attempts to marry in London. The wedding was stopped by the officiating clergy on more than one occasion: various impediments were the alleged reasons, but clearly race was a major factor in both the media attention and the clergy's reluctance to perform the ceremony. The couple finally did marry (in a registry office) the following year (Shephard 2003, 99–149).

The Literary Context of *Rupert Gray*

Caribbean Literary Traditions

Stephen Cobham published *Rupert Gray* in 1907, a mere two decades before the appearance of the first "barrack yard" stories by C.L.R. James in *From Trinidad* and the *Beacon* magazines. Cobham and James were the products of similar racial and sociopolitical milieux. Both had profited from the educational opportunities available in Trinidad to exceptional young men of African and mixed race by the turn of the twentieth century, and both took a partisan interest in the anti-establishment activities of the Port of Spain City Council. If anything, Cobham was more race conscious than James: an early pan-Africanist, his ideals of racial uplift, like those of his African-American contemporary W.E.B. Du Bois (1868–1963), drew on nineteenth-century assumptions about the unique contributions to civilization of each "race" within the human family, rather than on the claims of class solidarity, or of the shared oppression of the colonized, which underpinned James's later international socialism. And yet, these two early exponents of Trinidad writing seem light years apart in their aesthetic and literary sensibilities. Cobham's subject matter is the genteel melodrama of social uplift within the black and brown middle class; James brings to his portrayal of the same group the gritty prose and explicit sensuality of social realism. In *Rupert Gray*, the formal conventions of romance ensure that Cobham's hero gets the girl, the family business and the family estate, overcoming formidable obstacles of race and class. By contrast, in James's *Minty Alley*, a similarly black protagonist feels secure enough that he can exercise his *droit de seigneur*, at least socially, while renting a room in a barrack yard in order to pay the mortgage on the family property that underwrites his middle-class status.

James and Cobham do share, however, a remarkably upbeat investment in the comic resolutions of their plots. Cobham's cache of special effects – leaded coffins and plaster effigies – protects his star-crossed lovers from the inevitable doom reserved for "tragic mulattoes" and interracial lovers in nineteenth-century American fiction. Similarly, James ensures that the reversal in his hero's financial fortunes is mercifully brief, so that there is little opportunity for his cross-class slumming to produce murderous lovers, bitter fallen women or unclaimed bastards. In this respect, *Minty Alley* reads more like a throwback to the comic realism of novels such as Henry Fielding's *Tom Jones* (1749) – a genre on which Cobham also draws – than like the dour social realism of Theodore Dreiser's *An American Tragedy* (1925) or the Trinidadian writer Alfred Mendes's *Black Fauns* (1934).

Seen from the perspective of these differences and similarities, *Rupert Gray* can be read either as the forerunner of a twentieth-century Caribbean literary tradition, or as the last in a series of nineteenth-century ones. Although its tone is more Victorian, it invokes the same pre-war world in which H.G. de Lisser, in *Jane's Career* (1913), and Claude McKay, in *Banana Bottom* (1933), set their plots. In *Rupert Gray*, the black middle class that the later novels describe has already begun to challenge the white monopoly of law, medicine, trade and politics. Nevertheless, its allegiances to the British Empire remain unambiguous and its standards of beauty, culture and erudition clearly derive from the "mother country" (see the section "Race and Empire", below). That posture would have been unexceptionable at the turn of the century, when individual assimilation, for however tiny a cohort of black and brown West Indians, might well have seemed a more realistic goal than the alternative of full political enfranchisement.

Race and Gender

Shakespeare's *Othello* is an obvious literary context for *Rupert Gray*, and references to the play crop up throughout the book. Cobham focuses on the first act of *Othello,* involving the Moorish general who is made much of in Venice for his valuable services, until he presumes to cross the sexual colour bar.[19] Explaining how he and Desdemona came to love,

---

19. The term "Moors" refers to North Africans, though in Shakespeare's day they were often conflated with black Africans by the many who had never encountered either. In 1907, stage Othellos were almost always "tawny" rather than black, and always so in the United States; Henry Irving played the role in black makeup in the late nineteenth century in England, but no black or blackface Othello appeared on an American stage until

Othello emphasizes that her father Brabantio has often invited him to his home, and asked him to tell the story of his life, travels and adventures, while Desdemona listens "with a greedy ear" (1.3). Having finally heard the story through, she tells him that any friend of his who loves her need only learn to tell it as he has:

> She thank'd me,
> And bade me, if I had a friend that lov'd her,
> I should but teach him how to tell my story,
> And that would woo her. Upon this hint I spake:
> She lov'd me for the dangers I had pass'd,
> And I lov'd her that she did pity them. (1.3)

Like Gwendoline, Desdemona makes the first move, knowing that it would be difficult for Othello to do so given his race and hers, and he speaks his love only "upon this hint". The later part of the play – Iago's manipulation of Othello, Othello's jealousy and the murder of Desdemona – has no parallel in Cobham's novel (though the substitution of the statue for Gwendoline does recall another Shakespearian jealousy plot, *The Winter's Tale,* in which the "statue" of Hermione, the unjustly suspected wife, turns out to be Hermione herself).

Rupert, of course, is not a soldier like Othello with a tale of wonders and dangers to unfold, and in fact the first reference to *Othello* in *Rupert Gray* underlines the difference between the two protagonists. When Gwendoline asks her father if he does not think Rupert like Othello, her father laughs and reminds her that "Othello was a soldier . . . an exponent of strength". Mr Serle sees Rupert simply as "a faithful employé", overlooking his strength and the "strange magic" of his voice which attracts Gwendoline much as Othello's story attracts Desdemona. Like Brabantio, Mr Serle is unable to imagine his "tender, fair and happy" (*Othello* 1.2) daughter running "to the sooty bosom / Of such a thing"

---

19. (*continued*) 1930. The performance history of the play in the nineteenth and early twentieth centuries, especially in the United States, reflects anxieties about miscegenation; the very idea of a black man embracing a white woman on stage was disturbing, and Irving never included *Othello* in the repertoire of his American tours (see Kaul 1997). Gwendoline, however, does seem to think of Othello as black, and an apt parallel for Rupert.

(*Othello* 1.2), and so misses the hint entirely. To Gwendoline, though, the connection between Rupert and Othello is obvious, if also ominously prophetic of her father's murderous rage. Moreover, Gwendoline and Rupert cannot escape Mr Serle as easily as Othello and Desdemona can evade Brabantio. The Venetian authorities order Othello to Cyprus to assume the governorship and command the garrison there, so that he and Desdemona leave Venice almost as soon as her father discovers their marriage, but Rupert is less mobile, at least until his departure for England in the wake of Gwendoline's supposed death. Hence the focus of *Rupert Gray* falls on the battle against a white father's anger, not on a black man's jealousy. If, as it seems, the *Othello* references are in the book to lend cultural authority to *Rupert Gray*'s problematic interracial love affair, Cobham would naturally want to use them so as to avoid any suggestions of violent propensities in Rupert – a desire that may also account for Cobham's leaving him silent and largely passive in the shooting scene.

As noted above, Cobham probably modelled his protagonist's romance on the real-life marriage and career of Henry Sylvester Williams; throughout the region there were well-known cases of professional men of African descent whose marriages to white women, though at first the subject of scandal, eventually helped establish their social credentials. The best known such alliances helped found the first families of Barbados and Jamaican nationalism respectively. Grace Thorpe's 1929 marriage to the promising black lawyer Grantley Adams, in defiance of her affluent white Barbadian family, undoubtedly facilitated her husband's political career. And though the apparently interracial marriage between Norman Manley and his English-born wife Edna Swithenbank caused a stir – as much on account of their being first cousins as anything else – the dashing couple become the darlings of Jamaican high society when they returned to the island in the 1930s. Moreover, both Grantley and Norman were themselves the children of marriages between black men and white (or "near-white") women who would have been contemporaneous with the fictional Gwendoline Serle and Rupert Gray.[20]

---

20. Hoyos, in *Grantley Adams and the Social Revolution* (1974), explains that Grantley Adams's near-white mother had an acknowledged connection to two white half-sisters. On

Both formal and illicit sexual unions across class and colour lines, involving black women as well as black men, are as old as the plantation system in the Caribbean, although at different political moments some pairings have been more widely tolerated than others. However, the shift in literary emphasis between 1907 and 1936 – from marrying "up" the colour scale in *Rupert Gray* to cohabitation "down" class lines in *Minty Alley* – anticipates the shift in political consciousness within the region after World War II. Although they never fully rejected a vision of their future as bound up with personal advancement into the ruling class through marital and professional alliances, members of the black and brown middle class were forced to reassess their relationship to the folk, on account of the popular mass movements for democracy and self-determination spawned by the spread of pan-Africanism and international socialism at a grass-roots level during the inter-war years. Historically, we can see that move in the political realignment of men like Adams and Manley – from legal representatives of the Crown to political representatives of the people – over the course of their careers.

An interesting feature of Cobham's novel is the presence of two women characters, both British, who are highly educated, enterprising persons living very much in the public domain and, in that respect, defying Victorian gender conventions. Florence Badenock, a Scot, is a qualified medical doctor, still a rarity in Britain in 1907, an independent woman of strong character, even if she is ready to put aside her profession to help Gwendoline and then to marry Lionel Murchison. Lady Rothberry, an English aristocrat, is a great traveller, respected scientist and philanthropist, who seems to move all over the world on her own and interacts on equal terms with the great and the good of the British Empire. Even Gwendoline, though depicted as a conventionally accomplished "lady" with no career aspirations, is highly educated, with literary interests, and, of course, her active wooing of Rupert shows her to be a courageous woman prepared to defy her father and her caste, not the passive, swooning type of heroine so characteristic of earlier

---

20. (*continued*) the race of Edna's mother, Brown (1975, 18) states that family testimony is contradictory, but she was probably "coloured"; the important point is that the Shearer children could and did pass for white.

novels.[21] Far from swooning in the shooting scene, Gwendoline shows remarkable physical courage as she places herself between her father's revolver and a strangely passive Rupert; she does succumb in the water – inexplicably, since she is supposed to be a good swimmer – but that only allows Florence, in turn, to show her resolution and her professional skill as she works to revive her friend.

It is possible that Cobham had absorbed some of H.S. Williams's positive views about the role of women in public life; he involved women in his Pan-African Association, both locally – Mrs Philip John, a schoolteacher, was secretary of the Trinidad branch – and in London, where Jane Cobden Unwin – daughter of Richard Cobden and wife of the publisher T. Fisher Unwin – was a member of the executive committee of the Pan-African Association. Cobham's hero Maresse-Smith also had enlightened views, no doubt influenced by his mother, the Trinidadian bluestocking and writer Emilie Maresse-Paul; virtually alone among the "reformers" of the late nineteenth century, her son supported giving the vote to middle-class women if the colony received elected representatives.[22] But Cobham does not depict any non-white, middle-class woman in his novel; the female characters are either white (British or Creole) or working-class blacks. Did he see the independent and educated woman as a model suitable only for the metropolis?

To some extent the major women characters echo the heterodox attitudes and occupations of the "New Woman" novels of the 1880s and 1890s in England. Novels as different as Sarah Grand's *The Heavenly Twins* (1893) and Olive Schreiner's *The Story of an African Farm* (1883) attempted to move away from the plot patterns of conventional fiction, and from the passive female characters that tended to go with those plot patterns. Cobham may have had such novels in mind as providing precedents for Gwendoline's and Florence's unorthodox competence, though

---

21. Nineteenth-century novelists in fact often took aim at the "swooning woman" stereotype: the eponymous heroine of Charlotte Brontë's *Jane Eyre* (1847), for instance, rarely swoons and passionately rejects authority on several occasions. Jane has many more or less resolute sisters in nineteenth-century fiction, especially though by no means exclusively in novels written by women. But the stereotype persisted, in part because it remained a staple in popular art forms such as melodrama.

22. For women in the Pan-African Association, see Mathurin (1976, 80, 99); for Maresse-Smith's views, see Smith (2000, 346–47).

he seems to use their emancipation simply to make their resistance to racism more probable. Certainly some of the narrator's remarks show a fairly conventional sense of women as sexual temptresses, and hint that Gwendoline's love is at least a mixed blessing for Rupert, if not downright harmful. In chapter 4, for instance, after Gwendoline's gift of the scarf pin, Rupert thinks of her love uneasily as something that will cause a "blemish" in his relationship with Mr Serle (ironically the relationship the scarf pin points to, since it has been made from the coin that commemorates his first meeting with his employer). The narrator likens her image in Rupert's mind to that of a "mermaid" and a "siren", and exclaims against "woman" as Eve-like, "a temptress from the earth's natal day". Gwendoline is again likened to Eve at the end of chapter 6, where the narrator adopts the conventional idea of "the feminine nature" as dangerously mysterious, "appealing to no umpire but the instinct of Eve – unfathomable always" and fated to remain "half a puzzle". The chapter ends with a quotation from Tennyson's "Locksley Hall", applied in the original to a woman who has betrayed her lover for the sake of the same social rules that Gwendoline flouts: the quotation does not fit Gwendoline, but in its misogyny it echoes the earlier temptress/Eve comments. At this point in the text, before Rupert or Gwendoline has suffered any social consequences for their love, the narrator sees Gwendoline almost as a troublemaker who will destroy Rupert's prospects by her uncontrolled passion for him.

Cobham also demonstrates orthodox gender (and class) attitudes for the most part in his presentation of Edith, whose efforts to emulate Gwendoline's learning are mocked (albeit gently): she never seems to get much beyond the "comic servant" mode in which she appropriates "detrimental" and Dr Johnson to bolster her own opinions. Interestingly, though, Edith's role in the plot ends up resembling that of Florence and Gwendoline: for all three, development ultimately means little more than change in marital status. Their common destiny is to become wives and mothers, even though it is largely their loyalty and ingenuity that bring about the happy ending to Rupert's story. At the end, however, only Edith's voice is still heard, and she is the one who makes the most visible break with convention, if only in relation to her son's future: she wants him to study agriculture and botany, not a profession such as

Rupert Gray's, which would lead to the normative symbols of success –
"frock coats and beaver hats".

Race and Empire

An important feature of *Rupert Gray* is the expression of the author's
views about race and empire, views that, as we have seen, were generally
held by the members of the colony's middle class at the time, including
the men who may have been the models for his title character. Cobham
shows himself to be well informed on the history of blacks in the
Americas. The "Negro worthies" who are mentioned by Mr Serle (see
notes to pp. 58–59) include not only local men like Maresse-Smith,
Philip, Thomas and Brown, but also heroes of the Haitian Revolution
(Toussaint, Dessalines, Christophe, Jean-François, Biassou); and Booker
T. Washington, Edward Blyden and Conrad Reeves. No doubt speaking
on behalf of the author, Rupert Gray in London calls for the upliftment
of the race, not through special favours, but by the establishment of a
"fair field and no favour" on which blacks must (and will) prove themselves through their own efforts.[23] This would involve co-operation with
liberal whites (like Lady Rothberry and her heir) rather than separate
organization, a view strongly held by Williams, whose Pan-African
Association included white supporters and sympathizers

As the novel's several references to British history and literature suggest, the culture of the "mother country" could provide examples of
resistance to oppression, not only in the global imperial context that
Rupert invokes in his London speech, but also in the context of the
British Isles. The tour that Rupert takes with the Earl of Rothberry suggests an interest in the quasi-colonial relationships between England and
other nations within Britain (see notes to pp. 102–3). Substantial parts
of the tour focus on Ireland, Scotland and Wales rather than on England,
and there are several references to supporters of the Stuarts, the Scottish
and later British royal house finally deposed in 1688. Though they were

---

23. In Selwyn Cudjoe's view, "one of the major functions of *Rupert Gray* was to provide a literary vehicle to carry forward the sentiments about race pride and race development that were rampant in the [Trinidad] society" (2003, 371).

by no means always friendly to the oppressed themselves, the status of the Stuarts as exiles linked them symbolically with outsiders, especially with the Scots. That they were ultimately the losers may make Stuart history, and the sufferings of their supporters at places such as Glencoe and Culloden, all the more inspiring as tales of resistance against the odds. Similarly, although the Nine Years' War in Ireland – apparently in Rupert's mind, given the visit to Enniskillen – did not lead to victory for the Irish insurgents, it can be read as a heroic struggle against the advancing tide of anglicization. Like *Othello,* British history can offer something other than lessons in metropolitan cultural superiority, if only because the ethnic plurality of the British Isles, as emphasized by this tour, suggests the resilience of subject cultures and the potential for a national or imperial identity that can embrace many peoples.

Like Williams, Rupert Gray articulates an essentially positive view of the British Empire in his speech in London (see note to p. 101). This speech echoes a public lecture delivered by Cobham in Port of Spain in 1898, in which he linked the wealth and power of England and the empire to the admirable character of the British people and the virtues of the nation's men of action, science and literature over the centuries. Cobham ended his eulogy of England and empire by expressing the hope that "a thousand years hence, well-governed myriads of imperial and colonial subjects might stand up – all – even to the last man – and pronounce as I do tonight: – 'England with all thy faults – I love thee still' ". In fact, Williams, Cobham and most members of the Trinidad intelligentsia saw the empire as potentially a great force for good in the world; they believed in the possibility of a moral imperialism. They rejected the paternalism of empire; they sought to prove their "adulthood", their fitness to take charge of their own destinies and to achieve as any other human beings. Hence their race pride, their stress on self-reliance and self-help; hence, too, their anxiety to master British culture and civic forms, especially the English language and oratory (particularly salient to the lawyers). Certainly they raised issues of racism and discrimination, but they did not attack imperialism itself, nor did they question the superiority of Western values and culture. They always sought acceptance and respectability in a world where others held power and others defined the standards of respectability. Williams was, in many ways, an Anglophile, who (unlike Blyden) never challenged the superiority of British culture or the wisdom and necessity of christianizing Africans; and even Maresse-Smith, perhaps the most radical of the Trinidad intelligentsia in this period, took a prominent part in the local celebrations of Victoria's jubilees of 1887 and 1897. William Smith calls these men "Liberal Loyalists" who wanted to destabilize the colonial system in order to stabilize the empire.[24] Their views, shared by Cobham, were faithfully reflected in *Rupert Gray*.

The subtitle of *Rupert Gray*, "A Tale in Black and White", foregrounds both the race issue and the novel's polemical approach to it from the outset: the intent to state the case boldly – in "black and white" – underpins the novel's use of melodramatic events, narration, dialogue and typed characters (the stalwart hero, the spotless heroine, the treacherous villain and the violently angry parent) to tell its tale of love thwarted by racism but ultimately triumphant. The melodrama may put off twenty-first century readers – and indeed may have grated on many readers in the early twentieth century. But the extremes of melodrama have often been used to good effect in protest literature: the stronger the entrenched opposition, the greater the felt need to eliminate moral gray areas in the protest.

Apart from Rupert, Cobham introduces three significant black characters who augment the reader's understanding of the hero's complex social status. Edith Olliviere and François Pierre play the roles of loyal retainers to Gwendoline and Rupert respectively, while Rupert's nemesis, Jacob Clarke, is a fellow employee at Serle and Murchison. Edith's malapropisms and Pierre's stammering offset the erudition and eloquence of the protagonists, as their romance provides a humorous counterpoint to the elaborate courtship between Rupert and Gwendoline. Here, Cobham draws on a familiar technique in the comedy of manners, whereby the peccadilloes in the private lives of the serving class provide a foil to the high drama in the romances of their betters. In keeping with its theatrical underpinnings, the novel achieves this comic effect by distorting the speech codes of the minor characters. Edith's malapropisms

---

24. See Smith (2000, 371–80) and Hooker (1975, 73–74); for the 1898 lecture, see the *Indian Kohinoor Gazette* (Trinidad), 16 and 26 November 1898.

and hypercorrected English differentiate her intellectual capacities from those of her mistress, demonstrating for the reader the limitations of a smattering of book learning unleavened by refined cultural intercourse. Edith's characterization allows the author to demonstrate that cultural maladroitness is a defect of class and opportunity rather than race: the reader has no difficulty distinguishing between Edith's comic delivery and the unforced refinement of the local "coloured" thespians, who deliver their lines with distinction and poise in Gwendoline's amateur theatricals, even though they know that social prejudice precludes their mixing as equals among the white guests and actors. Pierre's speech defect and his use of Creole similarly underwrite Rupert's gentility. His stutter both performs and deflects the untutored passion to which Rupert Gray, as a more highly evolved black man, must never succumb. Cobham is explicit on this point: when Clarke complains that blacks resent taking orders from men of their own colour, he has Rupert respond that "there are negroes and negroes . . . bad and good in every race". And precisely because some of them are undisciplined and resentful, "you in authority ought not to show resentment. You are supposed to be the cream of your people crowning the lees and dregs below, tainted with the traces of narrow prejudices, which will only wear away with years. Use tact and mother wit and there's an end to it" (p. 17). Later in the plot the narrator makes a point of stressing how, even when Rupert is physically attacked, he never speaks or acts intemperately.

The instinctive loyalty that Edith and Pierre offer their social betters, both black and white, draws attention to the challenge more recent Caribbean writers have faced in representing and accounting for cross-class allegiances. Although more recent authors seem to have assumed that working-class black characters have more equivocal relationships with white authority figures than Cobham allows, their assessments of intra-racial solidarity across class lines vary. Merle Hodge, whose own novel, *Crick Crack Monkey* (1970), draws sharp distinctions between the values of upper- and lower-class black Trinidadians, offers a searing critique of *Minty Alley* when she points out in an essay called "Peeping Tom in the Nigger Yard" (1972) that James offers the reader no textual justification for the almost unanimous esteem in which the men and women in the barrack yard hold his middle-class protagonist, Haynes.

Indeed, from Hodge's perspective, Haynes shamelessly exploits their generosity. The Jamaican V.S. Reid's position in *New Day* (1949) is closer to Cobham's. His narrator associates lower-class origins with volatile rhetoric, suggesting that Paul Bogle's impassioned speeches are partly responsible for the tragic loss of life in the aftermath of the Morant Bay Rebellion. Moreover, the ageing narrator legitimates a younger generation's success in inaugurating a political new day in Jamaica by stressing how the restraint and cultural refinement exhibited by its leader, Garth, differentiates him in style – if not in substance – from the passionate but ultimately extremist politics of Garth's father, Davy.

The Barbadians George Lamming and Kamau Brathwaite take the opposing position. In their work, the most highly educated members of the emergent black middle class – such as the teacher-turned-politician of *In the Castle of My Skin* and the character Chalkstick in *Mother Poem* – earn the author's unambiguous hostility. Their lower-class supporters seem, at best, misguided. Like Cobham, these authors use stuttering, lisps and neologisms to indicate when lower-class characters struggle to maintain control of their passions. But they use that linguistic aphasia to mark the psychic cost of cultural repression as well as a residual Fanonian capacity for redemptive violence. More than is the case in Cobham's novel, racial tension is apparently superseded by class conflict in these later works. However, writers as various as Erna Brodber, Samuel Selvon, Derek Walcott and Earl Lovelace remain sanguine about the possibility of constructing a society in which Rupert Gray's virtues of "tact and mother wit" provide the basis for mutual, if not always harmonious, co-existence in a complex, multiracial space.

Cobham's most sustained focus on the intersection of class and racial privilege plays itself out in the novel's presentation of its villain, Jacob Clarke. As the classic evil twin of melodrama, Clarke plays a role similar to that of the near-white DeGuerinon in *Adolphus,* an earlier novel reprinted in this series. Whereas *Adolphus* exposes DeGuerinon as unworthy of whiteness, Clarke's downfall comes about because he betrays his black race as well as his native land. He repays Rupert's generosity in helping him find a job by conniving to expose the affair between Rupert and Gwendoline and he treats other blacks with contempt. He commits his most egregious offence, however, when he writes a letter to the *Daily Mail* in London, disparaging Trinidadian society. Its criticism of Port of Spain and Trinidadians recycles a familiar catalogue of woes levied against the island by writers from Froude to Naipaul:

> The town is close and hot, with low-roofed houses innocent of ventilation. . . . The squares and thoroughfares are disagreeable through the abuse of ill-kept urinals. . . . The blacks never work. Banana stealings and midnight visits to hen roosts they find more lucrative. . . . Every morning fashion-plated Grecian girls with their hair half combed, waddle about the stores. After being shown goods for an hour or so, they purchase half a yard of ribbon, or pay three cents for buttons, to the chagrin of practical salesmen. . . . The Portuguese coin money for the sale of weevil-holed biscuits. An ordinance is to be passed restricting their consumption of cabbage. . . . The East Indians are victims to yaws. Their cutlasses do not spare spouse nor estate managers. . . . The Chinese are gambling kings in whé whé palaces. . . . In short the only thing of value throughout the whole town is the legal eunuch whose forte is monkeyism. (p. 90)

The point here is not so much that Clarke invents these charges: Trinidadians still level them at each other in their more jaundiced moments. The more scurrilous jabs – like the one about laws against the Portuguese consumption of cabbage – were probably the subject of contemporaneous calypsos or running jokes. In fact, Cobham himself is clearly having a great deal of fun putting these slurs into print, even though he wants us to castigate the character who pens them. Clarke's offence is that he repeats these clichés out of context, thus exposing his society to the ridicule of outsiders. For Trinidadians, who are among the world's most sophisticated exponents of *mauvais langue* – a semi-ritualized form of criticism and teasing – such exposure remains paradoxically a national sport and the deepest form of betrayal. Indeed, that defensive closing of ranks against outside critiques was one of the earliest marks of an emergent shared communal identity in Trinidadian society. Cobham makes a point, for instance, of having his characters refer with approval to *Froudacity*, which J.J. Thomas published in 1889, to refute J.A. Froude's disparaging comments on Trinidad in *The English in the West Indies* (1888) (a book which is referred to positively only insofar as Froude's attitude that "nature in the tropics is always grand"). Clarke's vices and, conversely, Rupert's virtues have everything to do with how they measure up with respect to these two sets of social allegiances – a commitment to racial advancement and a wider patriotic allegiance to a multiracial Trinidadian society.

Cobham uses the tension between competing social allegiances to account for Mr Serle's behaviour as well. The white Trinidadian's commitment to an inclusive local professional community is expansive enough for him to consider making a black Trinidadian accountant his business partner, but he baulks at allowing that same black accountant his daughter's hand in marriage. As he explains to his dinner guests:

> We are ready to receive the black man with open arms into the professions, the services of the Crown, and in commerce, but when it comes to mixing up in the company of our wives and wanting to marry our daughters – I say, "No, sir." I say to them what Canute said to the waves: "Thus far and no further." (p. 59)

Serle's choice of Canute as his model already intimates that he will be powerless to stop this particular wave from crashing onto his shore. But his speech makes explicit the differences between his limited notion of community and the much more drastic forms of segregation upheld by his counterparts in Jim Crow America during the same period.

We must understand how these potentially contradictory allegiances to country and race intersect for the author in order to grasp how the marriage of a black man to a white woman becomes, without irony, the ultimate symbol of racial advancement in his novel. From Cobham's perspective, Rupert does not betray his race when he aligns himself with his boss's business interests or seeks to marry a white woman, because neither action compromises his commitment to his country. As a black man, Rupert supports racial advancement when he offers Clarke a helping hand in finding a job and when he treats the black workers under his supervision with compassion and respect. As a Trinidadian, Rupert upholds his society's honour when he refuses to wash its dirty linen in public by responding to the calumny heaped upon him by a fellow Trinidadian's libelous claims in the British press, and when he rejects emigration as a way of advancing himself. As he explains to one of his patrons, the young Earl of Rothberry, "England is already made. Trinidad needs her sons to make her" (p. 104).

The narrator's description of the Port of Spain wharves directly after Clarke has delivered his first contemptuous commentary on black people reinforces this image of a community whose cohesion is built around shared industry despite dramatic differences in its members' racial, cultural and economic attributes:

> Already industrious Indian matrons – red-spittled Madrassees – armed with buckets, were boarding the united chariots ere their wheels grew cold. A watering cart followed in the wake of a heavy stone-crusher along the convex street, improving on the recipe Sir John McAdam gave to the world. Groups of workingmen, idling for weeks together, were sauntering everywhere with thoughts of home upon their honest faces. The *Kennet* and the *Spey*, one on either side, hugged the herculean jetty.
>
> Wily fruiterers – white-aproned Bimshire wives – haggled over oranges and bananas with sailors and new-comers unused to local market prices. All is fair in the love and war of bargaining and barter, even on the wharf, where ragged urchins, scarce at years of discretion, learnt the ways of the world in this rough-and-tumble environment – this scrambling-ground for daily bread – this vortex of survival. The struggle for fortune shifts over to the water. Flatmen slowly hoist or reef sails. Pigmy steam launches and a fleet of boats of all sizes with oars like wooden fins, ply all day. (p. 18)

Cobham's panoramic sweep in this passage recalls E.L. Joseph's description of the same bustling Port of Spain wharves three-quarters of a century earlier in *Warner Arundell*. It celebrates Trinidad as a vibrant cosmopolitan society, at the hub of a global enterprise that brings to its shores an array of adventurers and entrepreneurs of all races, classes and occupations, united by their industry and the shared prospect of economic opportunity. The passage preempts Clarke's letter to the *Daily Mail* quoted earlier, in which racial and cultural diversity become synonymous with slovenliness and disorder. Despite its utopian elements, it constructs for the reader an authentic sense of place:

> Who can spare time to notice the long broadening tracks of foam across the bosom of the deep? Off yonder a stupendous crane wheels lazily for ever, its half-greased mechanism creaking and groaning. The blazing day star –

Phoebus Apollo – the sun-god of old, is careering in his chariot, high overhead, in all his torrid majesty, softening the asphalt between the tram lines and causing the surface of the flinty thoroughfare to burn quickening footsteps – boots or no boots. Smart-looking youngsters busy themselves between Customs, or bank and counting house, with red-marked paper bags of money. Tallying clerks keep feeling in the pockets of their coarse brown linen, or snow-white blouses, for notebook or monster lead-pencil. (p. 18)

Like the author of *Warner Arundell* before him, Cobham plays up the exotic attire and cultural variety his cosmopolitan swarm displays. But he also embeds his workers in an industrial landscape, signified by cranes, steamships and locomotives, all relatively recent symbols of a new industrial age at the time that he was writing. That modernist fascination with the phallic energy associated with machines is rare in Caribbean writing. It bears comparison to Paule Marshall's (1959) description of the New York factory in which the mother in *Brown Girl, Brownstones* works. The only comparable scene in a novel set in the Caribbean that comes to mind is Selvon's description in *A Brighter Sun* (1952, chapter 8) of Tiger's fascination with the power of the bulldozers that the US Army Corps of Engineers used to build roads and runways in Trinidad during World War II. Kamau Brathwaite's *Arrivants* trilogy (1973) makes memorable use of the rhythms of trains to indicate the ways in which the descendants of enslaved Africans have appropriated the power of the machine in their art, but industry *qua* industry resists representation in Caribbean literature. This absence may indicate how profoundly alienated many West Indians still feel from the industrial agendas carried forward by their labour. Or it may be that a nationalist literary tradition based on a nostalgic reclamation of the land has not provided the imaginative space for writers to deal with industrial landscapes. At any rate, the prominence that Cobham gives to this tableau of late nineteenth-century industrial vigour suggests that certain modernist preoccupations intimated in his novel have yet to be fully explored by writers from the region.

Introduction

Gardens of Empire

One of *Rupert Gray's* most significant subplots culminates in the hero's induction into the Linnaean Society. It is set in motion by his accidental encounter with Lady Rothberry, an amateur British horticulturalist. Rupert's ability to trade Latin nomenclature identifying the genera and species of the specimen plants in the Trinidad Botanic Gardens with a visiting aristocrat in disguise seems at first glance an unwieldy plot mechanism for attempting the hero's rehabilitation. However, it situates Cobham's novel securely in its historical moment, as well as anchoring its themes within a Caribbean literary tradition that extends back to James Grainger's eighteenth-century poem, *The Sugar-Cane* (1764), and forward to Jamaica Kincaid's *My Garden (Book):* (1999). In *Nature's Government: Science, Imperial Britain, and the "Improvement" of the World* (2000), the Caribbean historian Richard Drayton explains the crucial role that Britain's Kew Gardens played in orchestrating the nexus between gardens as ornamental pastimes, instruments of imperial consolidation, and nurseries for the emergent scientific disciplines of botany, ecology and evolutionary theory. Drayton's study ends at the turn of the twentieth century, around the period when *Rupert Gray* was written, but it affords us a clear understanding of the central role that the science of botany and horticultural innovation played in the construction of colonial subjects at the time that Cobham was writing. It also helps explain why gardening, in its broadest sense, remains a vivid trope within contemporary Caribbean literature.

Drayton argues that Kew Gardens served as the lynchpin of the imperial state, in much the same way that the position of the ruler between God and his natural creation was the lynchpin in the pre-Enlightenment ordering of society articulated by the great chain of being. In both systems, the management of nature in the service of the economic improvement and moral uplift of society became a measure of the success of the state in fulfilling its civic functions. Drayton also points out that Kew's central role in the proliferation and exchange of horticultural commodities was sustained by the botanical gardens at its periphery. Through the exchanges between centre and periphery that this system of global horticulture promulgated, these gardens transformed Britain, even as they altered irreversibly the landscapes of her colonies.

Introduction

Many of the historical developments in agriculture and horticulture that Drayton describes attained their most significant expression during the period in which *Rupert Gray* is set, and Trinidad had a distinctive role in some of the most important of these. In the first place, Drayton identifies the island's botanical garden, in which Rupert and Lady Rothberry have their chance encounter, as one of the oldest – and the oldest continuously functioning – botanical gardens in the Americas. Established in 1818 on plans first laid out by Governor Picton in 1802, it was a showcase in its heyday for tropical plants culled from all over Britain's tropical empire. Trinidad's own, often distinctive, flora and fauna were also noteworthy; its abundant varieties of orchids and hummingbirds, for instance, were among the earliest exotic specimens to attract the attention of British collectors and commercial interests. The island's geologically recent separation from the South American mainland had led to a unique set of ecological relationships, not unlike those in the Galapagos Islands that helped Darwin establish his evolutionary hypotheses. Consequently the island was – and remains – a favourite destination for botanists and ecologists.

The nineteenth-century writers on Trinidad flora, including L.A.A. de Verteuil (1858) and Charles Kingsley (1871), probably obtained much of their botanical information from monthly *Colonial Agricultural Reports* that were published to catalogue the progress of any economically beneficial findings for the colonies. The Scientific Association of Trinidad, founded in 1861, concentrated on agricultural and social matters, as well as conchology and geology. The Trinidad Field Naturalists Club, established in 1891, was a hotbed of investigation into many aspects of natural history. Walter Elias Broadway (1863–1933), its only specialist in botany, was the assistant to J.H. Hart of the Botanic Gardens, and had been recommended by W.T. Thistleton-Dyer, director of Kew Gardens (Baksh-Comeau 1992). The local flora had been fairly well catalogued in the first definitive *Flora of the British West Indian Islands*, prepared by August Heinrich Rudolph Grisebach, with the help of Hart and possibly Broadway, in several volumes published between 1859 and 1864. Founding members of the Field Naturalists Club, both first-generation immigrants and locally born creoles – including Henry Carraciolo, Plantagenet Lechmere Guppy, R.R. Mole, Thomas Irwin Potter and

Friedrich W. Urich – contributed greatly to the understanding of local and global tropical natural history. Although records of the club's membership are not available from the late 1890s to the 1920s, most club members were probably white or mixed race; nonetheless, it would have been possible for Cobham (and Rupert Gray) to have attended public lectures on agricultural and scientific topics. Cobham's interest in such matters would have likely been supported through his relationship with R.R. Mole, the publisher of the newspaper for which Cobham wrote, and the owner of the establishment that printed his novel.

On the agricultural front, cuttings from Trinidad cocoa plants, sent from the island's botanical gardens to Kew, were used to jump-start the cocoa industry in Ghana at the turn of century, with spectacular results. The agricultural institutes connected with the botanical gardens established in almost all of Britain's Caribbean territories trained native West Indians to take up posts as horticultural and agricultural officers in other parts of the British Empire while contributing to the development of new hybrid strains of such tropical staples as sugar cane, bananas and coffee.[25] Rupert's interest in botany, therefore, alongside his work for Serle as an exporter of agricultural commodities, places him at the heart of the horticultural ventures of his age, so vital to the imperial project.

Rupert's familiarity with the publications of the Linnaean Society (and, by extension, his creator's familiarity with that organization) locates him within another set of relations that Drayton describes: botany was among the last of the natural sciences to establish its academic credentials during the Victorian era. As late as the 1860s, even after the publication of Darwin's *Evolution of Species,* there were few chairs in botany at British universities and no graduate fellowships to support aspiring scholars. Consequently, serious botanists remained dependent for much longer than other scientists on private patronage. Founded in 1788, and named for the Swedish botanist, Carolus Linnaeus, who

---

25. The Imperial College of Tropical Agriculture, established in Trinidad in 1922, had no special connection with the local Botanic Gardens. Its purpose was to train experts in tropical agriculture for service in the whole British Empire, and relatively few West Indians, including Trinidadians, ever attended it. In 1960 it became the Faculty of Agriculture of the then University College of the West Indies, the first faculty of what would become the University of the West Indies at St Augustine, Trinidad, in 1962.

invented the system of taxonomy still in use today to order all living things into genera and species, the Linnaean Society was one of the leading organizations in Britain that facilitated such patronage. It brought together a hodgepodge of aristocrats and professionals, garden buffs and self-taught gentlewomen, whom one of the commentators Drayton cites dismisses contemptuously as "Horticultural and Gooseberry Societies, with their irregular troops, the tulip fanciers and prize auricula [primrose] men with their scientific arrangements, classifications and pruning hooks" (2000, 142). By the end of the nineteenth century, new publications by a younger generation of botanists and evolutionary theorists, as well as new uses for agricultural products like vegetable oils, plant fibres and rubber – as lubricants and insulation for modern technology – had secured a niche for the scientific study of plants within British industry and academia. Rupert's knowledge of plant diseases and his familiarity with esoteric botanical debates is a testament to that new scientific and economic order.

Such developments notwithstanding, the social face of botany and horticulture in a colony such as Trinidad would still have been associated with those mid-nineteenth-century amateur botanists in whose likeness Cobham fashions Lady Rothberry. Cobham describes Rupert and Lady Rothberry as being absorbed in deciphering curious name plates on plants "interesting only to the disciples of Bentham and Hooker" (p. 56) Yet at the time this novel was published, William Hooker, the director of Kew who succeeded the legendary Joseph Banks, had been dead for almost half a century. The topics of Hooker's epistolary exchanges with George Bentham had been superseded by new horticultural advances associated with his successors at Kew, Joseph Hooker and William Thistleton-Dyer. Moreover, William Hooker's dependence on aristocratic patrons like the Duke of Bedford (whose family's history sounds remarkably like the details from *Debrett's Peerage* that Cobham invents for Lady Rothberry) was no longer the norm.[26] Nevertheless, the fictional Linnaean Society's plan to finance Rupert's formal study of botany through the publication of his essay on tropical diseases suggests that

---

26. Drayton describes how the sudden death of John Russell, Duke of Bedford, in 1839 almost put an end to William Hooker's campaign to become director of Kew, until Hooker.

private patronage of botanists was still alive and well when Cobham was writing – at least in the imaginations or experience of colonial subjects who lacked more direct access to new avenues of imperial influence. It may be a sign of the changing political climate in the West Indies, however, that Rupert eventually elects to study law rather than botany.

But Rupert Gray's relationship to horticulture goes beyond the boundaries of imperial science and it is in this respect that Cobham's novel aligns itself most significantly with that of later Caribbean writers. Not only can Rupert recite the Latin names of the plants in the Botanic Gardens: he also knows their local names and usages. Like Laurine and Belfond in *The Slave Son* (Wilkins 1854) and the Romelia family in *Adolphus* (Anon. 1853) (both reprinted in volume 2 of this series), his mastery of both European and local garden lore establishes him simultaneously as a cultivated individual (in all senses of the word), as well as authentically West Indian: secure in his racial and cultural heritage, but able to benefit, like his contemporary, W.E. Du Bois, from exchanges among the "civilised races" of the world. Caribbean writers since Cobham have continued to invoke the garden as an ambivalent trope – a place that Jean Rhys's narrator in *Wide Sargasso Sea* associates with "the garden in the Bible – the tree of life grew there. But it had gone wild" (1966, 19): it is a site of esoteric, racial knowledge as well as the proving ground for cultivated refinement.

Kincaid's provocative engagement with horticulture in *My Garden (Book):* is the most sustained such performance. Like Rupert, she engages directly with the heritage of the Swedish taxonomist Linnaeus, establishing her horticultural credentials through her precise knowledge of his classification system. But Kincaid uses those credentials to critique the racist or imperialist underpinnings of the achievements of such famous horticulturalists as Thomas Jefferson and Joseph Banks. At the same

---

26. *(continued)* was able to use a memorial in his patron's honour to attract the attention and continued patronage of the new Duke of Bedford (2000, 162 ff.). The uncanny correspondences between this historical event and Cobham's plot twist of killing off Lady Rothberry when Rupert needs her patronage most, then arranging for him to memorialize her in a way that re-establishes his currency within horticultural circles in England, suggest that Cobham may have been familiar with the details of Hooker's biography from his own engagement with the study of botany and that he may have imported details of that story into his plot.

time, her writing tells another story, of the ways in which gardens remain for her – as for Rupert Gray – a site of intimate pleasure and pain, bound up with her personal history of colonization, resistance, repression, alienation and desire. Several of her essays in *My Garden (Book):* evoke a time during her childhood when both she and her stepfather were ill and she would accompany him to the Antigua Botanical Gardens to collect the leaves of medicinal herbs that he used to treat his condition. In *The Autobiography of My Mother* (1996), Kincaid's protagonist, Xuela, puts to work a similar indigenous knowledge of the properties of plants to abort her unwanted children and to poison the first wife of her English husband – a man she describes as either destroying or colonizing every living thing he encounters in the Caribbean landscape, with the aid of Linnaeus's taxonomy:

> He cleared the land; nothing growing on it inspired any interest in him. The inflorescence of this, he said, was not significant; and the word inflorescence was said with an authority as if he had created inflorescence itself . . . He made long lists under the heading Genus. He made long lists under the heading Species. From time to time I would release whatever individual he held in captivity, replacing it with its like, its kind: one lizard replaced with another lizard, one crab replaced with another crab, one frog with another frog. I could not ever tell if he knew I had done so. He was so sure inside himself that all the things he knew were correct, not that they were true, but that they were correct. Truth would have undone him. Truth is always so full of uncertainty. (Kincaid 1996, 222–23)

For Naipaul, in *The Enigma of Arrival* (1987), the encounter with Jack's garden in rural England undams a flood of difficult recognitions. He must acknowledge that much of the cultivated landscape he thought of as uniquely Trinidadian when he was growing up turns out to have been a transplanted version of an imperial idea. Yet, despite the inscription of his alienation in the artificiality of that landscape, Naipaul's narrator remains incapable of shaking the hold those colonial gardens exert on his imagination, as he struggles to construct a new relationship with the trees, flowers and shrubs of his exile. The garden theme in *Enigma* elaborates a struggle already enunciated in *The Mimic Men* (1967), when Singh's French Creole friend, Deschampneufs, warns him that his attempts to escape Trinidad will always founder on its landscape. In a passage shot through with bitterness and belonging, Champ ruminates:

> You know, you are born in a place and you grow up there. You get to know the trees and the plants. You will never know any other trees and plants like that. You grow up watching a guava tree, say. You know that browny-green bark peeling like old paint. You try to climb that tree. You know that after you climb it a few times the bark gets smooth-smooth and so slippery you can't get a grip on it. You get that ticklish feeling in your foot. Nobody has to teach you what the guava is. You go away. You ask, "What is that tree?" Somebody will tell you, "An elm." You see another tree. Somebody will tell you, "That is an oak." Good; you know them. But it isn't the same. Here, you wait for the poui to flower one week in the year and you don't even know you are waiting. All right, you go away. But you will come back. Where you born, man, you born. (Naipaul 1967, 171–72)

Walcott inverts many of Naipaul's garden tropes in *Omeros* (1990). Here, it is the expatriate Major Plunkett who first reads the landscape through its imperial signs. Despite his wife's attempt to recreate a Victorian garden in the tropics and his own determination to impose efficient First World standards on his farm, Plunkett comes to realize that neither an overarching taxonomy nor an imperial design for tropical horticulture can fully encompass the experience of life, work and loss in the St Lucian landscape that he finally embraces as his own. Conversely, for Ma Kilman to find an herbal cure for Philoctete's wound, she must establish a visceral relationship with the growing things transplanted, like her ancestors, into the St Lucian landscape. Unlike Rupert Gray, Ma Kilman never succeeds in recovering the name of the plant she needs in any language. It remains, like Pierre's stutterings, on the tip of her tongue. Instead, she follows the trail of ants whose language she understands "the way we follow our thoughts without any language" (Walcott 1990, 244) and the "reek of an unknown weed . . . [whose] pronged flowers / sprang like a buried anchor" (237). Through, smell, touch and primal sound, Ma Kilman reconnects with the properties of the plant that are part of an ancestral heritage for which she has no words.

The horticultural sites in *Rupert Gray* establish the coordinates of a convoluted trajectory of signification within Caribbean writing. From the garden of Gwendoline Serle as a symbol of her own cultivated refinement, to the agricultural estates her father exploits for imperial profit, to the Botanic Gardens, where Linnaeus meets Ma Kilman in the conversations of Rupert and Lady Rothberry, Cobham both continues and anticipates the uses to which Caribbean writers have turned this complex symbol of refinement and exploitation, intimacy and alienation, beauty and pain.

Notes on Editorial Procedures

The original novel was, not surprisingly given Cobham's profession, written in newspaper style: that is, with every sentence comprising a new paragraph. This gives the text the breathless pace of a fast-breaking news item but, in the longer fiction form, leaves the reader in a constant state of unfulfilled excitement rather than experiencing a more customary series of calms and climaxes. We have therefore glued sentences together into paragraphs in a manner that allows the reader to read with anticipation but not anxiety.

Several spellings which occur only once and which are not supported by other known practice or variation of the period have been changed to reflect correct modern usage: palet → palette (chapter 1); okre → ochre (chapter 8). Established variants, even if archaic, have been kept as in the original, for example, amuck (amok) (chapter 2); roll (role) (chapter 6); gutteral (guttural) (chapter 17). Names of scientific families have been corrected and capitalized: leguminosae → Leguminosae; rosasae → Rosaceae (chapter 9). A few obvious errors have been silently corrected: moslem → Moslem (chapter 9); terrible band → terrible bang (chapter 11); possibilties → possibilities (chapter 16); change of air, and of scene, dietary → change of air, scene and diet (chapter 18); and Jollyman → Jolliman (chapter 19) (as in two previous incidences). Plausible missing words have been supplied in "wild bulls from the mainland *that* escaped" (chapter 14) and "lights in the dwellings of the *upper* classes" (chapter 19), and on the very first page, we have completed Rupert's costume by providing him with the "glossy tan *boots*" – more likely than shoes – omitted in the original.

RUPERT GRAY.
A TALE IN BLACK AND WHITE.

BY

STEPHEN NATHANIEL COBHAM.

TRINIDAD:
MIRROR PRINTING WORKS, 27, CHACON STREET, PORT-OF-SPAIN,

1907.

"Secundus dubiisque rectus."[†]

— DEBRETT'S.[†]

DEDICATION.

———

To him, whose sympathetic and gentlemanly demand placed me on my
mettle together upon authorship, this short Story is gratefully, aye,
respectfully, dedicated.

S. N. C.

CONTENTS.

CHAPTER I

The Home-coming

It was afternoon – eleven minutes to four. The Port-of-Spain Railway Station was the scene of hurrying and hustling. Cabs kept arriving in an endless procession. Coolies† staggered in under heavy burdens which they deposited with a gesture of relief. Country belles, in the latest style, sent their young men – flannel and white boots wearers, in white tunics and sporting hooked walking-sticks – to purchase tickets. Men with umbrellas and hand-bags crossing from the restaurant opposite hastily consulted their watches. The gong clanged everlastingly of each tram car† as it circled past. Newsboys, stumbling after reluctant buyers, hawked the daily papers. A row of hucksters† made the entrance lively with their good-natured invitations, as they sat waving off the flies from discussing the contents of their trays. Then last bell, closed doors, late arrivals. At one minute past the hour the train would start – the last down-train to San Fernando.†

At a window of one of the first-class carriages sat a young girl. Her eyes wandered over the sea which sparkled in the blazing sunlight like a sheet of liquid silver. There out in the distance on the southernmost confines of the shipping, a great ocean liner rode at anchor; its long, black hull a decisive contrast to its huge, red-painted chimneys. So it must have looked a while ago before the young girl quitted its deck.

But why was she, to all appearance a stranger from a far-off land, sitting so still, heedless of the bustle around? In what could she be so absorbed? Perhaps she was thinking of the happy short days spent on board, and of the many friendships formed. Isolation and a common danger never fail to forge the links of friendship.

The bloom of a genial outward passage lay fresh about her. Evidently her reverie could not be due to the effects of her voyage. Not so she sat on board where she had been the life and soul of everything. Was it the features of that brilliant seascape which made her so reflective? And who could this young girl be? Truth to tell, none of these causes was responsible for her state of mind.

Gwendoline Serle – for that was her name – had just received an impression. A strange influence was upon her. Not an hour ago the poignant vigour of a man's voice – masculine, musical – floated around her, and turning – the voice spoke as she leaned against the deck rails – she faced a full-blooded negro. One look at him sufficed to tell he was a man who earned his bread at in-door work. There was character in that face of his, shaded underneath his panama. He stood tall and athletic. His manner bespoke refinement and habitual self-respect. He wore a tweed suit of sombre grey, and the rubber heels of his glossy tan boots yielded noiseless footfalls, as crossing the deck to where she stood, he whispered low, "Miss Serle, I presume."

She nodded and looked surprised.

"This will explain my errand," he said, handing her a slip of paper.

It was the copy of a telegram, "From P. Serle, San Fernando, to R. Gray, chief clerk and accountant, firm of Serle & Murchison, Port-of-Spain;" so it was headed. It simply said: "Close for the day. See daughter safe per afternoon train."

One of the passengers who had landed had called at the store to say the young lady was on board. Her father being out of town, his accountant received the message and went off in the firm's boat. Nearing the steamer, nobody had pointed out Miss Serle. His quick eye, guided by the striking resemblance to her father, traced her out at once, as straining her eyes shorewards, she had stood on the deck, crowded with incoming passengers, bringing with them smiles and happy greetings, affectionate embraces; joyous, tearful, firm, hearty grips and a thousand questions of welfare.

"Are you Mr. Gray?" she had asked, perusing the slip.

"Yes," he answered, slightly inclining forward.

"Then I am quite ready," she said.

The daughter of Mr. Primrose Serle had watched his accountant go through every detail of her landing, struck by his ease and quiet self-sufficiency; and now, as she sat in the train, his voice, with its rich baritone, once more trembled in her ear.

"I am at your service, miss; I wish you to know that I travel in this very compartment." And so saying, he retired to a corner of the saloon,† with the air of a man satisfied with having done his duty.

．　．　．　．

Mr. Serle was at the railway station at San Fernando to welcome his daughter. He shed tears as he folded her to his bosom. Now twenty years of age, she was but ten when she sailed for Europe. The Serles were a proud old family, without a trace of intermixture.† A fortune had been spent on the education of the girl, who, with her father, was the only representative of the stock; she had also travelled extensively in the British Isles, France, Germany, Italy and Greece. Her father's immense wealth and good connections placed her in smart society in England; her diverse gifts and winning manners did the rest; her accomplishments comprised a great many branches of study; her body was strengthened by every kind of exercise proper for her sex; she excelled as a horsewoman, at tennis and in swimming; she was an elegant dancer; she handled a fine palette and sang exquisitely; she held medals, had walked off with prizes galore. The local press used always to advertize her successes. She had come out to spend with her father the last few years of his life as a man of business, from which he meant thence to retire, and finally settle down in Europe.

"How silent you have grown, Gwendoline. You are not the chatterbox you left Trinidad. Have you no questions to ask?" said her father as they drove along.

"Papa," she said, "I feel queer impressions. Who is that black man with the metal in his voice?"

Her father laughed. "Your first impressions must be a little queer, darling," he said; "your long absence makes you almost a foreigner. That is Rupert Gray, our trusty chief clerk and accountant. For the past two weeks the junior partner and I have been in this district buying up cocoa and doing a lot of other business. In crop time we prefer to be on the spot ourselves. This morning, to my delighted surprise, the accountant telegraphed to say you had arrived. I telegraphed back to him my directions to act as he did. You never wrote to tell me expect you by this mail,† you naughty little puss."

"I wanted to surprise you, papa dear," she said laughing as the cab stopped at the door of the firm's premises.

"It is a surprise – and a pleasant one indeed," said somebody listening from the door and helping her to alight – helping out what dawned upon him as a vision of feminine charm – form, soul, deportment.

All life long some men affect not to love. Books, politics, wine, pastimes – these divide their attention. Others, after long association, succumb late in life, guided in their choice by a judgment matured. A third type love on an impulse, without rhyme or reason. The junior partner looked into the face of the smiling girl and love came to him then and there. True love, free from all taint of interest: free from the recollection whose daughter she was: full of the sense that he, Lionel Murchison, man, had beheld Gwendoline Serle, maid, and loved her.

The firm of Serle and Murchison had their place of business in Port-of-Spain; but to facilitate the cocoa planters of the Naparimas,† ran a branch down there, where they were licensed to deal. They also owned broad cocoa fields on the slopes, and in the glens of Gran Couva,† and where Manzanilla's coconut palms suck moisture from the spongy beach.† Above their store at San Fernando they kept several furnished rooms, two of which the partners were now occupying; while the others came in handy for the accommodation of any merchant or planter friends or customers benighted in the southern borough.

That night after supper the junior partner went over to the hotel and engaged sleeping quarters. Dinner was usually served from the town restaurant. To-night a special menu was ordered. The accountant carried out the arrangements. He was invited to sit down with the party. The newly-arrived came down to do the honours, and did them like a queen. The black waiter from the hotel resented what he saw. "Nigga too black," he grumbled; "set down close bakra gul, tink heself big guvanah."† He actually went on to mark his disapproval of what he deemed an uncalled for preference shown to one of his own race, by purposely neglecting sundry items of attention due to the accountant. The omissions were more than pointing.

At length Mr. Serle brought him to his senses with: "How long have you been in the serving line?"

"Ten long years, sur," said the waiter.

"You behave as though you became a butler ten minutes ago," observed the old gentleman, regarding him from head to foot.

"Butler, sur," the waiter assured him, straightening up with his hands behind, "to Sir Graham Briggs, and the Lord Bishop, sur – whichin he dead, sur. Ask the Lord Bishop 'bout me, sur." Then he altered his attitude towards the negro guest. Never before had the old gentleman appeared to be in such splendid spirits.

"To-night," he said, after he had done ample justice to the viands, "I feel the goodness of Providence; I am supremely happy. Every stage of life has its own pleasures – its own enjoyments peculiar to itself. The laughing schoolboy deems himself the happiest of all. So does the passionate youth as he hangs upon the smiles of his lady-love. The man in his prime – in the heyday of rejoicing strength, looks down from the adult summit of his years, upon the earlier stages, and laughs – laughs at himself for having once been satisfied with the childish entertainment they afforded: as with self-congratulation, and a mood staid and serene, he piles up competency, acquires influence and power, gives away his daughters in marriage, and starts his sons in life: watches his wife grow mature, and teases her about her fleeting youth. Then, as green old age creeps on, and he dandles his grandchildren upon his knees, his, he calls the happiest lot of all, to live again in the successes and the fame of his issue, inspiring them to emulation by recounting the deeds of his well-spent life. Murchison – Rupert, let us drink to the health of my only child. Hallo! Murchison, what's come over you? You look to be in dreamland. Come, come, let's have some toast or another. You, Mr. Gray, wish us good luck."

The waiters hung around the door, gaping and whispering, as the accountant rose.

"It must be very gratifying to a father's heart," he began, "to be where you are to-night, Mr. Serle." Then looking over towards the lady, he continued: "I hope ere our tropical breezes blow the English roses from fair cheeks blooming at this board, some Knight, as of old, may pass along to keep the crimson there. May it be your privilege, sir, to live to see."

The white men's faces were all aglow. The black man's words were sweet. The three men stood, glasses in hand, and so her health was drunk. The lady bowed her thanks, rose and retired above stairs, still feeling the heave and lurch of the vessel, as when it traversed mountain waves, and glided up from Neptune's yawning troughs† – retired to rest but not to sleep. The strange magic of a black man's voice kept echoing in her ears, blended with the fancied roaring of winds, and the noise of mighty waters. It ranged itself around memories that would live – memories of the first impressions of her home-coming beneath the sunny skies of her native land – the land of the Humming Bird.†

CHAPTER II

Chief Clerk and Accountant

By first train next morning the accountant left San Fernando, where he had slept at the hotel after supping with the partners and the fair young lady. Quite a crowd lined the pavement in front of the block, enclosing the establishment of the firm of Serle and Murchison, in Port-of-Spain. Customers were there, clerks, work people, porters in groups or in pairs, in every variety of posture: their faces showing all shades of expression, from laughter to gravity. Many were the conjectures as to the cause of the late opening that morning. One man gave it as his opinion that it was the earliest symptom of bankruptcy. A second, taking up that cue, declared: "Ef me was marchant nevah keep black book-keepah."†

A third put it in this way: "Daughter, come, you understand me; overhaul de books, you understand me; find money missing, you understand me; no wuk to-day, you understand me." A fourth was more personal: "Dat fellah Ubut Gray, way he know? P'raps self de gal go keep de books. Old fahdah sen way Gray. Serve he right. Have fo' haul molasses fo' a livin' now."†

A fifth, more generous than the rest, a man of few words, delivered himself thus: "N-n-no. D-d-dat en fair. D-d-de boyo know 'e wuk. Is because he black. Au-au-all you nigga cuss. Bet you white dog never eat white dog. Who way don' like it g-g-jump;"† and doubling his fist, he swung his brawny right in true pugilistic fashion.

The other speakers, thinking discretion the better part,† let the stammerer have the last word.

"Hooray, hooray, book-keepah comin'," shouted a sixth, running amuck of the crowd in his boisterousness.

All eyes turned in one direction. There, in truth, the accountant, hurrying in from train. One loud "Ah!" escaped the lips of most.

"Good-morning, good-morning, everybody," he said cheerfully.

"Now, boys," he continued, producing large, heavy keys, "let us open up; and if things go right you shall have some beer to-day. The chief's daughter is come, and he is standing a treat."

"Hooray!" they shouted.

"Au-au-all you nigga cuss," opined somebody – hands a-pocket, back against a post surveying all.

Within five minutes work was in full swing. The men had set-to with a will. Reward, or the hope of it, acts like a charm on our frail natures. Even the patriot with his singleness of purpose has his reward. Let him but think of the approbation of posterity, the gratitude of his nation, and he will make superhuman efforts to achieve the almost impossible. The accountant before sitting at his desk set out on a round of inspection. He looked in, everywhere. The saw mill, the lumber yard with its busy labourers lifting while they sang, the rattling ice-machinery, the ship chandlery† branch with its dozen or so requisitions, the cocoa store† whence were being carted load after load, the wholesale provision store, ironmongery, patent fuel department, all came in for a share of attention. This firm's trade was colossal. Even sugar was one of their commodities. They came the biggest consignees in the colony.† The painstaking chief clerk returned to the starting point. At the door stood someone.

"How is the chief clerk and accountant?" the person asked.

"Hallo-o-o, Clarke," exclaimed the other in a tone of surprise, "glad to see you, Clarke. First time we've met since school days. How are times, old chap?"

"As you see – no work, no cash," said Clarke.

Rupert Gray surveyed his shabby outfit. Silence fell between them. The accountant was thinking how best to help him. Presently, he said, as though he had at last hit upon the right thing: "Say old chap, would you do tallying?"

"Do tallying," gasped Clarke clutching at his companion's hand, "do anything, any blessed thing."

"Well, then," continued the accountant, rising and opening a drawer labelled "Workpeople's Advance Loans",† "here's some money. Get a new outfit and come on at once."

While Clarke was murmuring thanks, Gray led him upstairs. Walking to an open window overlooking the Gulf of Paria,† he took down a long spyglass, and for a second or so, searched the horizon. Then handing it to his companion, said: "Do you see that schooner† yonder? She is a fortnight out from North Carolina with five hundred thousand feet of pine."

Clarke took the glass, and pointing it in the direction indicated, said: "Yes, I see her upon the skyline bearing into port."

"Before noon she will want a tallying clerk on board of her," explained Gray.

Without another word Clarke bounded down the stairs, skipping four, five at a time. Within two hours he re-appeared, transformed from head to foot – hat, suit, boots – thanks to some ready-made clothing department.

"Bravo, lad," said Gray in astonishment; "bound to succeed in life. Commend me to men of swift action. Drones call that impulse. Your personal appearance is in your favour, old boy." Rupert Gray took Jacob Clarke aside and initiated him into the shallow mysteries of tallying. Meanwhile the schooner, after tacking the whole morning, came to anchor.

"Now, the next thing," said Gray, "is that you get on board of her without delay. Of course you shall be at it all night, you know. You will get your meals on board. No trouble whatever. The cargo being ours, you are entitled to get alongside in the firm's boat. Pierre———"

"Ah-ah-comin', boss," shouted Pierre as he lumbered up.

"Place this gentleman alongside the *Mary Sherman*."

"R-r-r-right, sir."

Clark sank into a chair quite overcome. All this seemed like a dream to him. Letting his head fall towards his knees, he wept for some time. Sympathy, sweet and kind, generosity and unselfishness, these reach the human heart, and bring out that sense of indebtedness, that desire to repay, that despair at being unable to repay, the sum total of which is gratitude, a magnificent quality in any man – a "touch of human nature which makes the whole world kin."

"B-b-b-but, Mr. Gray, O, an you s-say you done help you cullah, c-c-c-since d-d-dat last f-fellah p-p-put you in,"† remonstrated Pierre.

"Silence, Pierre, and know your place. Go and wait outside till the gentleman is ready."

Pierre, wearing quite an injured look, did as he was told.

"Buck up, Starch-Nose," said Gray in a jolly tone slapping his friend on the back as hard as he could. "Starch Nose" was Clarke's nickname at school. "Come this way," continued the accountant "and bathe your face. Use my napkin. Put back your handkerchief. That's something like it. Now you look fresh. Pierre————"

"Ah-ah, an you sen' me outside, boss? Ah-ah must t-take time to reach," answered Pierre in a far-away voice as he rolled in looking quite logical.

"Get us something to drink," said the accountant, handing him the coin.

Pierre's eyes brightened. He took the money and darted off. In a few minutes he was back. "B-b-b-boss, O," he called, "l-leave my sh-share in the bottle."

"Come, Starch Nose," said Gray, "take a good one – keep your courage up."

"I owe you a debt of gratitude, Gray, which I can never adequately discharge. The man who puts a penny in another's way is the friend," said Clarke, pouring out a stout lot.

"Rupy Gray, old boy," he continued, holding the accountant's arm, "you are an exceptional negro. Men like you we don't come across every day. Here in Trinidad you find a coloured man moving heaven and earth to do those a good turn who neither need nor care for it. He thinks it nothing to turn his back against true merit, aspiring, striving, battling bravely through good and evil report, with every good intention, every noble impulse. Nay, your purse-proud underminer goes a step farther. He is careful to pile every possible obstacle upon the agony. His pulling of strings, and stirring up of wavering fires, he nicknames diplomacy. He wants to befriend you without your knowing, he says. How he trots about minimising your virtue, and multiplying your rare vices: scattering broad-cast as he goes, poisonous seeds of slander, grains of cruel detraction. Then, throwing up both hands with a look of horror in his innocent face, he exclaims: 'What a prodigy of iniquity!' No matter how his own dunghill festers he pelts his neighbour's glass-windows like a madcap rioter. Another type – poor tool – does not remember how tribulation pounded him in days of yore. Re-instated at last by smiling fortune, see him expand, or rather contract into a mercenary oppressor – a blindfolded shylock – a miserable exacter of his pound of flesh![†] Mark his loud strutting – shoulders affected – false face in the air – head twisting and turning to the cardinal points – O ye shades of Crusoe's man![†] – rejoicing in the thought that God has spared even him to gain some notoriety by being mischievous and naughty. What admirable scrupulous greed: what decent lust after coin! Mark his averted guilt looks as, grabbing his victim by the throat he blurts out his reasonable demand: 'Make bricks without clay – blood out of stone.' Gray, my friend, thanks for your goodness, and excuse my warmth, my justifiable contempt, my righteous indignation."

"Don't mention it, old boy. Don't mind these things. There are negroes and negroes. There are bad and good in every race. This is your chance. Go in and win," said Rupert Gray.

They drank together.

"Pierre, the gentleman is ready," called the accountant.

"Ah-ah, running back wid d-de two glass fuss: an aftah ah comin' " explained Pierre, as he cleared the table – Dawson[†] and all.

"Gray, my dear friend, have you any straight tips to give me, going out to work as I am, among the shipping for the first time?" added Clarke.

"No. None that I can think of," said Gray – "except perhaps this – but it applies generally – handle your authority mildly. That's the great lesson West Indian natives have yet to learn. Never be a screw upon men. The best employers glory in a merciful under-servant."

"Yes," replied Clarke, "but have you noticed that our people do not – will not respect men of their own colour in authority?"

"True," urged Gray, "and for that very reason, you in authority ought not to show resentment. You are supposed to be the cream of your people, crowning the lees and dregs below, tainted with traces of narrow prejudices, which will only wear away with years. Use tact and mother-wit, and there's an end to it. *Au revoir.*"

The signal of a schooner still dangled from the lofty staff before the

Custom House door. Locomotive engines, flying vermillion flags, shunted their after-math of trucks over-laden with reeking puncheons.[†]

Already industrious Indian matrons – red-spittled Madrassees[†] – armed with buckets, were boarding the united chariots ere their wheels grew cold. A watering cart followed in the wake of a heavy stone-crusher along the convex street, improving on the recipe Sir John McAdam gave to the world.[†] Groups of workingmen, idling for weeks together, were sauntering everywhere with thoughts of home upon their honest faces. The *Kennet* and the *Spey,* one on either side, hugged the herculean jetty.

Wily fruiterers – white-aproned Bimshire wives[†] – haggled over oranges and bananas with sailors and new-comers unused to local market prices. All is fair in the love and war of bargaining and barter, even on the wharf, where ragged urchins, scarce at years of discretion, learnt the ways of the world in this rough-and-tumble environment – this scrambling-ground for daily bread – this vortex of survival. The struggle for fortune shifts over to the water. Flatmen slowly hoist or reef sails.[†] Pigmy steam launches and a fleet of boats of all sizes with oars like wooden fins, ply all day.

Who can spare time to notice the long broadening tracks of foam across the bosom of the deep? Off yonder a stupendous crane wheels lazily for ever, its half-greased mechanism creaking and groaning. The blazing day star – Phoebus Apollo[†] – the sun-god of old, is careering in his chariot, high overhead, in all his torrid majesty, softening the asphalt between the tram lines and causing the surface of the flinty thoroughfare to burn quickening footsteps – boots or no boots. Smart-looking youngsters busy themselves between Customs, or bank and counting house, with red-marked paper bags of money. Tallying clerks keep feeling in the pockets of their coarse brown linen, or snow-white blouses, for note-book or monster lead-pencil.

To-day a new man joins their ranks. Jacob Canaan Clarke, tall and unstately, swaggers across the broad, white quay towards the boat in waiting. His body sways pompously from side to side like a ship at sea. He refuses to pause, will not yield to the rattling carts whose drivers, swearing angrily at him, are forced to slacken pace, while they gibe him for a gait naturally restless, and made more so just now by a sense of present success, finished off with a good glass of ardent spirits.

CHAPTER III

The Last Lesson

Two weeks had flown since Gwendoline Serle had joined her father in the Naparimas. His engagements having all come to a fulfilment, Mr. Serle brought home his daughter. In the interim, his house outside the suburbs of Port-of-Spain underwent the repairs necessary to her comfort.

The house, built for ease in the tropics, was beautiful for situation. It stood on a knoll, hidden among ancient trees, in the centre of a broad cocoa field, parted by a river which leaped and danced in its course to the sea – now over rocks in Cascades[†] – now lost in glade – now meandering through open country, a streak, twixt rich verdure – now a crystal current along pebble-bed – now smooth water under bridges – now imprisoned in overflowing reservoirs by the artifice and the hardihood of man – but ever issuing forth in quest of the open sea in obedience to the law of level.

The fortnight had proved a time of busy preparation. A lady's maid joined the staff of servants. The house was freshly painted throughout; the furniture varnished; beautiful plots formed of the greenest turfs were laid out; to the left of these, near an inward curve of the river, was the tennis court; high over-arching bamboos shaded seats around their immemorial clumps; garden parties were frequent.

Gwendoline Serle was all refinement and kindliness; she grew very popular. Some people have the gift to be sought after by one sex only. Gwendoline attracted both. "Sunflower Manse"[†] became a social shrine of pilgrimage. "Sunflower Manse" was how she baptized her home; and with her own artistic brush, painted that legend on the front of the veran-

dah, round whose marble pillars stephanotis[†] clambered. In the centre of
the garden grew a great colony of sunflowers[†] – the largest ever seen
here. Their brilliant yellow would have baffled the skill of the most fas-
tidious colourist; the patch fringed with myrtle[†] was heart-shaped,
enclosed by upturned bottles, blue, green, and colourless,[†] following in
order. From this the house derived its name, "Sunflower Manse."
Gwendoline's hand had a marvellous effect upon plants; before long her
garden was "a thing of beauty."[†] It was a pleasure to her father to spend
hours in it.

The old man lived anew, her sunny nature cheered him, he wished to
live to enjoy his child, she was to him "a ministering angel,"[†] she talked
and read to him. He would sit at times when the moonlight fell on hill
and river and listen to her singing till his eyes moistened. Sweet in a parent's ear is the earliest cry of the babe. Sweet the reckless laugh of romp-
ing childhood later on: but who could tell what exquisiteness welled up
in the soul of this honest-hearted old widower, as his daughter's music
awakened slumbering emotions, and made his heart yearn after

> "The touch of a vanish'd hand
> And the sound of a voice that is still."[†]

"Do you feel lonely very often, Gwendoline?" he asked one morning,
as, arm in arm, they neared the gate. Her father lingered. The carriage
was in waiting.

"O, no, papa dear, not very often. My time is pretty well taken up. I
have to be in the garden at sunrise. My next pleasure is to take leave of
you here, every morning. Then in less than an hour Mr. Gray is here to
inspect my shorthand and typewriting exercise.[†] How kind of you, papa
dear, to spare your busy clerk three days in each week that I may extend
my knowledge. I must say, he is a very conscientious and exacting
instructor. Papa, I actually fear the accountant. I never met such serious-
ness before. He behaves in such a silent way, you know, with a sort of
faraway semi-respectful hauteur that puzzles me."

Her father laughed outright: "Search the world through," he said,
"and you will never find a more faithful employé."

"After the accountant is gone," continued Gwendoline, "I am then in
a frame of mind for mental work. I do some light reading. First, I read

romance, then poetry. I am doing my Shakespeare over. Papa, does not the accountant remind one of Othello?"[†]

Her father looked amused: "Rupert like Othello. Murchison must hear this joke. Othello was a soldier, Gwendoline, an exponent of strength," he reminded her, laughing.

"But, papa," she protested, "Mr. Murchison himself said that Mr. Gray knows fencing and pugilism; that he is as strong as Sandow;[†] that his muscles are so well developed as to have enabled him to lift a heavy load of something or other and toss it on to a cart."

"That is a fact," answered her father, a little more serious, "that boy does not shame the food he eats. But finish telling me of your day's fixtures,[†] little daughter."

"I read till luncheon," she went on, "when some of 'the girls' are sure to be here. Some hours later we have pastime. Then it is dinner time, when there is always more news about the doings of your stand-offish accountant: and here my programme ends. Amen."

"I was thinking, Gwendoline," said her father gravely, "you might be happier, if you had some friend of yours to stay with you at "Sunflower Manse." Why do you not send for your friend, the lady doctor – Miss – Miss Allcock?"

"Miss Badenock, you mean," laughed Gwendoline. "Thanks, dear papa, I shall think it over," and she waved her tiny kerchief till he was out of sight.

Gwendoline ran back to the house, and in no time type-wrote a letter of invitation to Florence Badenock. The thought had occurred to her pretty often. Her father's suggestion this morning decided the matter. Having completed her letter, she hurried back to the gate. Evidently she was quite anxious. Leaning her chin there upon the back of her hands for some time, she became lost in thought; let us hope over the letter just written!

The rolling of carriage wheels soon recalled her out of dream-land. The accountant was coming. The landeau[†] which took down her father always fetched him up. Seeing the young mistress of the household, the coachman pulled up his pair. The accountant looked out and bowed.

An impulse seized Gwendoline Serle. Impulse, that pitfall of the unwary – that initial prompting of the heart – many times wrong, sometimes right, inwardly impelling women, less often men, to act naturally. No sooner the carriage stopped than she stepped into it and seated herself beside her father's accountant. Homeward thundered the spirited steeds, their hoofs ploughing up the new-laid gravel. The house stood a long way in.

All the servants noticed them. The maid, under pretence of airing a carpet, popped her head out of a window. The cook came to the kitchen door stripping a fat bird. The under gardener looked after them wonderingly as bareheaded Miss Serle alighted and led the way through the verandah, the hose in his hand, by some mischance, drenching the Portuguese† head gardener as if his beard was on fire. This unexpected face-bath caused that frightened horticulturist to leap sky-high in spite of his heavy clogs.

The maid came downstairs, passing and re-passing the groom. "You and I next," he remarked to her, unharnessing the horses.

"I am the least of the apostles,"† she replied, shaking her head in the negative, not looking right nor left, as she purposely swept past him; "and furthermore," she added at the last, condescending to turn her head for an instant, "Dr. Johnson wrote in the days of King George the Third that that is detrimental."† Heaven only knows where she picked up that from. Once having got hold of the idea that her mistress liked books, she affected literature.

"So this is our last lesson, Mr. Gray," said Gwendoline, leading the way to the library which was situated in the mid-eastern wing of the building.

"Yes, indeed, Miss Serle," he said, "how time flies. To-day is exactly three months since we began. May I have your exercises?"

The pupil produced them. First he looked through her shorthand. There was no fault. "Excellent," he wrote across it. Next she presented her typewriting. "This," she said, "is the result of my first trial at the new typewriter with the silver keys papa gave me on my birthday. How pretty, Mr. Gray, does the script type† look! These are invitations to some theatricals† I shall be having soon; these are visiting cards; these are invitations to Miss Muriel Onslow's wedding next September; this last is a letter hurriedly done to a friend of mine – a lady doctor in Scotland – specialist in tropical fevers – I am inviting to come out to Trinidad, though not to practise. Your name is mentioned in it, do you know that, Mr. Gray?"

"My name!" he asked in surprise, adding, "what a pity Miss Serle, I have spoilt your letter by scribbling the word 'Excellent' in red lead across it."

"It doesn't matter," she assured him, "I shall explain it in a post-script."

"And now, Miss Serle," he said solemnly, "this brings our relationship of instructor and pupil to an end; you have done well; you have been very apt; your grasp is admirable; you never had to be told twice; I respect your intellect."

A blush of earnestness suffused her face. "My grateful thanks are due to you, Mr. Gray," she said. "You have not taught me shorthand and typewriting – you have done more than that – you have taught me how to teach myself those subjects. You have communicated power to me. All that remains now is that I should plod on alone. You have not instructed me in knowledge; you have educated me to the acquiring of knowledge. With knowledge we triumph. Knowledge is an iron-bound coast against which the waves of ignorance and spite vainly spend their force. Help some people to acquire that, and you have a friend for life. A good teacher can never be forgotten. The plastic minds he moulds carry the impress of his hand throughout life. Pray accept this slender gift," she continued, unclasping a tiny box, which encased in its satin lining a gold scarf pin. Its head was a half sovereign.

"Can you guess what coin is this?" she asked.

The pathos in her voice held him mute. He could only shake his head in the negative.

"This coin," she explained, "got you into my father's service. Do you not remember how fifteen years ago he dropped it in the street, and you, then quite a lad, picked it up and restored it to him?"

"Yes, yes, I remember," said the accountant, "and do you mean, Miss Serle, that Mr. Serle kept the piece of money all the time?"

"Yes," she answered, "he declared he never meant to part with it. It was to have gone down for an heirloom."

"Fancy that," said the accountant, visibly touched.

"Let me settle it into your tie with my own hands," she said, removing the pin from its case, which she gently placed on the typewriter. She had first to undo his necktie, and to arrange it in the form usually adapted to wearing scarf pins. While thus engaged, the pin lay thrust under the lace of gossamer fringing her low square fronted bodice. Her hands trembled a good deal. She was longer at it than she bargained for. Her colour came and went. The wind swelled out her bishop's sleeves, short only to her elbow.[†] The cream lace curtains flapped loosely about the library windows; through them the morning sunlight kept working and weaving on the green walls around, on her pretty head, her sad pale face, and the light blue folds that wrapped her "form divine."[†] They looked to be of even height, both tall and stately. He felt her fragrant breath laving his brow as her respiration came deep and full. A canary bird, perched within a large cage, was flooding the room with melody.

At length, completing her self-imposed task, she stepped back to view the effect. "There," she said, as their eyes met. "I had to plead very hard before papa would consent to part with that half sovereign, Mr. Gray; nobody else could have got it from him. The gift is but a commonplace one, but there is merit in the intention; wear it for my sake as long as you live." And before he could make reply she fled from the room.

CHAPTER IV

Cupid's Bow Did Carry a Twin Shaft

Like one in a dream, Rupert Gray left "Sunflower Manse." He declined the coachman's offer to run him down. "No, thank you, Lewis," he said; "I prefer to walk."

"But the sun is stinging, sir."

"I shall catch St. Clair car.[†] I am a negro born in the tropics, one of those who do not regret their colour," said the accountant, making a show at lightheartedness and tossing him a tip.

Rupert Gray wanted to think. His feelings were mixed. Uppermost were thoughts of loyalty and attachment to his master, coupled with deep regret at the blemish now threatening. He could see clearly what was what; had seen it long ago. The woman to conceal her love is not yet born. A man may try not to conduce to, nor foster and increase it, but detect it he must, unless he be a blind hypocrite. Again, once let it dawn upon her, that her love is, or can be returned – and sometimes even when it cannot be returned – and "not gods, men, nor columns,"[†] will avail to bar the rising tide. Just you season your self-control with some spice of good manners, and you are safe. Precisely the opposite of what you expect will happen.

What was now to be his line of conduct, the accountant was musing. Surely, knowing Trinidad as he did, was it not hopeless to entertain such a notion? Neither her father nor society would be for it. His own people, those of his own colour, would be the first to scoff, to taunt and insult, to wound and shatter the feelings of the sensitive creature who was brave enough to entrust her happiness to his guardianship. What was he going to do? Might he not, as far as gallantry would permit, continue his plan of passive resistance? Is such a course manlike, chivalrous?

But wait. After all, might he not be mistaking friendship for love? Her treatment of him might only be the counterpart of her father's benevolence – the kindliness of a generous nature? But what of the scene just enacted? Clearly that meant something – something calling eloquently from swimming eyes and quivering lips, from her nervousness, as she smoothed back the stray hair frizzled by the breezes: something in the words spoken, that now kept recurring to him. "There is merit in the intention. Wear it for my sake as long as you live." Words which gave him secret pleasure. Remember he was a man. A woman of worth had said them.

Again and again he resolved no harm could come of it. Again and again his conscience warned him there would be harm. Ever and anon the sweet, pale face of Gwendoline Serle rose up before him like that of a mermaid out of the sea, haunting his pity – appealing to his vanity, stirring all the great depth of love in his nature, and scattering to the four winds of heaven every resolution ere it took shape. O woman, woman, a temptress from the earth's natal day; a siren luring life's mariners devious, spreading witchery with her beauty and conquest with her tears!

Meanwhile, Gwendoline Serle had sought the privacy of her boudoir. Turning the key, she threw herself upon a couch, and burying her face in the cushion, found relief in a hearty outburst peculiar to temperaments like hers. Repentance, pride of sex, struggled against love and struggled in vain. Doubts, fears, hopes, knocked alternately at her heart's door. How little she dreamt to what extent the other was impressed. Our means of knowing things are limited. Good for us it is so. Limit of the scope of human ken is incidental to mortality – is a law of our being – underlies all energy and activity – makes for progression. All nature depends upon each single law and each single law upon all nature.

Blinded by her own great love, it did not occur to her that men also are weak. It did not occur to her that Cupid's bow did carry a twin shaft, which, with unerring exactitude, hit two marks. Let none despair, who, loving first, awaits the final issue. Love sleeps in every bosom. The trouble is to awaken it. The human heart is a musical instrument: touch but the relative chords, and life's discord vanishes. Be a heart never so hard – a nature never so cold – a character never so eccentric – somewhere in God's world there breathes a kindred spirit, whose breath could soften, whose warmth thaw, whose intuition decipher, the refractory tone. It is in selection the success seems to lie. Each soul, on earth has its counterpart. To hold otherwise would be to challenge the skill, the workmanship of God. You postulate Deity looking down upon his creatures – a multitude of misfits – seeking in vain to conform to the laws of a non-existent adaptation. But it is otherwise.

She had met a kindred spirit – so thought Gwendoline Serle – a God-given second self, made up of a cluster of the finest qualities, underneath a dark complexion. But what would society say? What would become of her? There are times when every woman, no matter how far lost, sits and thus questions herself. Fancy, Gwendoline Serle loving a black man! She had declined to marry Captain Polo. Lord Trotter, the harum scarum young English patrician, pleaded in vain. In vain he promised to give up gambling on Sundays. She sent him and his offer to the right about. Then there was old Sir Graham Sprightly, C.M.G.,[†] who never tired of persuading her to be an old man's darling. Last of all was good, honest, steady Lionel Murchison, who adored her from the day of her homecoming. He was her father's junior partner. His father and hers had started life together in Trinidad, in the days when sugar was king.[†] To all these suitors she gave the self-same answer: "A loveless marriage is a torture."

Her eyes fell upon her father's accountant with the cultured looking face of ebony. Her pity went out to him in his proud humility, his civility. Her spirit rose in revolt against colour distinction. She flung away regard for the rules of her order. He was worthy, she felt, of any sacrifice to be made.

Albeit, the thought kept haunting her, that she had given herself away. She had paid the purchase money before the article was forthcoming; and now she was at the mercy of the other side. At least so she thought. Had she remained passive and endeavoured to hide away her sentiments, what then? Would he have sought to discover them? What did he think of her, now, she wondered. Were there any other white girls in Trinidad in a parallel situation? These were her reflections, as at that early hour she dressed for the evening, and seated herself in the library with her Shakespeare open before her.

"Edith," she charged her maid, "I will see no one. I am indisposed to-day, do you hear?"

"Yes, miss," said Edith, sympathetically.

Edith carried out her mistress' instructions to the letter. In vain pretty little Muriel Onslow tried to "see dear Gwen about the prints."

"She is not at home, Miss Onslow," insisted Edith, "the poor creature are interposed. She were typewritering in shorthand since God made morning: and Dr. Johnson wrote in the days of King George that that is detrimental."

CHAPTER V

"All Will Be Well with Rupert Gray"

The next day was a busy one at the store. Customers were coming in from all parts. The accountant had not had time even to have his breakfast. The two partners upstairs were engaged in a long conference with a stranger. During a lull in the rush of business, the senior spoke to the accountant through the tube.†

"Can you spare time to come to me?" he asked.

"Very well, sir."

Gray's heart leaped; had anything gone wrong; could it be about Gwendoline he wished to speak? Jacob Clarke sat at the desk; whenever not out among the shipping, he was sure to be at the store where, the typewriter having been placed at his disposal, his fingers soon learnt how to fingle† the keys of the mercantile piano. "I must go and see what the chief wants," said Gray, "bring over all these items to the debit, and carry forward the total."

The accountant went upstairs; his misgivings were awful; nevertheless he must endure. The stranger was an American – a man with a clean-shaven, practical face.

"Take a seat, Mr. Gray," said his employer.

The accountant winced at a handle being put to his name. When your employer puts a handle to your name, contrary to his wont, look out, as sailors say, squall ahoy. Serious business was really in progress.

"Now, Mr. Gray," began the strange gentleman, in the real nasal twang† of the out-and-out New Yorker, "we Americans believe in brains; I guess and calculate you have a big lot of it; out there in the States a man like you will shine; your ability to converse in German, French and Spanish would stand you in tip-top stead. Come out to the States with me for three hundred and fifty dollars per month, and a house to live in," and the speaker fastened upon the accountant eyes of will power.

The accountant thought for a while. There was this peculiarity about him – when his mind was at work his face then seemed to be in repose. Nobody spoke. The senior partner sat at his desk on a low dais, where also on his left the stranger sat tilting his chair back to the newly white-washed wall, and bringing off the lime upon his coat sleeves.

The junior partner sat on a table with one foot still resting on the floor, a couple of feet before the dais. Between the dais and this table, against which he leaned his elbow, sat the accountant considering the tempting offer. The United States always held a fascination for him. He longed to walk among the negroes of the South; to study them at home, to compare them with their West Indian brethren, and to make himself useful and famous among them. That was his inclination.

Now, inclination is the heaviest drawback to the drawing of correct inferences. A man may be inclined to do a thing for which he is not fit, or disinclined where he is totally fit. Inclination is not fitness. In the process of reasoning one has to be careful to keep it clear outside the ring. Chronic inclination becomes bias or prejudice. This mental disease finds a genial habitat in the mind's eye, and partial or total mental blind-ness is the result. Such minds are warped badly, are weakened. The fac-ulty of dispassionate judgment grows clogged. The form of the disease varies. It may be a dislike, a distrust, a fear. It may be the result of a wild rumour, of a baseless accusation lodged in the mind. It may be an influ-ence by a stronger will, or a certain belief, the popular opinion – noth-ing more is needed. The conclusion is jumped. The accountant weighed the *pros* and *cons* nicely, and without flurry.

Then, regarding the New Yorker steadily, he said: "I thank you very, very much, sir, for your generous offer; but I have no mind at present to change my situation."

"Sentiment, I guess," said the New Yorker, bringing down his chair as it creaked under his weight, and talking in his nose more than ever. Then, as if half soliloquising, he added: "Sentiment. Don't want to leave Mr. Serle, I guess. Three hundred and fifty dollars per month, with the chances of becoming a black millionaire some day! You British negroes will die of sentiment. The Uncle Sam negro[†] has less book-learning, but I guess and calculate he is deucedly more practical."

"Would you like to try Jacob Clarke," asked the accountant; "he has just passed his examination for a chartered accountant."

"Who coached him?" asked the New Yorker.

"I did."

"Did he pay?"

"No, he got it free."

"Well," said the American, "I guess and calculate he was the first to approach me, application in hand – four pages of foolscap. Look here, Esau Clarke,[†] says I, life is too short to spend time over that paper. You're a bit too previous. You gallop ahead to collar that job. You're no friend to your pal."

The accountant showed no surprise. He felt none. Clarke had every right, he thought, to try for himself. One circumstance, however, was against him. It was known that the American capitalist was trying hard to secure Gray's services. That was no secret. Why, then, did Clarke make a secret of his applying?

"My spirit never went with that man's, somehow," observed the junior partner.

"That sort of sharp practice will not succeed in the end," said the senior.

"Shan't see New York at my expense, anyhow;" jerked in the New Yorker; "have him at tallying, keep him at that. That blooming noisy haw-haw style[†] tells us he is nothing but an empty vessel. Good-bye, gentlemen. Mr. Gray," he added, turning back, "anytime you hit New York, just look up the Sherman lumber depôt and you'll be welcome," and away he strolled.

"Now, Rupert," said the senior partner who had refrained from interfering with the New Yorker's proposal, "we, too, have an offer, not an offer exactly, but an invitation to extend to you. Soon I shall be retiring from business. Mr. Murchison is thinking to buy in the goodwill. He desires to admit you into partnership. The four thousand dollars now standing to your credit with us will constitute a large enough sum for the purpose. A very goodly saving that, for a young fellow – a man of colour besides. You ought not to feel hurt, if I say your people have yet to learn how to be provident. They live too much in the present, preferring fine clothes to Crown lands; large rental to small freehold.[†] They imitate the extravagance of the rich, but avoid making the sacrifices whereby riches accrue. Of course, you will be held out as a partner. We are not ashamed of the association in the least. I had my solicitor prepare the deed before he sailed for Europe. It is very elaborate and will take time to peruse.

"That you can do at your leisure. Blank spaces are left for names and dates. It will be executed on the day of my retirement: and now, my young friend, let me be the first to congratulate you," he continued, with apparent feeling; "you have worked well in your time. You never found yourself above reproof. You ever paid us the respect due from a subordinate. Honesty, truthfulness, strict integrity, marked all your dealings. Through you, we have great hopes in the future of your people, for nature never throws away the mould in which good samples are fashioned. My boy, seeking as you are, the summit of life's success, it behoves you to be circumspect. You shall have to think, think, think. You shall have to know when to, and when not to act. Mistakes you must make. The late Bishop Hayes[†] always said 'The man who makes no mistakes, makes nothing.' Great men rectify their mistakes, and turn them to advantage. Enemies must abound. They are a necessary evil. Thank God for enemies. Never mind for an instant. Give them the go-by. Caesar burnt his enemies' letters falling into his hands. The man with the fiercest enemies gets the truest friends. In the world there will always be good men and true, unwilling to be tools in the hands of wicked conspirators. Men who are willing to see merit in every case, and with that end in view, look clear over the heads of those bent on another's ruin. I hope you will live to be all that you expect to be."

The accountant thanked the senior partner.

"Promotion," said the junior partner, addressing Rupert Gray, "spoils some men. I hope it will not be so in your case. You have obeyed well, you ought to command well." And rising, he grasped the accountant's hand in a firm grip, each looking the other straight in the face, while the old head of the firm, his face beaming with that satisfaction born of being instrumental in helping others, came and stood between, a hand on the shoulder of each, and said: "O, all will be well with Rupert Gray, already weighed in the balance a thousand times and never found want-ing.† No, not once."

33

CHAPTER VI

The Bachelor's Button, White

The private theatricals Gwendoline was preparing would be coming off in a few days. The stage was already fitted up at the northern end of the spacious hall at "Sunflower Manse." The decorations were superb; flags of all nations were willingly lent by Mr. Murchison. Never before were colours so blended; here her artistic taste had full scope. All the girls flocked to help. There would be two rehearsals before the event.

The play was written by a native; none of his people therefore cared to read it, and the books lay unsold at the booksellers.† Gwendoline thought to help the discouraged author, who in his misery sought her out. If people once got to know that the play was staged at "Sunflower Manse," the books would sell; so she sent invitations to Press representatives, and devoted much time and labour in perfecting herself in her own part.

"Papa," she said at night, handing her father the book, "follow my passages," and she began to interpret them by voice and gesture.

"Very fine," remarked he, when she had concluded, more pleased to watch her than listen to the lines.

"I do admire the verses of that song from the head of Abbotsford,"† she said; "I should enjoy hearing them rendered by an elocutionist of the stamp of Mr. Gray. What a feast would his rich voice make of them."

"I will send him to you to-morrow," said her father; "it will be a welcome change for Rupert, from the counting house to the stage." Mr. Serle did not forget his promise. His word, once given to his daughter, he never broke.

The landeau that took him down fetched up the accountant. His pulse quickened as he neared the familiar mansion. How sweet is that sadness one feels on revisiting familiar places, linked with pleasant memories of what has ceased to be?

Since the morning in the library they had not met. Gwendoline sat before the stage awaiting him. She had summoned up all her powers of self-control. Their meeting was formal. Both were guarded; each seemed to be playing the same game. The accountant was smitten with admiration of the decorations.

"Now, Mr. Gray," said Gwendoline, placing the book into his hand, "I want a model; I sent for you to interpret my part."

"Who is sustaining the role of Ethelred Wencelas,† the hero of the story," he asked, turning over the leaves.

"That inimitable Irving† of Trinidad, Mr. Johannes Warbattleton;† and he it is who has also very cleverly dramatised it," she said, handing him a programme very creditably typewritten.

"I see," said Rupert Gray, "you have borrowed some of the "greater lights" of the Port-of-Spain Theatrical Club.† He with the eagle nose will look down from the boards. The dapper little St. Maryite† will hold his own. That talented artist, called after him who doubled the Cape of Good Hope will treat the audience to an exhibition of orthodox gestures. That Arima star, named after the hero of Barra,† will be there. A graceful lady will, in musical accent, sustain her reputation. Miss Le Purple will preside at the instrument, improvising on the melo-dramatic idylls as in her Brussels days. Scenery and stage effect will be entrusted to the care of Mr. St. Philipot St. Jin. I see there will be dancing afterwards. How will you manage, Miss Serle, with your coloured guests?"

"O, Mr. Gray, I am so sorry," she said. "In England that could never happen. It was with great difficulty I managed to prevail upon the whites to take part at all in the performance. There was an ugly hitch at the last rehearsal. One of the coloured players had to lead in the gipsy – Miss Marion Allwhite. She drew herself away with such scorn that after the practice Mr. George Hubert,† the author, told me the coloured players had decided not to stay for the dancing."

"I am sure the coloured players do not care to be deemed guests. They consider they are lending their talent for the benefit of the author," said

Rupert Gray, trying to dissipate her genuine uneasiness, as he mounted the stage and commenced reciting.

She seated herself at a table on the stage, propping up her chin. Her eyes were fixed steadily on him. As he warmed to his theme he seemed to grow forgetful of her presence.

Here was a picture! The speaker, standing midst a blaze of colour with the lady for all his audience, his sombre garment forming a contrast to every hue around. A disappointed love-match was the subject-matter of the play. The heroine seemed to take comfort from the thought that fate and not falsehood had made the severance. She was made to sing, on the eve of her dying, verses of a threnody found in Walter Scott.† The words were those of the self-same roundelay Fitz Eustace sang to beguile the tedious hours of Lord Marmion after his all-day ride across "the heights of Lammermoor."†

Rupert Gray's gestures were few. His matchless voice rang through every shade of sentiment. He lifted it as he reached the climax till all the silver in it seemed to chime like fairy bells challenging the acoustics of the fretted roof: then slowly, gradually, it fell away, as, fully and clearly, the author's meaning walked out in every phrase, concluding with the romantic refrain:–

> "Eleu loro, Eleu loro
> Never, O never."†

Gwendoline sat rapt

> "As it were,
> Nerves . . . all chained up in alabaster
> As Daphne was.
> Rootbound that fled Apollo."†

Not Vishnu, with the flame flashing out from finger tips, could have rained more magnetism around upon his Brahman votaries,† than did this dusky master of the histrionic art, in one superb sweep of his extended arm from right to left.

Lord Byron sings that–

> "Women, like moths, are caught by glare."†

Gwendoline Serle truly acted like a moth. Here, of her own accord, she had again placed herself under the subtle fascination of a voice and presence which did havoc to her self-control. Her pride and admiration deepened into awe, which gave place to a feeling of unworthiness, which in its turn gave place to doubt and uncertainty – which developed despair. Silently, silently, her tears began to flow; he set down her emotion to the pathos in the passage.

"Edith is coming, do not let her see your tears," he said.

Before Gwendoline could get behind the scenes Edith was upon them, followed by a lady looking like a foreigner, with a touch of command in her bold, free stride, and a slight bend of carriage.

"O! Gwendoline, dearest Gwendoline," exclaimed the stranger, springing on to the stage; "are you not glad to see me?"

Florence Badenock, the lady doctor from Scotland, and Gwendoline Serle, were folded in each other's embrace.

"My dear, dear, Flor, I am overjoyed – a thousand welcomes – I wrote you a letter – now on its way – you have anticipated my wish – you understood I wanted you – we spoke to each other at a distance – true telepathy, real communion of mind. What further proof is needed of our mutual sincerity? I have someone at last in whom I can confide. I have hundreds of acquaintances and not a single friend. Poor, fragile Muriel, leans upon me. I never confide my own troubles to those who look up to me for guidance. It makes them doubt my strength. How fit and happy you do look, Florey, – Mr. Gray will you excuse? Many, many thanks for your pains. I shall expect you to the play on Friday evening. Mind you come, do you hear, Mr. Gray?" said Gwendoline, looking back over her shoulders, and smiling through her tears, as she led away her newly-arrived companion.

"If I do come, it will only be to witness your triumph," he said, as he prepared to leave.

Miss Badenock studied the negro.

Edith busied herself with getting in the stranger's baggage. Edith was a jewel of a maid – a servant who could always guess at the right thing. She liked the newcomer at sight.

Florence Badenock was just in time. Before the play came on she had explored every cranny of the house, established herself in the hearts of all the servants, earned from Mr. Serle the sobriquet of "doctor daughter," made the acquaintance of all "the boys and girls," scored a victory over half of them at tennis, caught over a dozen lobsters and crayfish in the river, and learnt the topography of every square inch of the ground.

Rupert Gray had never attended any function at "Sunflower Manse" before. Once, and only once, was he introduced into his master's inner circle, namely – the night at San Fernando.

The accountant went to the play. He, however, kept himself in the background, sitting in the last row of seats against the wall.

The play – "The Violet of Oropuche,"† as it was called – came off with eclat. All the players – as well coloured as white – vied with one another in trying to excel. Lord Trotter was so pleased with Gwendoline's performance, that he presented her with a bouquet that stood on a piano near by. This was the signal for renewed applause.

Next day all this appeared in the papers. There had been a crowded house. The tickets were sold for the author's benefit. Even Miss Badenock paid for hers. Mr. Serle bought his for five pounds. In addition to that, his daughter every morning thrust a few into his pocket, requesting him to sell them to his friends. In the afternoon he paid over the value of the tickets and kept them without her knowing. Lord Trotter, not to be outshone, paid a ten-pound note for his. Government House† bought ten dollars' worth in tickets. All "the girls" sold to all "the boys" at a crown each. Dancing at the tail-end ensures the sale of tickets. After this function the books sold with surprising rapidity.

The play ended, the company broke up into little groups. The coloured ladies were busy adjusting their mantles, preparatory to leaving. A bevy of other ladies moved about the stage humming pretty tunes and stamping lightly to test the boards. These were mostly the home set whom Gwendoline called "the girls." "The boys" smoked in the vestibule. Here and there an exchange of graceful compliments. Here and there whispering flirtation. Here and there a pair of cosy lovers.

Suddenly the strains of a magnificent waltz burst upon the air – the southern door of the drama hall opens, disclosing a spacious, airy room, cleared for dancing. Mr. Serle, looking a score of years younger, led out with the Colonel's lady.

Miss Badenock, tripping it with Lionel Murchison, was summoned in the glory of the waltz to give first aid to a hysterical young lady who had

decided to faint. Gwendoline, vainly endeavouring to escape the impor-
tunities of Lord Trotter, had at length to gratify that nobleman's insistence upon having the first waltz. All His Lordship's talk about his
invincible team of cricketers fell upon deaf ears. Her heart was not there.
She deprecated the snub to the coloured party – the people of Rupert
Gray. The ball-room was to her a vacant space. She felt the regret of
camaraderie at the exit of the outcast amateurs. They had shown no
pique – these coloured ladies and gentlemen. They partook of the refresh-
ments pressed upon them with reassuring grace. Their ease of manner
went far towards alleviating her embarrassment. Her ethics clashed with
the social rules of her caste.

While Miss Badenock was unlacing the stays of the hysterical damsel,
her waiting partner engaged the accountant in conversation. The
coloured party therefore left him behind a couple of minutes' walk. At
length, tearing himself away, he stole off, as he thought, unobserved. As
he reached halfway down the gravel-walk, he paused. The waltz was
playing fine. Its music arrested him – compelled him to listen as it leav-
ened the entire soul – telling of

> "Old, unhappy, far off things
> And battles long ago."[†]

Light footsteps on the gravel, and the approaching rustle of a woman's
dress caused him to turn; and there, flushed, from the whirl of terpsichore[†] in all the loveliness of youth, grace and beauty, stood the daughter of the house. In her hand she still carried the trophy of flowers won
by her dazzling genius, laid at her feet by an English laird, who, at her
slightest nod, was willing to share his honours with her, to clothe her
with his ancient title, and endow her with princely manors.

"Mr. Gray," she called, approaching him, "here is a present for you,"
as, deftly drawing from the cluster a white bachelor's button,[†] she handed
it to him saying: "Think of the signification," and without pausing she
hastened back.

Gwendoline Serle rose to the occasion. She was queen of the art of
entertaining. She dispensed hospitality like an ideal hostess. Her radiant
face lit up the shining hall. Round her, as centre of attraction, the
crowded function revolved. Howbeit, her gaiety was only apparent – her

debonair attentiveness a veneer – her geniality conventional. A tremor of loneliness warped her whole soul. A millstone of sadness weighted her drooping heart, as at intervals her thoughts reverted to a solitary wayfarer journeying to Port-of-Spain along the smooth white road.

Lord Trotter laid no great stress upon her asking to be excused from completing that first waltz. She was a pre-occupied hostess, he thought, good-naturedly. The calls upon her time were responsible for her absent-mindedness in conversation. He was ready to forgive anything – everything.

Pity lovers do outgrow this spirit, when passion waxes stale. He deemed nothing amiss in the charming girl who recked not for, heeded not, his well-bred attentions. With her, coronet and rent-roll counted for chaff – pageantry and pomp for a void. What matters rank, what matters title to a woman in love? What cares she for wealth or fame? Irresolute and fickle when caring for fortune – devoted and true when loving for love.

Governed in its fancies by a law of its own – appealing to no umpire but the instinct of Eve – unfathomable always – often misunderstood – unreadable but to few – the feminine nature will ever remain half a puzzle. Here and there a dowager-empress weds her private secretary. Here and there my lady in her prime dotes upon a stripling. Woman's mode of loving knows no law, obeys none, save perhaps the law of evolution and reversion.

> "Woman is the lower man, and all her passions matched with mine
> Are as moonlight unto sunlight and as water unto wine."†

CHAPTER VII

The Dream

A friendship sprang up between Florence Badenock and Lionel Murchison – a friendship far from superficial. How could it be otherwise? Who in the world showed him more sympathy? Who smoothed by tact, healed by solicitude, every wound suffered by the rejected worshipper of Gwendoline Serle? Why should he not appreciate Miss Badenock? Was she not ever seeking to lead him to forget his pain, ever furnishing him with dissipation, that splendid antidote for love-sickness?

Friendship is the stepping-stone to love. The world laughs at platonic friendship. People baptize it "love in disguise." They define friendship between two of opposite sex to be the name given to the period during which one party waits till the other catches love's fever.

Life held some consolation now for Lionel Murchison. No wonder he spent all his evenings at "Sunflower Manse." Intercourse with the strong-willed lady doctor did him good. It is difficult to prevail upon some men to continue mixing in the society of a woman who has once rejected them. Miss Badenock encouraged the junior partner. He thought a world of her. Taking sympathy for her ladder, she climbed up into his estimation. As the starlit nights came and went her ascendency over him grew. She administered real comfort.

"Gwendoline may learn love's lesson yet," she would say; "love, you know, is a climbing plant which needs much cultivating. Time, patience, determination, will bring you off the conqueror, and if even disappointment comes," she would laughingly say in Gwendoline's own presence, "why, there is as good a fish in the sea as caught. At least, George

Withers thought so, and sings it, too:

> If she love me, this believe,
> I shall die ere she shall grieve.
> But if she slight me when I woo,
> I can scorn and let her go,
> For if she be not for me–
> What care I for whom she be!"[†]

All this came like healing salve – fell like balm upon the blistered spirit of Lionel Murchison.

Miss Badenock interested herself in everything about him. She never seemed to tire hearing all he had to tell. His history, his hopes, his fears, his aspirations, his successes, and his failures, were the favourite topics pursued.

Effort spent must yield fruition. Slowly but surely as the love-vine[†] spreads its tendrils over yonder hedge – softly as rose petals kiss the earth, falling before the rollicking zephyrs – sweetly as angels whisper in the ears of dreaming childhood – her womanly influence clothed his soul.

Let wives and matrons but dream what potency they may wield. Let them be at pains to find the way to the heart – with only a little close observation – only a little selflessness. Let them but remember that the pleasures of the senses are the grossest of all means and lead to the hearts of the minority of men. Let them but learn how to unlearn: and they would soon achieve an ascendency at once surprising. Their every word would be a law at a fireside where, in the incandescent light of purity of conduct – a check upon desire – each can reign a queen.

Florence Badenock played her cards with the skill of a goddess. What did it matter that she held a physician's diploma. Profession or no profession, women's profession is marriage. Good bread-winners, but better home-spinners they always are. The best redeeming feature – the brightest phase in the lot of women bread-winners, may be the deeper insight they get into men.

Gwendoline Serle was not a hard taskmistress. She had said "no" to Lionel Murchison's offer very gently. Her attitude towards him was always humane. She knew the pangs, had suffered the aches of a throbbing, shackled love. She accordingly did all that in her power lay to promote his intimacy with Florence Badenock. Woe to that man whom one woman resolves at any cost to annex, but wooer he becomes when two unite to further the self-same object.

One dew-bespangled morning the Scotch girl rose with the dawn. She wandered forth into the garden among the flowers. Her lofty air showed pure ideals and a set purpose to live for virtue. She looked more like a sylvan nymph or "glassy wave" Sabrina,[†] than the bonnie lassie she was from the land of the heather bell. The thought on her brow lent majesty mellowed into beauty by her fervent love for Lionel Murchison, into grace by her devoted friendship for Gwendoline Serle.

Gwendoline Serle came down near sunrise. As she stood under the verandah, training the stephanotis, one looking at her would perforce exclaim: "Pity such clay must die." If Florence Badenock inspired respect and admiration, Gwendoline Serle drew love and attachment – the kind of woman to win hearts without trying. A feminine sweetness – a receptive yielding was hers.

She moved out into the open, lithe of limb. At the head of the sunflower patch she stood, herself a flower. Clinging becomingly to her voluptuous outline, hung the folds of her matin gear.[†] Gems sparkled on her fingers. The clinking of golden bracelets beneath her Japanese sleeves,[†] seemed designed to wake the flower sleepers she tended from beds all drenched with dew. Frank and confiding, she appeared wholly unconscious of her worth. How had nature dowered her with hair and eyes and silken lashes – damask, mobile cheeks – a dash of character in the underlip and intellect on the brow!

The two girls moved among the flowers till at last they came together. Among lilies and roses, the rose met the lily.

"O, Florey, Florey; why so pensive this morning? Has Lionel done you aught?" asked the rose.

"Lionel? No! I am thinking of you, dear," said the lily.

"Of me and I am here? It seems presence makes the heart grow fonder in these later times," said Gwendoline Serle, growing serious as she looked into the troubled eyes of her friend.

"Last night – or rather this morning, I dreamt a curious dream. O, Gwendoline, dear, I dreamt a mysterious dream;" said Florence Badenock.

"Tell it to me, if that is all your trouble; I am a modern Joseph.[†] Interpret it, I shall," said Gwendoline, laughingly.

"I fancied, in my dream," Miss Badenock began, "that I saw you in bridal attire. You wore light cream-flowered silk with a snow-white collaret of ruching.[†] Your hair was a study, and the natural orange blossoms were just lovely. A queen might have envied the abundance of dainty muslin veiling your figure on every side. Your sleeves and train were a gorgeous piece of finery. On your splendid chest there nestled a cluster of the largest bachelors' buttons, white, I ever saw."

Gwendoline's lips grew pale. "Bachelors' buttons, white," she said mechanically; "no, one bachelor's button, white."

Without noticing her, Florence Badenock continued: "But the strangest part of it all, my dear, was that your papa came shielding his eyes with one hand, while with the other he sprinkled the lovely bridal costume all over with blood. As you moved near to lean upon his arm he gave you his back. Then you seemed to laugh aloud, like one delirious, you know: merciful heavens, how I shuddered at your shrill voice. Your dead mother ran to your assistance. I recognised her in the resemblance. She looked sad as she paced to and fro, saying: 'Gwendoline, that poor child of mine, is too good to suffer.' "

"Dear me," said Gwendoline; "Flor, it is a remarkable dream."

"It is ominous," said Miss Badenock. "I do not like the dream."

"There is something in dreams," said Gwendoline: "our fancy traverses in sleep the unexplored regions," she said, heaving a long drawn sigh, adding, "there is telepathy between the living and the dead. My poor mother is distressed for me."

The Scotch girl looked at her long and earnestly. Then she said: "Gwen, my dear, I take the liberty to speak to you. Is it not possible for you to bring your feeling under control? Could you not try just a wee bit to forget this Rupert Gray? Perhaps the dream has reference to him. I have thought over your love story night and day. I cannot see how it can end well. Advice is no use to lovers. I myself would listen to none. But, dear, it is my duty to point out to you your danger. This match will not, cannot answer."

"The only way I can forget him is to cease loving; aye, cease living," she said.

"O, Gwendoline, darling, do, try," pleaded her friend.

"It is too late now," she said; "it was always too late."

"What will your papa think of me? I shall surely come in for a share of blame," said Miss Badenock.

"How can you?": queried Gwendoline. "I will exonerate you by explaining you met me already loving him."

"Your father did you a wrong to throw you both together," sighed Florence Badenock, with a look of sound judgment in her face.

"Papa does not even dream of such a thing. He has not the remotest idea," explained the other.

"Mr. Gray is black, you see, there's the trouble," said Miss Badenock. "No such obstacle lies between my marriage with Lio, nor Edith's with Francois Pierre. The whites will never be reconciled to making inter-marriage the *via media*.† Rigid exclusion is sure to be the social outcome of such a union. The blacks will keep shy of your house. A great gulf will be fixed. Rupert Gray will go to them but they will never come to him. Yours will be a selfish happiness. That wife whose husband cannot continue being useful in his generation is an encumbering parasite – a woman born to old-maidenhood."

"I answer you in the words of Byron," said Gwendoline:

> 'Here's a sigh for those who love me
> And a smile for those who hate,
> And whate'er sky's above me
> Here's a heart for any fate.' "†

All that day the lady doctor pondered over her vision. She could not for the life of her shut out from her imagination the pathetic figure in bridal costume gleaming with spangles of gore.

When Mr. Serle came home Florence Badenock confided her trouble to him. She told him the dream simply. He laughed at her fears and tried to dissipate them as they walked about the grounds within sight of Gwendoline at tennis.

"Never fear for Gwendoline," he said, "she is no putty head – young head on old shoulders. She should have been a boy."

"True, papa," assented Miss Badenock, "but love does not come under the dominion of reason. Here the cleverest is but a fool. Cupid's mistakes are those of the heart, not of the head. The moment reason comes in, you do not love, you like."

"Gwendoline is the kind of girl to look before she leaps," boasted her father; "she is a girl whom title, rank, or wealth cannot tempt."

Miss Badenock sighed. Would she could tell Mr. Serle the true state of affairs.

"Papa, women frequently go from the sublime to the ridiculous in matters of love, and that too with their eyes wide open," said the troubled dreamer.

"Flor," said Mr. Serle, pausing and facing her, "whomsoever my daughter likes, I shall. Surely, she will not bring us a nonentity. Let him be poor, young or old, so long as he is rich in qualities. You share Gwendoline's confidence, do you not? You ought to have some influence over her. Surely you would not encourage her to make that dream true."

"Though our best friends may know, they cannot always direct our wills, is it not so papa?" asked Florence Badenock anxiously.

Little did he dream of the import of her remark as he stooped for a stray tennis ball, and made everybody laugh with his comical throwing.

CHAPTER VIII

Two Men Shall Meet

Serious developments were meanwhile getting ahead down at the store. Not that the business of the firm showed any symptoms of unsoundness. On the contrary, these were its halcyon days. All went well – clockwork business – devoted employés – punctual customers – regular and well-selected consignments – skilful and transparent book-keeping – preponderance of credit over debit–enormous profits. The partners were happy. Contentment and cheerfulness pervaded their atmosphere. All the subordinates caught the contagion. A woman had entered into the lives of two – and a child, a daughter, into that of a third. "Cherche la femme,"† runs the French proverb; so it ever will be; we see traces of a woman's hand, as good or ill should chance. The developments were from another cause.

From the day the New Yorker told how Jacob Canaan Clarke tried to get to America, he grew very sullen. Whenever the accountant met him there was a dark squint in his face. How he got to know that the outspoken Yankee had sold him never transpired.

Trinidadians have a proverb: "When you spread cocoa in the sun look out for rain."† Clarke spread plenty of cocoa. He noted the strained behaviour – the painful toleration in the accountant. Gray was still kind, obliging and polite, but Clarke's quick eye soon detected effort. The man who inflicts the injury jumps first to be revengeful. Heed him not: his industry is but evidence of the revolt of conscience disapproving self – the disagreeable whispering of the still small voice, crying out in the mental hearing of the traitor like "Abel's blood for vengeance"† – demanding wherefore all this "envy, hatred and malice, and all uncharitableness."[†]

Jacob Canaan Clarke hated his friend, his benefactor – for what? For having stretched out his hand and rescued him from cruel privation; hated the man who did him good; who felt that doing good to his fellows was the better prayer; who loved the whites not the less but negroes more. Jacob Canaan Clarke forgot the past. Forgot how he sat before Rupert Gray, beaten by misfortune – moaning out his piteous plaint "no work, no cash." Forgot the manly generosity of that true negro who, each time Clarke attempted to utter thanks, placed his palm over the ingrate's mouth, exclaiming: "Don't mention it, old boy. We must forward the race. We must do good, and if we cannot, we must do no harm to other negroes. We must see after correcting our own vices. We ought not to expect reward. Race-uplifting should be our reward. We must proffer the sympathetic grip as we confer the knighthood of encouragement, saying: 'Take heart, brother; rise up and prosper.' " There are men with bad memories all the world over.

One day, at the store, as he shivered under the cold contempt of the accountant's manner, Clarke broke the ice: "Mr. Gray," he said, "I understand that you accuse me of trying to oust you with the New Yorker."

The accountant made no reply. He simply looked into the eyes of the speaker, whose gaze quickly fell. Mr. Serle was at a meeting of the Chamber of Commerce. Clarke did not observe that Mr. Murchison was within hearing. The junior partner walked up. Clarke returned to the attack.

"Mr. Gray," he said, "upon what grounds do you base your charges?"

"Who is your author?" asked Mr. Murchison.

"That is best known to me," said Clarke. "This man is always villifying me. I may tell him frankly I have consulted my lawyer, and I mean business."

"Your threats tell me you have fear – you have qualms of conscience," said the accountant, speaking for the first time.

"I have none," said Clarke; "you are mistaken."

"None of what?" asked Mr. Murchison. "None of conscience, I suppose. Gray's silence has beaten you. Had he taxed you with your sharp practice you had not been ill at ease."

"Mr. Murchison, does this concern you?" asked Clarke.

"None of your impertinence, young man; you cannot be wrong and strong at the same time," said the junior partner energetically.

"Wrong and strong," repeated Clarke. "Mr. Murchison, you are dreaming."

"Am I? Now tell me, did you not apply to the New Yorker?" asked the junior partner.

"No."

"Did you not apply in writing?" asked the accountant.

"I tell you no," said Clarke.

"Mr. Clarke," said the junior partner solemnly, "did you not present your application written on four pages of foolscap?"

"I am a stranger to what you are saying," said Clarke.

"You are a stranger to truth," said the accountant emphatically.

Clarke turned on his heels to leave. An impulse turned him back. He felt awkward. He feared the opinions they would express after he was gone. "Will you promise to advise your accountant, Mr. Murchison?" asked the embarrassed man.

"I should like to advise you," said the junior partner, "to set aside those disagreeable tendencies and adhere to the sound views you were wont to hold about the unpatriotic throat-cutting among coloured men."

"If you wish to see mutual throat-cutting go to Europe, the white man's home," retorted Clarke; "it is merely the presence of rival races – subject races, which keeps the whites clannish out here in the colonies."

"Why don't you Africans pull together also, in the midst of rival races?" asked the junior partner. "Here you are," he added, "without invitation, fighting hard at picking a quarrel. Did anyone trouble to tax you with duplicity and ingratitude?"

"Nobody taxed me openly, you mean," said Clarke. "That snake in the grass sitting there," he went on, pointing towards the accountant, "I shall have to get even with him. His civility is but a veneer. Smooth water runs deep. You may smile as scornfully as you please, my good man, I shall make you feel me yet: I tell you, two men shall meet, and terrific will be the impact."

"Do your worst," muttered Rupert Gray in a guttural of a contempt also visible in his face. "Plan destruction as you can. Conspire with the assiduity of Guy Fawkes and his crew:† you be active, I am passive:

aggression yours, defence mine. Wake up at midnight and I look you in the face, a compliment you dare not return. You may win skirmishes, but the final victory belongs to me. Let the man who molests Rupert Gray expect war to the knife."

"And who is Rupert Gray?" asked Clarke sarcastically. "Man, what airs are you assuming? What role are you playing?"

"I will not waste time to ask who is Jacob Canaan Clarke. I am not anxious to know," observed the accountant with a sneer.

"Mis-mis-Mistah Murchison O, ah-ah always t-tell Mr. Gray d-dis m-man is a crab – can't t-tame," said someone highly annoyed. "P- put d-de m-man out d-de store," and, so saying, Pierre started from among the barrels to carry out his suggestion.

Clarke was no physical coward, he moved slowly forward to meet Pierre. Mr. Murchison held a large pot of red ochre wash[†] in one hand and a brush in the other, as he moved among the barrels. Placing himself between Pierre and Clarke he raised both hands to keep them apart. Somehow, in trying to duck under, Clarke's head knocked the marking pot from the junior partner's hand, its whole contents anointing his pate.

There was no stammering in Pierre's loud laughing as he stooped, caressing his abdomen. The accountant was quietly splitting his sides over his books. The red ochre ran all over. Jacob Clarke looked like a living advertisement of red wash. In walked Mr. Serle.

"What's all this?" he asked quietly, as he passed hurriedly by.

"There now," said the junior partner, apologising profusely, "I always said you would one day come to grief."

"Somebody will pay for this, two men shall meet!" said the red-crowned scold.

How he kept his word, and what events it bred, time shall unfold.

CHAPTER IX

"My Name Is Gray – Rupert McKinley Gray"

The band discoursed sweet music at the Botanic Gardens.† Beauty and fashion filled Trinidad's Eden. Little children with chubby limbs and faces gambolled round the fountain. A long row of carriages, wherein reclined the rich, was drawn up before the Governor's palace.† Opposite, on the savannah which stretched away like a miniature prairie, there was a parade of the Local Forces. These comprised a motley group of fighting units representing every shade of colour. The gallant Colonel, a soldierly looking Scotchman, with a hooked nose, galloped about, first spurring, then reining in his charger, as he shouted to the nervous Constabulary: "Why don't you keep back the *hoi polloi?*"†

Most of the spectators forsook the cricket. Alone the panting willow-wielders wearied every nerve. "See Naples and then die," runs the Italian proverb. "Play in England and live," dreams the average Trinidad batsman.†

The savannah† was all animation. A lady, evidently English, of the tourist type, wearing a snow-white turban fluttering from her broad brimmed straw,† walked across from the Queen's Park Hotel.† To her this was no novel spectacle, yet long she lingered some yards west of the race stand. She was no stranger to gorgeous pageants. Her eyes had looked at ceremonial drill of the mighty legions of empire arrayed in Hyde Park.† She had viewed from the Viceroy's palace† windows the manoeuvring of India's dusky battalions. Yet here she lingered.

A negro lieutenant led the Artillery, almost a purely native corps. As they marched past there was clapping of hands.

The stranger seemed to evince the interest of a critic, as she plied one of the bystanders with questions. Then with rapid strides she continued across the park, careful to keep on the outskirts of the crowd. She walked in the direction of the gardens.

Purple streaks lay across the sky from Maraval to the Naparimas. The northern heights, stretching away to westward, faded into blue behind Mucurapo and Diego Martin[†] like endless graves of giants. The stranger entered the gardens by the westernmost gate, a little above the car terminus. Away in, behind the nutmeg grove, south of the burial place, there towers a gigantic specimen of the "Hog Plum" tree.[†]

Against its grand old trunk, there leaned with upturned face, crossed leg, and folded arms, a typical negro. The air was redolent of the fragrance of spices. The marble columns before him recorded the memory of the illustrious dead beneath. Meditation sat upon his brow. His soul, upborne on the wings of harmony, floated towards the spheres. Away there from the haunts of men – alone and not alone – his consciousness steeped in the sobering process of introspection, leaned Rupert Gray.

"Fine afternoon, sir," said a female voice; "a fine afternoon, I say."

"O – I – excuse – thanks – O, yes, a very fine afternoon indeed," returned Rupert Gray, bowing slowly to the stranger. "Excuse my absent-mindedness. I was not aware of your presence."

"The apology is mine to make," she said, coming upon the sward from the narrow path leading east from the main way. She halted at the foot of the Bushes' tombstone.[†]

"I must apologise," she repeated; "first for taking a snapshot of you leaning against this noble trunk, and then for disturbing your thinking; but I felt I could not go away without speaking to one – a native besides – who knows how to think so well. The natives have impressed me favourably. As I crossed your park a while ago I was struck with the precision the volunteers displayed. One corps especially – the artillery – seems as susceptible to trained movements as any white soldiery. Can you tell me what specimen of tree is that you are standing under?"

"We call it 'Hog Plum,' " he said. "Its scientific name is *Spondias graveolens.*"

"What a thick cluster of rope-like lianes trail from it," she said admiringly, walking round the trunk and looking up; "*Tanaecium,* they look like."

"Yes," he replied. "*Tanaecium jaroba.*"†

"Your tree reminds me of a young *Wellingtonia gigantia*† I saw in New Zealand last winter. Do not the lianes resemble the ropes of an eighteenth century wooden wall? Mr. Froude is right. Nature in the tropics is always grand.† Where is that delicious odour coming from?" she asked, drawing a deep breath.

"Yonder," he said, pointing towards the nutmeg grove watered by bamboo aqueducts, "and from those stripling trees there," as he turned and pointed to the right. "They are cloves," he continued, "*Caryophyllus aromaticus.*† I believe this month they commence to flower."

"I recognise," said the stranger, "the cinnamon specimens – a fine sample of *Cinnamomum zeylanicum.*† They compare very favourably with those I saw in Ceylon; and those shrubs down there under the hillside – *Coffea arabica,*" she suggested, moving on to the stony path.

"No, *Coffea liberica,*"† he corrected, crossing among the tombstones and pausing with his left hand resting on the iron rail enclosing a grass-grown plot.

"Yes, yes, Liberian coffee," she said, returning from out the hollow whither she had hastened to pluck a few of the leaves which she now crushed in her hands: "*Coffea liberica,*" she explained, "was the topic for discussion among the members of the Linnaean Society.† Pray, excuse me, but which in your opinion is the deadliest enemy to coffee-trees?" she asked, glancing at him with increased confidence.

"The pest," he answered, "known as coffee leaf fungus, the *Hemeliae vastatrix,*† I should say."

"The very same – just the same – that's exactly what Miss Forestier contended in her paper!" she exclaimed, with genuine approval, as she walked right up to him. "Let me introduce myself to you," she said, laying her kodak† and a little lap dog she petted, down on the sward. "I am the Countess of Rothberry," as she handed him a card, bearing the arms and crest of her house.

"Lady Rothberry," said the negro, bowing low: "my name is Gray – Rupert McKinley Gray."

From far away, among the branches of the poui-tree, whose eastertide blossoms flared out yellow† from the shaggy uplands, came the sighing of some lonely passerine,† sinking below the symphonies from the bandstand. The "cigale's" endless monotone, silvern or graterlike,† aided a variety of tenor. Semp, acravat and picoplat,† perched on spice tree† twigs or among dwarf mango branches, accorded harmonious soprano. Among the palmfronds blue-birds† gleamed. Kiss-ke-dees† challenged "king-page" butterflies† and yellow-winged "zabuecoes"† for violating the sanctity of their leafy domain.

Here, at the foot of Charles Warner's grave,† was made this self-introduction – here, betwixt nature's concert and man's – 'twixt sylvan music and artificial harmony – the dulcet carolling of piccolo, the euphony of flute and clarion, the triumphant drawl of cornet, the tiny tinkling of steel, the weird clashing of cymbals – Zion's own instruments, and the martial base and drum. Betwixt these, and the honey-throated chirping and whistling from vale and hillside, stood Europe and Africa upon the ashes of the dead. West Indian native and English noblewoman meet, fact to face, on the common ground of science.

She was a daughter of the Teutons,† a blue-eyed, fair-haired Aryan, whose Anglo-Norman ancestry had bequeathed to Great Britain a line of warriors bold. It was Bertrand de Rothberry who dashed with Coeur de Lion through the Moslem's bristling centre. The blood of Seigismund de Rothberry enriched the wreck-strewn field of Crecy. Talbot de Rothberry's intrepid escutcheon parried the bowsmen's onslaught in the breaches of Agincourt where the chivalry of England crowded to victory under the standard of Harry of Monmouth.

The stately form of Cawdor of Rothberry was conspicuous in the retinue of Fidei Defensor, at the field of the Cloth of Gold, where precedence was accorded the peerage of the realm by the rules of Grand and Petit Sergeantry. Rothberry blood and Rothberry treasure were spilt and spent in the cause of the fated Stuart. Glenullin of Rothberry found a soldier's grave outside the ramparts of Malplaquet. De Courcy of Rothberry danced in Brussels overnight, to perish on the morrow, covered with glory, where the fastnesses of Planchenoit frown on Waterloo. Rockdale of Rothberry rode in the Light Brigade. Noel of Rothberry marched to the relief of Lawrence, where the minarets of Lucknow sheltered a beleaguered garrison. A scion of the house was present at El Kebir; saw

Metemneh's sunrise: his victorious sabre glittered around the blood stained wells of Ablu Klea. When the folds of dominion were flung out over Pretoria, another son of this historic house joined in the "tremendous cheering" that echoed far away, beyond kopje and veldt.†

Thus her house had fought and died for their country, from father to son. The male heirs of the line all slept. She, the living representative, was herself a soldier – a soldier of peace, helping science and learning to overcome ignorance, virtue to overcome vice, the wretched, squalor, the weak, the strong. A patroness of letters she, a friend of subject races. What a meeting with an ideal native who could entertain her on the recondite topic of the flora of his country – a gentleman with no ancestry – no history – no past. It is idle for coloured people to boast of parentage in the West Indies where emancipation is the common stock.

The peeress was delighted. "Where did you learn botany?" she asked.

"Mainly by reading. I do not profess to know botany," he said.

"Are you a Trinidadian?"

"I am."

"Are there any more natives like you?"

"There are hundreds in this city alone. My people, Lady Rothberry, are striving to advance."

"I do believe you," she said; "I was never in Trinidad before. I was under the impression the natives were savages. While in New Zealand I heard a story about your Carnival. Somebody said the natives here were far behind the Maoris.† That after playing Carnival for the two days prescribed by law, they insisted playing on the third day also, which was Ash Wednesday. So they went parading the streets on the first day of Lent. At last they wound it up by swarming around the Government Buildings in a mad fury clamouring for the key to the reservoir. The dear, good Governor was forced to seek shelter in a cupboard in one of the offices. At last the native police felt so sorry for him that they broke loose from discipline and rushed through the streets, bayonetting pretty mulatto girls."†

"We had three days' Carnival in honour of the relief of Ladysmith.† That is the only ray of truth in the whole story. Your mind by this time, Lady Rothberry, is entirely disabused, I hope," he explained, vainly endeavouring to suppress a smile.

"Entirely disabused," she assured him: "and I am glad: seeing is believing; but I may tell you, I had my doubts early. If that is a faithful account of the state of the natives, I said, then what were the churches doing?"

Laura Lucretia Emma Lucy Arabella Winifred, twenty-third Countess of Rothberry, was said in Debrett's to be a peeress of Great Britain in her own right. She always travelled incognito. At the Queen's Park Hotel, where she was staying, her name appeared on the list as Mrs. Kathleen Hill. She came touring these islands in search of specimens, taking notes and snapshots. She was careful to avoid local society, preserving her incognito inviolate.

To-day, in a gush of graciousness, she was pleased to disclose her identity, among gorgeous flower beds sparkling with scented "stars of earth,"† or fringed with green or silver-bladed tufts; under shady palms, or giant forest kings, decked with the red and white flowering of climbing plants; around neat pagoda pines,† or across level sward at the back, where art combines with nature to make vegetation happy.

Through all this organized profusion she followed her dusky cicerone,† examining fruit and blossom – pistil and stamen, primary and secondary branches, leaf, stem, and gnarled roots, deciphering curious name-plates interesting only to the disciples of Bentham† and Hooker;† classifying, discussing the technicalities of *Leguminosae* and *Rosaceae,*† admiring the beauty and the bounty of tropical nature; and lingering till the last strains of music died away, and the red-braided bandsmen had folded up and were gone, till the shadows deepened into twilight, and great, clumsy bats were wheeling athwart the park, whence the sea sloped upwards to the clouds through glimpses of foliage behind St. Clair.†

CHAPTER X

"Thus Far and no Farther"

It was Mr. Serle's birthnight. The dinner was a family one. Covers were laid for five, namely: the old head of the house, his junior partner, the two girls, and Mr. Serle's eminent school-fellow – Sir Humourous Southfold,[†] the Chief Justice. Mr. Serle, who was a splendid table companion, was in high spirits. He and Sir Humorous had exhausted their whole fund of pleasant anecdotes and reminiscences of Eton.

"We must let the young ladies have their fling now," suggested Sir Humorous, whose sallies had kept the board lively all the time.

"I do not expect to spend a night like this in a hurry," said Mr. Serle. "Sir Humorous, though it's premature, here's to the law," he said, raising his glass of sparkling beverage, adding, "This is an informal supper."

Sir Humorous was responsive.

"Toasts after soup, what an anomaly," laughed Miss Badenock.

"You will soon feel as jolly, papa," said Gwendoline. "You have to attend a wedding: there will be a wedding soon."

"Who and who?" enquired her father, helping himself to a beauty of a drumstick after despatching fish.

Mr. Murchison turned all colours. Florence Badenock sat fathomless like a consummate actress.

"The contracting parties will be Mr. Rupert Gray, of the firm of Messrs. Serle and Murchison, and one Mrs. Kathleen Hill, of the Queen's Park Hotel," explained Gwendoline.

"Who is Mrs. Hill?" asked Lionel Murchison.

"One of our tourist visitors," said Florence Badenock, greatly relieved.

"Why is it," asked Mr. Serle, "that a native seeks a wife as soon as he leaves school. Bad policy that, very bad. Sir Hume, try some roast. Rupert Gray would make a mess of his future, should he marry now. It would be a queer thing too for this Mrs. Hill, whoever she may be – a European lady marrying a black. It may obtain in Europe where the black man is not known. It is not fashionable out here in the black man's home. Mrs. Hill's own people would cut her right and left."

"You cannot cut a Hill right and left," chimed in Sir Humorous, "you shall have to cut a tunnel right through."

"I think she deserves to be cut," continued Mr. Serle, as the merriment over the witticism of the Judge lingered in his face. "For my own part, I do not believe in such marriages. The lady must sooner or later regret: this isolation soon brings her to her senses."

"Rather her senses bring her to this isolation, for she must love with a deal of feeling, you know, and feeling is one of the senses," said Sir Humorous mischievously, looking quite comical.

"Remember, you wear the ermine† now, Sir Hume; you're no longer the wit of a lawyer you were," said Mr. Serle, as he whispered in the ear of the gliding butler to bring on something strong. "Now, I believe that our coloured people are enlightened enough to form an aristocracy of their own. Let them cling to their people. We whites respect the negro who clings to his people. Booker T. Washington,† their present leader, says: 'In all things that are purely social we can be as separate as the fingers, yet one as the hand in all things essential to social progress.' "

"All men are equal," said Miss Badenock; "that is the opinion of many whose best study is mankind."

"Mr. Maresse-Smith† once said that the best study of mankind was womankind,"† observed the Chief Justice.

"I do not deny the equality of man," said Mr. Serle, "but I do think that the West Indian negro barely stands within the threshold of culture. There is no greater admirer of the race of Ham† than I. That a great future is in store for them I am certain. But I deem it childish to try to force the game. They must bide their development. We all respect the fertility of their virgin brain-power, we look with pleasure at the distinguished sons they have produced. The world at large must bow before the genius of Toussaint L'Ouverture the brilliant slave of Breda† – warrior and statesman – the founder of the Haytian commonwealth. Then there are Jean Francois† and Biassou.† There is King Christophe,† "the Henry I of the North" – the sole black royal head outside Africa – the rival of Dessalines.† There is Edward Wilmot Blyden,† M.A., D.D., LL.D. – author of "Islam" – sometimes Plenipotentiary to Liberia at the Court of St. James† – a negro scion of the Island of St. Thomas, Danish West Indies. There is Booker T. Washington, whose name will be his monument – a modern Moses leading the Black Belt to the promised land of labour – wealth – prosperity. Sir Conrad Reeves,† that star of Little England† – that child of opportunity – that eagle whose pinions flapped out fame all round the Caribbees. Michel Maxwell Philip,† the demosthenic† lawyer, who in Trinidad's pantheon fills his niche: where John Jacob Thomas† already is; and Vincent Brown,† a titan at the forum, and Edgar Maresse-Smith, true lover of his kind, will one day be. Thomas, spite of mistakes, a sturdy race-vindicator. Brown, now acting, is destined to be Attorney-General some day. Who but he could have climbed to bar-leadership under Crown Colony† form? Philip could not. Reeves did not. Brown alone "arises like a giant refreshed with wine,"† and walks off with the gates of nominative hindrances. Maresse-Smith, the idol of the average native, shall be called a philanthropist without having ever crossed the Bocas.† All this is as it should be. We are ready to receive the black man with open arms into the professions, the service of the Crown, and in commerce, but when it comes to mixing up in the company of our wives, and wanting to marry our daughters – I say, 'No, sir.' I say to them just what Canute said to the waves: 'Thus far and no farther.' "†

"Miss Serle, are you ill?" asked Lionel Murchison.

"You have grown quite pale," said Sir Humorous.

"Sip a little wine, Gwendoline," said her father.

"Murchison," he continued, "do you remember that night at San Fernando. I can never forget Rupert's allusion to roses in Gwendoline's cheeks. Rupert Gray is my negro accountant," explained Mr. Serle, looking at Sir Humorous.

"What I do remember," said Lionel Murchison, "is the circumstance of that stubborn butler sulking to wait upon a black man like himself."

"Exactly," continued Mr. Serle; "why don't these people respect one another? They lack cohesion. Their spasmodic efforts sicken one. Debating and cricket clubs and dancing classes that never last, bickering, litigious friendly societies wanting to be under government audit all point to their helplessness. The Working Men's Association stands out the one exception – thanks to the unostentatious public spirit of a gentleman of Chinese extraction.† Even this institution is yet to gather in the printers, the salesmen, the porters, the labourers, the plantain men in the street.† These have no guild of their own, yet day after day studiously neglect to join a body striving to be in touch with the House of Commons. Let them remember that a kingdom against itself cannot stand. Let them learn to unite, not against any other race, but against their own selfishness. Booker T. Washington himself says: 'The greatest enemy of the negro is the negro.' "

"They will lose all that in time," pleaded Miss Badenock. "O, pa, Rome was not built in a day."

"That is so, Flor, my dear," said Mr. Serle, "meanwhile let them marry one another and give the West Indies a breed of pure-blooded leaders."

"What would you say," asked Mr. Murchison, "if your daughter – Miss Gwen – Miss Serle, I mean, did fancy a-a-man of col – a black man?"

"What," hissed Mr. Serle, fairly rising and upsetting his drink, "I – I should shoot any such scoundrel."

"Papa," asked Gwendoline without looking up, "would you shoot Rupert Gray?"

"Rupert has better sense than that," said Mr. Serle, subsiding into his former self. "I am not an Englishman, nor was my father before me, nor my grandfather. But with the exception of these three generations – Creole born and English bred – my entire stock is English.† Why should I or my daughter affect their posterity with an admixture of blood? Let Mrs. Hill please herself. That is her affair."

"That story about Mrs. Hill," explained Miss Badenock, "is all a joke. That is how your imaginative daughter chose to put it. Mrs. Hill is collecting specimens. This Gray is a kindred spirit. Chance throws them together at the gardens. Gray has the gift to quickly ingratiate himself with strangers. Since then every moth, butterfly, beetle, or orchid he can lay his hand on gravitates to the Queen's Park Hotel. Naturally now and then the lady detains him to supper. It is true the man is black, but his accomplishments are not black."

"He is only a black-mail, that is all," put in Sir Humorous.

"He and this Mrs. Hill are always together," remarked Gwendoline.

"Mrs. Hill, as a bird of passage, can well afford to do that," said Mr. Serle. "Of one thing I am sure, no white woman in Trinidad will envy her. Our women-folk fear these people who are always cutting one another's throats. Eventually they must run to the white man for mutual salvation. Talk as you like, we set them a splendid example of esprit and mutual justice. Take for instance that recent scandal of that coloured professional and his apprentice. Fancy one coloured man checkmating another on the eve of his promotion, merely for the look of a couple of guineas. Do you think any European, Indian, or Chinese would have so treated a countryman? I say no, a thousand times no," said the old gentleman, thrusting away his plate of dessert with a look of disgust, as if its contents were tainted with the magnanimity of the professional in question.

"A gentleman could never have done it," said Lionel Murchison.

"The apprentice himself would be a coward to swallow any further impositions," opined Miss Badenock.

Sir Humorous Southfold expressed no opinion. He looked grave and thoughtful.

After dinner Gwendoline sought solitude. She was sick at heart. Her father's views on the colour question came to her like a revelation – a painful awakening. Every word fell like a bombshell in her hearing. What a problem, she thought – this colour line drawn taut all round the West Indies. How would it all end?

She fell upon her knees, and prayed to God for help, beseeching Him to open a door of mercy for her, and if ill would be the outcome of her love, then in His great mercy to call her away before. Pure love borders on piety. That love is a failure which does not draw us nearer to God.

"Edith," said her mistress next day, "take this note to the store, and hand it to Mr. Gray. Mind you give it to no one else," as she handed the maid a letter addressed in typescript.

"To-day is Santa Rosa Races,† miss, the stores are all closed. Mr. Gray is at Arima,† I suppose," said Edith.

"Do as you are told and don't go supposing. You will find Mr. Gray there. Monday is mail day. Deliver your message and fetch a reply, and do not go pestering the gentleman about Dr. Johnson and detrimental. Here is a shilling for your tram tickets," said her mistress.

Edith carried out faithfully the instructions she received.

The accountant having finished what he was engaged in doing, was about locking the great heavy door, when Edith handed him the letter.

It read as follows:–

"SUNFLOWER MANSE,

"31st August, 19——

"Dear Mr. Gray, – For sometime past I have been expecting to hear from you relative to several matters. Last night I made up my mind to write you, though I know I am doing wrong. Months ago I handed you a flower. You were so busy with the tourist you made no sign about it. If you can come, meet me this evening at half-past eight o'clock on the grounds, near the fishing basin.

"Yours sincerely,

"GWENDOLINE SERLE."

"Say to Miss Serle it is alright, Edith, please," he said, when he had made an end of perusal.

Her father's ire of the night previous, instead of proving a deterrent, had had the opposite effect. Dinner was announced half an hour earlier than usual. As a consequence all the servants, save Edith, who slept on the premises, left early. Gwendoline, who appeared not to have been well overnight, bade Mr. Murchison good-night, and, kissing her father several times, retired. How in after years she recalled that affectionate embrace, the last he ever bestowed on her!

Jealousy in a woman runs through three stages. In the first stage she hates her rival. In the middle stage she dotes upon her lover and makes surprising sacrifices to keep him. The last stage sees love turned to hatred and revenge cruel, though wavering, her ruling motive.

Many an afternoon Gwendoline, with Miss Badenock, had watched from her carriage Rupert Gray and this English stranger in the gardens – and watched them narrowly. Her eye noted every detail, as only a woman's can. She measured every probability. Her instinct told her there was danger, and she had great faith in her instinct. She was of the type with the gift of prophecy. Whatever they tell you turns out true. They do not give their reasons – indeed can find none to give.

Intuition leads them by her mystic light and never leads them wrong.

CHAPTER XI

'Twixt Love and Duty

Rupert Gray was at the trysting place half an hour before the time appointed. It is in the fitness of things that Romeo be more punctual than Juliet. Around the fishing basin the darkness was dense by reason of the arcade of foliage. It therefore took sometime before his vision grew clear. He knew the spot well, though he had never had occasion to keep an appointment there before.

Back in the shorthand and typewriting days he had heard much about the fish-producing pond. It was a lake of goodly size, scooped out by the river falling over a ledge of rock in a noisy, copious sheet during the rainy season. Now that it was dry season the flow was but slender, in consequence of which the surface of the pool fell a couple of feet below the edge.

For hours during the long, hot days Gwendoline and Florence used to sit on the bank angling for crustaceans which made its waters their home. Mr. Serle heartily relished these dainties, for the reason he would declare "that they were taken by his two fisherwomen." His daughter caused him to have the side dug steep, raising the bank from time to time with sand shovelled up from the bed of the torrent. The opposite side of the basin, where was the clump of bamboos, needed no such improvement. Slippery, slate-coloured rock of aqueous formation, almost perpendicular and barely sloping inwards, formed this side.

A solitary bamboo reed, broken low, lay across the basin. The clump itself was enclosed by four long seats firmly nailed together in the form of a square. It was on that side of the seats between the clump and the river the girls were accustomed to sit with their lines. The space around the clump was hard and bare from constant friction.

Rupert Gray stood behind the clump, out of view of the first half of the gravel walk. The lights at "Sunflower Manse" glimmered through the lower windows. Their rays, darting along the dank leaf-covered field, had not the energy to reach the river's brink. He strained his eyes in every direction.

The uncertainty of expectation was within him. Would she walk down the gravel path, or, favoured by the deep, broad shadows of massive immortelle trees,† cross the cocoa field. The gravel walk leading from the verandah ran at right angles to the river, which was crossed by a bridge some distance from the gate.

Once he thought he heard footsteps as of someone crossing the bridge. He looked and listened, but heard nothing more, and, retreating behind the clump, waited for half an hour.

Precisely at half-past eight – the hour fixed – he thought he discerned an object moving under the cocoa,† some distance in parallel with the gravel walk. "She is coming," he whispered to himself. The river divided them.

Nearing the bank she paused for a moment; then turning abruptly to her right, stepped lightly on to the gravel walk and crossed the bridge; and, turning sharply to her left, she entered that half of the cocoa field, between the road and the river. Rupert Gray, advancing, led her by the hand towards the bamboo clump.

"How long have you been waiting?" she asked breathlessly.

"Half an hour," he said.

"I named half-past eight," she replied, dropping on to the seat.

"Where is Mr. Serle?" the accountant asked.

"Sitting in the verandah with Mr. Murchison."

"What are they doing?"

"Talking about to-day's races at Arima."

"And Miss Badenock?"

"Knitting," said Gwendoline, fanning her face with her scented hand-kerchief after settling more securely the lace hood she wore.

Then there was a pause – the pause that ensues when a woman waits upon a man. She had done all that feminine delicacy could permit; she could do no more. There he stood like a tower – all strength – all muscle – ever silent – ever wise. It seemed as if the weal or the woe of a nation hung on his word. Why was he so loth to speak? The very stars overhead, shut out above the arcade of leaves and branches, were not eye-witnesses. The fireflies glittered among the foliage. Here and there in the cocoa, a dewdrop pattered down from leaf to leaf. Save for the distant barking of irate watch dogs, and the everlasting sound of running water – silence reigned.

"Gwendoline," he said at last, in a subdued tenor. It was the first time he had so addressed her.

Beneath that outward calm her heart was wildly leaping.

"You presented me," he continued, "with a bachelor's button, white, upon terms of signification. The request you make through the flower is that I should let you know my mind. I hesitate to do so, Gwendoline, for your own sake. I feel it to be morally wrong. It would amount to a betrayal of the confidence your good father reposes in me. I am a poor negro boy, you a highborn lady. Race distinction divides us, as yonder river did a while ago. I love you, Gwendoline, God only knows how dearly. I loved you when first we met. I shall love you till I die. Your father and your friends would never countenance such a thing. Let us stifle, let us strangle this mad love of ours ere it be too late. Let us make a sacrifice. Come, lay your head upon my bosom and list to the heart that beats only for you. Let me steal but one kiss, sweet girl, and then say farewell forever."

Holding both her hands, he raised her to a standing posture; then with masterful gentleness, drawing her to his breast, he upraised her face and kissed her. Kissed her till her frame quivered like an aspen leaf, and her warm tears flowed fast and freely as hope, long congealed within her soul, thawed into realization.

O, the sorrow – O, the joy of it all – O, earth – O, heaven – O, life – O, death. A hurricane of emotions kept tangling up her nerves. Her great love, intensified by long secrecy, overflowed, overwhelming her senses. Her soul, steeped in a trance of the present, was delirious – intoxicated with happiness. When at length she returned from the astral plane of ecstasy, her emotions sought the outlet of speech as she nestled at his breast.

She was wiser now. His caresses had oped the rosebud of her experience of love's first kiss. Their souls were knit. The idea of severance staggered her.

"And must we part forever, you say?" she asked in tremulous reproach.

"It will be for your good," he said.

"To live without you cannot be for my good."

"It is your duty – part of your religion – to obey your father. What does the Bible say: 'Children obey your parents.' Remember, I am a black man," he said.

"I have never read in the Bible 'Thou shalt not love a black man,' " she said.

At that instant a whisper floated across the river; just a name lightly pronounced: "Mr. Gray – Mr. Gray."

Gwendoline strained her ears and listened. "We are discovered, Rupert. Do not answer," she cried.

Somebody crossed the bridge.

"Mr. Gray – Mr. Gray," came again, as the figure approached.

A cold perspiration bathed her face. She sank back to the seat. Rupert Gray moved forward to meet the person. It was only Edith, breathless and excited.

"Mr. Gray, is Miss Gwendoline here?" she enquired.

"Why do you ask?" he said, concealing his own surprise.

"Her father is searching the house upside down for her. He is unlocking every room," answered Edith.

"Why is he doing that?"

"A strange man came a while ago and asked to see him. I called him from the verandah," said the maid.

"What sort of man?"

"A black – a man of colour, sir."

"Do you know him?"

"I have never seen him before."

"Would you recognise him?"

"I think so. He whispered something to Mr. Serle which made him mad, mad. If you remain on the grounds much longer it will be detrimental," said Edith, wringing her hands and flying back across the bridge.

"What has happened?" asked Gwendoline, excitedly, as Rupert Gray rejoined her.

He had not the heart to tell her. He only drew her close. She understood it all in a flash – a flash of woman's wit.

"O, Rupert, Rupert, what should we do? Kiss me, darling, for the last, and go quickly," cried the agitated girl.

"I will not leave you now," he said; and there was force in his resolve.

"Rupert, we are lost – do, fly – I hear papa's footsteps coming down the gravel," she cried.

"I cannot run from danger," said the negro.

"Gwendoline, Gwendoline," called Mr. Serle, crossing the bridge with a vengeance. "Gwendoline – why do you not answer? Let me see whom you have here," he said, as he drew a match and held up its evanescent spluttering between the lovers.

The girl sat speechless. Her face was like that of the dead. The old man peered into the face of the accountant, who fixed him steadily as a traveller does a lion. For a moment Mr. Serle received a shock. He seemed electrified – dazed – lost. From his trembling hand the match-box fell, and with it something else – something heavy that went off with a bang – a loud, sudden bang. It was the report of a revolver-shot, and it re-echoed far away in Debé and La Civa.†

Gwendoline leaped forward. With one frightened scream that rose clear above the silent night, she sprang between. At once weak and strong, some women are quick and resourceful. The blood of both the Serles was up – father to destroy, daughter to save. Shielding Rupert Gray with both arms thrust behind, she faced her father.

Mr. Serle, having somewhat overcome his first shock, stooped quickly and took up the firearm.

"Papa, what are you going to do?"

No answer.

Each side step the old man made to get at the accountant, Gwendoline met with agility. At one time he almost got around her. She was barely in time.

"O, God, papa," she said; "you are planning murder. Think of the consequences."

"You will be the cause," was the only reply, and his voice was awful to hear.

"Well, then," she cried in desperation, "shoot both of us. Shoot me first, and shoot him after." Again she gave one scream – one loud long agonised scream.

Mr. Serle's eyes, now inured to the thick darkness, could make them out plainly.

She looked as she stood with her arms tightly folding her lover behind her, her full chest curving outward, like a maiden-martyr tied to the stake, in dark mediaeval times. Her lace mantilla had slidden to her shoulder. She was panting. Her eyes dilated like a lynx's.[†] She looked the black man's guardian angel.

The sound of hurrying footsteps came along the gravel. Gwendoline gave several shrill screams.

Her father made a last supreme effort. Quick as thought, he clapped his left hand upon her shoulder, and, pressing her down with all his might, while she screamed whole-heartedly, reached over and discharged two shots, in rapid succession, into Rupert Gray. The target never flinched nor fell.

At that instant Lionel Murchison pinioned Mr. Serle from behind. Florence Badenock tried to bring away the kneeling girl, who tightened her hold upon her lover, her sleeve all drenched with blood.

Edith bounded forward, lantern in hand, shouting: "Fire – somebody is –" and, raising the light aloft, cried: "Look, look, Mr. Gray is burning."

Gwendoline relaxed her hold with a start. The flush of the firearm discharged point blank, had set the accountant's dress on fire. With great presence of mind he tottered past the clump and let himself down into the pool.

The three women made after him. Gwendoline, first gaining the water's edge, flung herself in. Miss Badenock stood seized, with hands clasped overhead. A gurgling sound, as of someone vainly struggling to scream, was issuing from the water.

"O, God, O, God," she cried, "Gwendoline is drowning."

Edith, bringing up the rear as fast as she could, stumbled and fell. The lantern rolled from her hand into the lake. Its light went out. All this happened quicker than could be told. Darkness veiled the scene.

"The bleak winds of March
Made her tremble and shiver,
But not the dark arch
Nor the black flowing river.
Mad from life's history
Glad to death's mystery.
Swift to be hurl'd
Anywhere, Anywhere
Out of the world."†

"Let me go, Lion Murchison," roared Mr. Serle, struggling and stamping desperately: "Let me go, I say. Knew your father before you – think Tom Murchison would hinder me from shooting a d——d nigger?"

"Never mind – never mind – let it all pass," said the younger man soothingly, as he manacled the angry speaker more securely about the middle.

"Let it pass the devil!" thundered the enraged father, "all well and good to talk that way. Stand in my shoes, see how you'd feel."

"Yes, yes, I feel – I am sorry – old friend – but you have to reflect, you know. Think of the town-talk to-morrow."

"I do not care one brass button – town-talk the dickens. Never one of all the babblers will step in to help you bear the pinch," said Mr. Serle, a little cooled down.

"Reflect upon the consequences," said the junior partner, as he forced the revolver from the old man's hand, and, stooping quickly, rested it on the ground, – "murder, criminal sessions – the gallows."

"By heaven," swore Mr. Serle, "prefer to swing the gallows any day, than have a black son-in-law."

"Mr. Serle, is that you? You surprise me. You are mad to-night – yes, you are mad."

"Mad, aye, and with good cause. Not one in a thousand of all the whites in the island would condemn me. Two-thirds of the blacks would vote solid against that scoundrel, who, under the guise of subordination and uprightness, betrayed trust. Favoured by opportunity – access and intercourse – acquires influence over my child, and abuses it by tampering with her feelings, by trading upon her weakness, her kindness of heart, her unprejudiced tendencies, her innocence. Then induces her to steal out by night, from under my protection, to be kissing and cooing in the dark – what! a nigger kissing my daughter – no, sir, I must l ynch him, O, yes, bound to shoot him, let me go," he said in a fresh paroxysm of rage: "you may as well not hold me back. End his life I must by –"

"A rope – a light – for God's sake, somebody. Gwendoline, Gwen. Gray – Mr. Gray. They are drowned. They are dead," cried Miss Badenock from the riverside, interrupting Mr. Serle's oath of vengeance, as she walked off several paces, and then returned in doubt whether she herself might not run to fetch what was needed.

"Mr. Murchison – Mr. Murchison – do! Edith, where are you, Edith. Run for another lantern, girl. Will you not try to save Miss Gwendoline. She was good and kind to you, Edith. She loved you, loved your race. Edith, go, do you hear?" said Miss Badenock incoherently. Poor Edith, kneeling just where she fell, could not, was too frightened to rise.

"Lord have mercy upon us," she kept ejaculating. "From battle and murder and from sudden death, good Lord deliver us."†

Miss Badenock's call for help alarmed Lionel Murchison. "Let us leave here," he begged Mr. Serle, now somewhat pacified; "something has happened to your daughter and I must render assistance."

"It's all her own seeking," the old man said, with just a shade of uneasiness in his tone; and he allowed himself to be led back to the house at no slow pace.

Lionel Murchison ran back quickly with the stable lantern and some rope. Miss Badenock hastened as far as the bridge to meet him. Her face was sad to look at. Her cheeks had grown hollow. Her eyes were sunken. As she was hurrying back to the pool, her foot struck against the large revolver still lying where Lionel Murchison had left it.

Again the terrible bang broke the hushed night. The poor girl almost collapsed. Lionel Murchison supported her, relieving her of the lantern.

The bullet, grazing along the earth, sped through the coagulum of blood which marked the spot where Rupert Gray was shot.

Mr. Serle's revolver shooting Rupert Gray's blood as though the two men, but yesterday the best of friends, meant to prolong the feud by proxy.

As the echo fell upon the ears of Primrose Serle, pacing his room, the door of which Lionel Murchison had been careful to lock from the outside, the stern old man started – paused, wheeled round – stamped his foot, clenched his fist and ground his teeth audibly as though labouring to subdue the bitter throes within.

Lionel Murchison took out the four remaining cartridges from the vicious instrument.

On reaching the pool, Miss Badenock held up the lantern with feverish impatience. Its powerful rays illumined the whole scene. There, clinging to a fallen bamboo that lay across, was Rupert Gray with Gwendoline Serle in his arm, her head barely above the surface of the water, which was deeply tinged with blood. Their weight caused the bamboo to bend downwards.

Mr. Murchison could not swim, and the basin was very deep. He therefore made the rope fast round three stout bamboos of the clump, and then around his waist. Not a word was spoken. Taking hold of the fallen bamboo which bent dangerously under his added weight, he swung himself slowly towards the pair. Relieving Rupert Gray of his fair load, Lionel Murchison began to work his way back.

It was a perilous moment. He was at a disadvantage. With his fair burden in his right hand, he had only the use of his left. At times the bamboo threatened to break. Hugging it under he propelled himself shorewards with extreme difficulty. The two women on the bank held their breath. After each push forward Lionel Murchison paused and rested. At last he gained the side.

Miss Badenock set down the lantern carefully, and with the help of Edith, tried to draw the body out. The body of Gwendoline Serle was a healthy, well-developed one. Lifting it was no easy task. As they bent over, its weight well-nigh carried them off their foothold. The tears almost blinded Florence Badenock.

"Come, Gwen, darling, come to Flor," she said, addressing the lifeless form. "Give her to me so, Mr. Murchison," she said, lifting the body with its face turned from her. Then clasping it round the middle, she let the trunk fall forwards and the head hang downwards. "Do up her hair, Edith," she said.

"She is dead, Miss," said Edith, as she fumbled at the lank tresses.

Doctor Florence Badenock was no novice to work of this sort.

Stretching the unconscious limbs prone along the seat, where but an hour before the wave of love's tumult surged through them, Miss Badenock applied all the recognised methods for resuscitating the drowned. Edith was engaged in running to and from the house for such things as were needed.

Meanwhile Rupert Gray, weak from loss of blood, and unable to speak owing to his jaws being locked, clambered out with the help of the junior partner. Dragging to the seats he stretched himself on one side of the four, his head almost touching that of his lover as she lay on an adjacent side. Alas, for the uncertainties of life. From a lover's rendezvous the bamboo clump becomes a surgeon's operating chamber.

Dr. Florence Badenock worked for an hour. Slowly, as the dawn dapples the morning, returning animation showed in the face of the unlucky girl. Her young life, well-nigh extinct, was wooed back by skilled, loving hands. At length she opened her eyes.

"Where am I?" she asked. "Rupert – papa – is Rupert Gray dead?"

"Thank heaven, darling, you are alive," said Miss Badenock evasively, kissing the cold, pale forehead. Gwendoline Serle was borne to the house.

Leaving Edith at the bedside with directions how to act in case the patient swooned, the doctress returned with surgical apparatus to render the accountant first aid. Mr. Murchison held the light while she examined the wounds. Rupert Gray's was a powerful trunk, every muscle being at its thickest.

One shot had passed clean through the fleshy ligaments of the left arm, while another ploughed a deep furrow along his side, grazing off the flesh. He sustained no further injury, save the copious loss of blood from the side-wound.

The doctress, after dressing the wounds, ran back to the house and telephoned the livery stable for a carriage. She also rang up the Colonial Hospital, requesting her friend Dr. Lamaralle to admit, as a private patient, the accountant, who had accidentally received some slight injuries while out hunting with Messrs. Serle and Murchison at the backwoods of the "Manse." "Mr. Murchison," she said, "would speak to the doctor when the carriage fetched there." She also took the opportunity of inviting Dr. Lamaralle to tea the next afternoon. "Although Miss Serle, whom the doctor admired so much, was laid up with a nervous attack, in consequence of the accident, Miss Badenock hoped to substitute her in entertaining him." She did not fail to put Mr. Murchison on his guard.

The carriage arrived in due time. As the two men stepped in, Edith appeared on the scene quite out of breath.

"Is Miss Gwendoline worse?" asked Miss Badenock and Mr. Murchison simultaneously.

"She is come to herself altogether. She is anxious to know about Mr. Gray," explained Edith.

"Edith," said Rupert Gray, who had not spoken before, "did you notice any peculiarity in the walk of that strange man?"

"As I watched him advanced up the passage," said Edith, "he tossed from side to side;" and she illustrated her meaning by swaying her own body.

"It is Jacob Canaan Clarke," said Rupert Gray, sadly.

"We must be certain," put in Mr. Murchison; "I'll get it out of the old man to-morrow," he added, as he directed the man holding the reins where to drive.

Kind wishes were exchanged. Miss Badenock and Edith turned in from the gate. One o'clock struck.

CHAPTER XII

The Anonymous Letter

The morning dawned bleak and cloudy – the grey September morning. In the distance the sea reposed underneath a mist. From a hundred kitchens smoke was spreading slowly upwards. The chiming of church bells trembled from afar, calling early worshippers to the shrine of the man of sorrows. It was Sunday – the Lord's Day.

Everywhere in Christendom to-day the souls of millions feast upon the flesh and blood of the Son of Man: gaze with the eye of faith at His glorified form standing on the right side of the altar, whereon falls the amber light through multi-coloured glass, *clair-audient*† as they seem to hear His mandate down the long centuries:

"This do in remembrance of me."†

Then with sweet peace within, "which passeth all understanding,"† repair homewards for repose and recreation, hallowed rest, infused into the Lord's Day in analogy to the Jewish Seventh – the Sabbath. To-day the human race do ease their aching limbs. To-day the devotees of mammon† kneel the worshippers of God. To-day the labourer sits outside his shanty, singing beautiful hymns; the working man, dressed as smartly as his employer, goes visiting his friends. Shop-clerks assemble back of their establishments for refreshment and fun. It is Sunday everywhere. In the harbour, the local mariners – our brawny flatmen, after meals, stretch themselves about the well scoured deck. The business portion of the city wears the look of a civilised wilderness.

Alas two stricken hearts are also a dreary wilderness. Upon them the sunrays of luxury and splendour fall in vain. Joy is fled. Is human happiness or misery the deliberate counsel of God? No need propound a problem a little observation will solve. Doubt predestination as you choose: spite of the woe lying between the cradle and the grave. You cannot doubt that man's final weal is his final lot. If it is not so, why then is deity ever pleased to draw good from the evil heaped up by the wrong exercise of free will; else we mar His eternal plan. Positive evil is self-inflicted – that is to say – by human agency – a man's own hand or that of his fellows.

Jacob Canaan Clarke sat in his house looking through the columns of the *Port-of-Spain Gazette.*[†] He was a cold black – smoothed-skinned, sleek. A casual look at his face could never bring out its deep-lying cunning. In those reddish eyes of his all the trouble lay. He was addicted to the habit of pouting his lips up to his nose while inhaling heartily. The constant attempt at this feat lent a look of snappishness to the lower part of his face, spoiling its repose.

He laughed with a haw-haw, and in lieu of the inevitable word practised an accent, increasing the speed of his delivery all along. "To-morrow," he promised himself, "the whole stinking affair will fill a column and a half. In my account "I've omitted no detail. Let me see how he'll flounder out."

His eyes wandered from column to column. No headline seemed to invite his interest. Not so to-morrow. He would gloat in secret over his diabolical mischief. Ah, Jacob Clarke, doomed to disappointment! You shall not see what you want to see.

"The best laid schemes of mice and men gang aft agley."[†]

Mr. Murchison forestalled you; the editors of both dailies have the very version Miss Badenock gave the doctor. That is what will greet your eye to-morrow.

Newspaper editors are men, not things going on two props called legs. His eyes still scanned the pages of the journal. Here was a caption at last – large, bold type – no overlooking this –

"HONOUR FOR TRINIDAD"

"Trinidadians will be pleased to learn that Mr. Rupert McKinley Gray, of the firm of Messrs. Serle and Murchison, has recently been elected a member of the Linnaean Society.

"A paper written by him 'On the diseases of tropical plants,' was read before that body by the Vice-President, the beautiful, gifted Countess of Rothberry, who was out here not long ago under the assumed name of Mrs. Kathleen Hill.

"The meeting unanimously resolved that the paper should be printed and circulated among the members, numbering over a thousand, at a guinea a copy; the proceeds to be applied towards defraying Mr. Gray's expenses in going through a regular course in botany in England.

"Lady Rothberry has been appointed treasurer.

"We beg to offer Mr. Gray our warm congratulations. We are sanguine that nought but success can be in store for him.

"We look forward to the day when he will by consent be acclaimed an honour to his country and one of the stars of his race."

Jacob Canaan Clarke flung down the paper. "By gully – that man is never beaten – has nine lives;" and for half an hour he paced the room, his face portraying the bitter feelings of his heart. At length he stepped abruptly – "I've got it," he soliloquised, snapping his fingers; "I'll put a spoke into his wheel. He never gets that profession."

Jacob Canaan Clarke sat down – deliberately sat down, – and, taking pen and paper, wrote a letter. Wrote with care – drafting, and then re-copying, clean and fair, and pausing at times to consider the appropriateness of certain expressions. He, a negro – writing down a negro – prostituting the talent God gave him to the base end of trying to stand between a man and his bread and butter.

Insatiate with his dark treachery of only the night before, his remorseless conscience upbraided him not for the cruel blow he dealt a girl whose only sin lay in loving one of his own race. He sets himself now to shed more blood – the notional blood of a man's reputation – to belittle and bespatter a fame he could never hope to emulate – to be a viper in the bosom of him who had been his good Samaritan.

This is what he wrote:–

"Port-of-Spain,

"1st September, 19——.

"To Sir ASKINGALL CLUBBOCK,[†]

"President of the Linnaean Society.

"Sir, – Relative to the election of Mr. Rupert Gray to be a member of your society, I beg, in the interest of its numerous and respectable personnel, to furnish you with certain information. Mr. Gray now lies a patient at the Colonial Hospital, suffering from pistol-shot wounds received in the act of attempting to seduce the daughter of his employer, Mr. Primrose Serle, of 'Sunflower Manse.' No sooner did the enraged father shoot at him than he flung the hapless girl into a pool of stagnant water infested with eels. The distracted parent, in the wildest agony, leaped in to rescue his child. Your member seized that opportunity to make good his escape. I happened to have been an eye-witness, riding past from a place called Arima, where were held races that day. Seeing his condition, I placed him on my beast – not for his sake, but for that of society – Mutual Friendly Society,† and conveyed him to hospital. Should you require further information, write to Mr. Serle himself, or to Mr. Lionel Murchison, Miss Florence Badenock, or one Mr. Jacob Canaan Clarke, his best friend.

<blockquote>

"Hoping this will be of some service to you,

"I beg, sir, to subscribe myself,

"Yours very respectfully,

"SAM."

</blockquote>

Sir Askingall was at the rooms of the West India Committee when he received this letter. There was a meeting of the West India Club that day to consider complaints about the tardy promotion of natives in the Civil Service. He made haste and showed it to the good Countess. Great were her consternation and embarrassment.

"She did not credit one word of it," she said. "She would write out to the West Indies at once to Mr. Gray. He was a man of too high character to stoop. 'Black, and that was all,' she said; 'but comely.' "†

Meanwhile, Sir Askingall, as in duty bound, wrote to Mr. Serle. That gentleman's reply did not improve the situation. In fact, it decided the matter. It ran thus:–

<blockquote>

"Sunflower Manse,
"22nd October, 19——

</blockquote>

"To Sir ASKINGALL CLUBBOCK,

"President, Linnaean Society.

"Sir, – In answer to your letter to me enquiring as to the truth of certain allegations against my late accountant come to your hand, I have to state that I do not elect to take the Linnaean or any other society into my confidence. No society in the world is entitled to enquire into my private business.

"Whatever reverses I may have met – and any member of your society is liable to meet the same – I can bear without the aid of your august assembly.

"PRIMROSE SERLE."

Rupert Gray's answer to the Countess was even more laconic. It said:–

"Colonial Hospital,
"24th October, 19——

"Mr. Gray regrets he is unable to send Lady Rothberry the explanation, she invites. Such secrets he feels ought to be buried with him.

"Perhaps in the natural process of time truth will come to light. Till then, Lady Rothberry will, he hopes, be content to wait."

Her ladyship's reply to Rupert Gray was the last she ever penned. It read thus:

"ROTHBERRY TOWERS,
"11th December, 19——

"It comes very painful to Lady Rothberry to be obliged to write Mr. Gray the sad news her letter conveys. The Committee feel they must respect Mr. Serle's feelings. They have decided to withdraw from all they meant to do for Mr. Gray. Mr. Gray's name has also been struck off the roll of members, Lady Rothberry being the only dissentient at the voting. The thousand guineas they have handed over to the Indian famine fund. Lady Rothberry, however, has herself stepped into the breach. Enclosed is a cheque for a thousand pounds as a gift for Mr. Gray. Mr. Gray would do well to sail for England at his earliest opportunity. Lady Rothberry does not find it just to join in this hue and cry against Mr. Gray merely upon accusations contained in an anonymous letter. In the absence of anything more convincing she deems the charges malicious. Mr. Gray may continue to number Lady Rothberry among his truest friends."

The negro's rejoinder was characteristic:

"Colonial Hospital,
"1st February, 19——

"Mr. Gray thanks Lady Rothberry for her munificence. He agrees with the Committee that a man's feelings ought and must be respected. In declining to accept Lady Rothberry's kind present he wishes her to know that it causes him pain. He hopes Lady Rothberry will see how undesirable his adopting any other course would be. He begs to return the check enclosed, with a thousand assurances of gratitude to Lady Rothberry for her graceful patronage."

This letter never reached the hand of the liberal noblewoman. Before the mail reached England she was dead. She died of a chill taken in inclement weather whilst laying the cornerstone of a home in London for stranded natives from the colonies and Africa. Her death was a loss to science. She was accorded a public funeral and a monument was to be erected to her memory.

Her executor showed the letter to her lawyers who advised that the thousand guineas fell back into residue and went to the residuary legatee accordingly.

> "Howe'er it be
> It seems to me
> 'Tis only noble to be good,
> Kind hearts are more than coronets
> And simpler faith than Norman blood."†

CHAPTER XIII

"He Never Smiled Again"

THE day after the shooting Miss Badenock lost no time in telephoning to the village for the sergeant in charge. Sergeant Jolliman, spic and span, moustache waxed, rode over. He spent a respectful time wiping his boot-soles on the door mat.

"Riding in such close weather," Miss Badenock said, "was very fatiguing, the sergeant must need some light refreshment." Sergeant Jolliman acquiesced.

Miss Badenock waited upon him herself. The peeler[†] did not love whiskey and soda a little; when Miss Badenock placed before him a bottle of old rum and "morbey"[†] he of the white tunic saw glimpses of paradise. After he had well partaken of the dainties in silver salver, his hostess explained all about the accident.

"Did you not hear the report of a firearm?" she asked.

"Yes, ma'am," admitted the guest in uniform, "but we is familiar with hunting bouts in this 'nighbourhood,' and alluding to loud screaming, I guarantee you it is the fashion for parties to hail out one another in the woods. The high folks seldom gives trouble, they understands the law. I wish everybody in this district wur high folks," said the non-commissioned officer, almost filling his glass with brandy from a decanter. Miss Badenock was all graciousness. The sergeant went away highly pleased: pity there could not be some more shooting.

The wounded accountant lay in hospital during all the correspondence set out in the last chapter. The wound in the arm was now healed, but the side took a longer time. At one time the doctors were thinking seriously of granulation.† Mr. Murchison visited him frequently. He kept him posted in all the concerns of the outer world.

He was surprised to hear that Mr. Serle had not broken voice to his daughter since that fateful night. The distressed girl never quitted her room when he was in. Her life was all spoilt now.

She became quite thin. All that remained of the Gwendoline of old were the luxuriant tresses, and the expressive eyes so full now of unutterable woe. Her memory waned. Nothing interested her. She passed hours in silence, resting her head on Florence Badenock's lap.

All her friends forsook her – all the gay company of Creoles. Muriel Onslow, now Mrs. Faithful, alone clung to "poor, dear Gwen." Is not that gifted creature Ella Wheeler Wilcox right?

"Laugh, and the world laughs with you.
Weep, and you weep alone."†

"The girls" and "the boys" all shunned her. A dark whisper went round. The sympathy of numbers was lost to her.

She had sullied her escutcheon,† they thought – humbled, sold her caste; exposed the vulnerables in their armour, and she must be punished. Like the miserable lepers in Jewry, ostracised to camp out in the wilderness for a lazaretto, crying "tame – tame," she was deemed unclean.† How could it be otherwise? Hers was not simply love of a man in defiance of public opinion. It was more than that.

It was love of a black man in violation of the usages of her order – the fashionable community – the ruling race. Her father, as a gentleman of the old school, was a true type of that order, or community. He was really a link-man† There are some men you cannot oppose without incurring unpopularity. He was one.

Many, smarting under a sense of her superiority, hastened to condemn her. Many, thinking to advertise their own supposed virtues, plunged through her fair name "coach and four"† and all. Many whom the world never noticed before, tried to become cheaply conspicuous by blabbering out her failings. Many disdained the fallen queen because they could not reign in her stead. She had ceased to reign abroad. She no more reigned at home.

Alas! Gwendoline Serle, for the false step taken – the irreparable self-wrought mischief. How have you abdicated the empire of your father's heart? How have you flung the diadem of affection at the feet of love! Aforetime your slightest wish was a trident swaying him to dotage – your nod imperative. Lo, now, you forfeit all esteem. The floodgates of his resentment are broken loose.

> "And to be wroth with those we love
> Doth work like madness in the brain."[†]

Though time may assuage his anger, "For blood than water is yet more thick,"[†] still the delicate link betwixt father and daughter is sundered beyond repair. Trust in your integrity has taken wing. Henceforth your erstwhile happy life shall be a desolation. Pillow bedewed with tears – stifling, sleepless nights – fitful, restless slumbers late in the early dawn; these shall be your portion.

Besides Mr. Murchison, another visitor went frequently to the hospital – François Pierre.

"B-b-boss, O!" he asked on the occasion of his first visit, "when d-d-de m-man sh-shoot you, why you en s-s-sen fo' me? T-t- tonnier, crazay, moi gad, *c-c-c-se moi ta la*. E- - - -eef ah – ah was d-day,"[†] swore Pierre, rising from his chair at the bedside and dashing down his soft felt hat.

"Mr. Gray," remonstrated Dr. Lamaralle, who chanced to see Pierre's display, "Dr. Florence Badenock requests that you be kept quiet. You should not excite yourself."

"Doc-Doctor," said Pierre, "ah-ah is a pure Trin-Trin-Trinidadian b-bred and b-born. Me fahdah is b-bajan, me muddah yarabah. Ah-ah is man to stan fo' me cullah. Exvantage is a bad have it. Feah play is a jewel."[†]

After the occurrence nobody dared mention the accountant's name to Mr. Serle. The deed of intended partnership he tore into fragments which were consigned to the waste paper basket. "If that villain ever ventures near my store door I will blow his brains out," he had said. Primrose Serle was a man who never threatened in vain.

The junior partner did his diligence that the two should not meet. He acted as middleman. The patient grew convalescent and was discharged from hospital. He did not sever from the firm without a pang. For many a day he felt awkward.

The entire mercantile community regretted the loss of him. They declared that the Countess of Rothberry was depriving them of the services of an able man. He was to have been the recipient of a purse and an address on the eve of his sailing for Europe. The work people, like the bulk of shallow wits they were, never realised his true worth till then. They spoke of him on every occasion. Everything was Mr. Gray. Mr. Gray never did this – Mr. Gray never did that. If Mr. Gray was here, so and so could not have been.

The post of accountant at Serle and Murchison's was a coveted sugar plum, though the office was no sinecure. Jacob Canaan Clarke lost no time in applying. The senior partner would not even listen.

"No, thank you, sir," he said, "no.black man ever sits there again," pointing to the desk.

Mr. Murchison was indignant. "Sheer audacity I call this – brass-faced gumption," he said. "My good man where's your sense of propriety? Were I in your place I should poke my head into a tar-barrel," as he followed him to the door.

"Why don't you first set the example," was Clarke's retort, as he walked out, not looking very pleased.

"Ah, my man, your day of reckoning shall come," said the fair-spirited Englishman.

As Lionel Murchison stood looking after Clarke, his thoughts travelled to "Sunflower Manse" – to the silent, suffering girl there pining to a shadow – to the father whose pride was humbled – whose life was embittered – whose outraged feelings went nigh leading him to the gallows.

Lionel Murchison's mind dwelt upon the happy past; and the dreary uncertain future. He sympathised with the wordless grief of the old partner. He watched with alarm how rapidly the old man aged. The impetus sorrow gives to decrepitude sprinkled frost upon his hair and beard. His was a grief that never complained; an eye that ceased to twinkle: a heart whose comfort fled. At table he knew no jollity. He lost weight perceptibly. From robust, healthful enjoyment of life he shrank and shrivelled into an uneasy, distrustful misanthrope, tottering under stooping shoulders. His face forgot how to smile.

Not all the efforts, the dutiful attentions, the hundred and one little tactful plots and ruses of Florence Badenock could avail to rekindle the spark. Long and earnestly the junior partner thought of the womanly doctress, capable and sympathetic, now the mainstay of what was once a home. That night bravery descended upon him. He waxed bold and aggressive. What writers call "the psychological moment" had arrived.

"Come into the open," he said to Miss Badenock, "that I may tell you how much I love you"; and he led her forth.

"You do not love me," she said, "you cannot love twice. You feel a weakness which you miscall love. I came in at a time when you needed sympathy."

"First love comes to discipline the heart," he pleaded. "My fancy for Gwendoline disciplined mine. Few ever do wed their first lover. Suppose I were a widower?"

"I should never think of marrying you then," she said. "I must be the first or none."

"Such widowers," he said, swinging both her hands the while, "are men of valour. Mr. Serle always says it takes a brave man to marry twice."

In the end Florence Badenock promised Lionel Murchison to be his wife. It was a moonlight night – a happy season for lovers. There was the old, old story of the pleasant first stroll – of the trifling small talk interesting only to lovers, of glances and caresses and long spells of silence broken by the expression of sentiments of hope and joy, doubt and fear, and of assurances of lifelong fidelity. Thus these two embarked upon life's perilous sea – already traversed by millions with entire, partial or indifferent success – whereupon millions before had sunk: where shoals and sandbanks had detained the crafts of millions more: where other millions had come to shipwreck, foundering against the rocks of incompatibility, wantonness, selfishness, ignorance and superstition.

Whatever the weaknesses residing in human nature the union of the sexes has to continue. Selection, the perpetuation of the species, the Creator's palpable design – vegetation, water, animals – ingress and egress of being: so it was, and so it ever shall be, till our planet, waning bald – passes like the moon into that stage of barrenness – the consummation of the world.

When Florence Badenock returned indoors she found Mr. Serle in a state of intoxication. That was how he went to bed each night. Next morning he would awake with the vertigo. The club monopolised a deal of the senior partner's time. For days together the store did not see him. For whole weeks he never went near his dwelling, where desolation reigned. There the voice of music was hushed. Laughter amidst a happy family group died away, and noiseless footfalls went along the thick, spongy carpets.

Gwendoline wasted. One afternoon Florence Badenock succeeded in persuading her to try a walk in the garden. She looked like a gaunt spectre. Her father came along driving home from the store. As his eyes fell upon her she tried to smile. He gave a start as though he had received a dagger-thrust; then he turned quickly and looked the other way. Miss Badenock felt it.

The old man went upstairs, both hands pressing the pit of his chest, groaning audibly as his faltering footsteps dragged form stair to stair: like the "monarch minstrel" of old, weeping for him who drove him from his throne at Salem.[†]

"O, Absalom, my son, my son."[†]

> "He liv'd for life may long be borne
> Ere sorrow breaks its chain.
> Why comes not death to those who mourn?
> He never smil'd again."[†]

CHAPTER XIV

The Junius of the West

Pierre – François Pierre – was a typical working native. Conjure up before the mind's eye a broad-shouldered semi-giant standing well nigh six feet – heavy boots – broad belt – shirtsleeves turned up – hat turned off forehead à la panama, and you get an idea of our man.

Pierre was easily understandable. He did his work, smoked his cigarette, and drank his grog. He fed himself well. Now and then, not very often, he assured you, he did a little gambling. He reverenced his mother's memory. He never let a funeral pass without uncovering. Once in a way, after some sudden death or accident, he would attend Mass outside the church door. His proud boast was that John Jacob Thomas was his schoolmaster. "Défin Tammas ta led, mai de bwes, neg la ta savant,"† he would say. Nothing pleased him better than to listen to stories about Maxwell Philip. "Avocah fama mon ami,"† he would interject.

He believed in the accountant. Of an afternoon when young men flocked at the store, Pierre would stand by swallowing every word his hero uttered. Then turning to the bystanders, he would exclaim: "Is man way talk, you hear!"

Lately Pierre went frequently to "Sunflower Manse." Mr. Serle drank so copiously now, that more than once a week Pierre could be seen shouldering a box of drinks up the gravel walk. He liked Edith to answer his call. She looked so trim in her white muslin cap and faultless apron, tightly drawn round her slender waist and strapped down over her shoulders. At last one day Pierre ventured some remarks:

"G-g-got cool water?" he enquired.

"I should not advise you to drink cold water walking in this heat, – seize your blood," she said.

"Ah-an if you seize me blood," said Pierre, scarcely stammering.

"That wouldn't be good," said Edith, looking away. "Dr. Johnson says it is detrimental."

"Don' know no doctor cau-call Johnson. Known Johnson d-de lawyer," said Pierre, turning away, and drawing with his index finger the sweat off his brow, while Cupid whispered to the negro maid – manly honesty – strength – independence of character. Falsehood formed no particle in his composition. Jacob Clarke hated him, and there was no love lost.

Stooping to conquer† was not in Pierre's dictionary. Few Trinidadians have it in theirs. "Prompt to ire,"† describes them well. Let an employer but raise his voice a little higher than usual, and off strolls your native, hat in hand, not even waiting to be paid.

Jacob Clarke believed in stooping – and that too – very low. He went back and apologised to Mr. Murchison. He tried to conciliate the partners in every way. He meant only to apply to act, he explained, till the English accountant came out. He had earned his best bread with the firm, and would go his neck in blood to serve them. All this failed. Jacob Clarke was determined. He made his pen fly.

Several letters began to appear in the English papers, warning Europeans against risking the climate of the West Indies. Trinidad came in for the most disparagement. Yellow fever, wild animals, savagery and bad rum were declared to be her chief features. The West India Committee† became alarmed. Several members took up the cudgels. Great was the controversy. The writer styled himself, "The Junius of the West."† No clue lay as to his identity. One thing was certain. There was internal evidence that he was unfamiliar with most of the islands, excepting Trinidad. Pity some people ever learn to scribble.

The firm of Serle and Murchison remained without the services of a book-keeper. In the end the junior partner was obliged to sail in quest of one, leaving things at sixes and sevens. The senior partner drank harder than ever. Jacob Clarke kept coming day after day. How he fawned upon the weak-minded inebriate. How he gulped down rebuffs. How he dissembled; how he cloaked up his ill-will: how he lauded himself to the skies, extolling his own capabilities like a ranting auctioneer.

"Good as Gray, or better," he told Mr. Serle. "Shorthand and typewriting, double and single entry, posting and all the rest of it were child's play." In fact he had invented a new system of book-keeping which he meant to publish to the world later. Talk of inventing! he was a master at inventing new strokes in practice. "He had specialized in tallying," he said.

Mr. Serle confessed he did not see wherein the mystery lay as to this branch. Truth to tell, Clarke could not tally better than anybody else. Many clerks around there were, without doubt, his superiors, and he knew it; knew his ability to be below mediocrity. He therefore must needs roll in huge boulders of braggadacio to swell it nearer water-mark.

Mr. Serle's aversion could not be overcome. Clarke was the newsmonger who had destroyed his peace of mind. He used the information, but hated the informer. One day, in a sober moment, the old chief told him: "You seem fond of dispraising others. You desire to be the only courtier at the throne of admiration. With you, to be unique means prominence."

The junior partner's arrival in England would soon neutralize the effect of those bad letters. Junius came out for the last time with a beauty for pessimism. He dipped his pen in gall. This last epistle ran thus:–

"Caribbean Sea.

"To the Editor of the *Daily Mail*.

"Sir, – With my last letter on the subject of the prevalence of yellow and black water fevers[†] in the region of the pitch lake[†] at La Brea and the oil wells at Guayaguayare,[†] in the Island of Trinidad, B.W.I., I had decided to close the series.

"The departure, however, from the West Indies of a canvassing agent for white commercial emigrants calls for another epistle dealing with Port-of-Spain, the capital and trade centre of the island.

"This city stands on a plain sloping from northern and eastern heights down to the haven called the Gulf of Paria, an enormous mud-hole swarming with monsters. Here boats capture 'cascaladoo'[†] at the estuaries, and what is called deep sea fish within bail of the sewage.

"Among the highlands overlooking the town roam fierce wild bulls from the mainland that escaped the lasso at landing.

"The town is close and hot, with low-roofed houses innocent of ventilation. Sometimes the thermometer is one hundred and twenty in the shade!

"The intense heat keeps white faces indoors all day, or sunstroke will lay them low. The squares and thoroughfares are disagreeable through the abuse of ill-kept urinals.

"As wide as the streets are, white cyclists lose their lives in the open day by reason of the recklessness of the very police.

"In the crowded tramcars natives purposely sit on the laps of European gentlewomen, the only apology being a broad grin.

"The blacks never work. Banana stealing and midnight visits to hen roosts they find more lucrative.

"Every Monday morning fashion-plated grecian girls[†] with their hair half-combed, waddle about the stores. After being shown goods for an hour or so, they purchase half-yard of ribbon, or pay three cents for buttons, to the chagrin of practical salesmen.

"The Portuguese coin money for the sale of weevil-holed biscuits and indifferent salt-fish. An ordinance is to be passed restricting their consumption of cabbage.

"The East Indians are victims to yaws. Their cutlasses do not spare spouse nor estate managers. They monopolise the milk trade and cleanse their vessels in gutter water.[†]

"The town is honey-combed with their hotels interspersed among the dwellings of the Westerns. Sanitary officers have a hard time of it with them.

"The Chinese are gambling kings in whé-whé palaces.[†] The poorer ones sell coal or parch coffee at twilight. Others are itinerant vendors of ochroes,[†] tomatoes, pepper, cucumbers and watercresses, the names of which they bellow out in Anglo-Oriental gibberish on Sunday mornings, so loud as to disturb divine service and make the parson laugh. In short, the only thing of value throughout the whole town is the legal eunuch whose forte is monkeyism.[†]

"Rates and taxes are appalling. Quarantine, like the poor, is always there. Beef famine, ice famine, plantain famine, cocoa disease, beet root bounties,[†] thirty per cent differential,[†] and a scarcity of white women, render life unendurable in the capital of the land of the humming bird.

      "I am, sir,

        "Yours truly,

           "THE JUNIUS OF THE WEST."

CHAPTER XV

"Wait Till the Clouds Roll By"

Florence Badenock felt keenly the parting from Lionel Murchison. They spent the eve of departure together.

"You seem glad to go from me," she said, noting his attempt at appearing cheerful.

Often had he tried to persuade her to name the wedding day. "Theirs could always be a quiet little wedding," he would tell her.

"Not yet, Lion," she would say very coaxingly, "not till Gwen recovers."

"That may be in Neverwary," complained the impatient lover.

"Dearest darling love," she said, "wait till the clouds roll by."[†]

Miss Badenock was left alone. Gwendoline, now a silent invalid, was no longer companionable. The far away look in her eyes told the story of mind wandering in conversation.

Dr. Florence Badenock administered no drugs. She saw that the mind it was which kept the body weak. Time was the best medicine she could prescribe. So she waited and watched for the crisis – for the turn in the tide of the mental ailment, when nature herself would make an effort to throw off the incubus.

One day Miss Badenock entered Gwendoline's apartment with tears in her eyes. In her hand she carried two letters. "O, Gwen, dearest, whatever shall I do? Truly Shakespeare is right. Troubles do come in battalions,"[†] she said, seating herself beside her sick friend, who was amusing herself with turning over the leaves of some journals.

"What is it, dear?" asked Gwendoline, looking up without the least flurry. Having grappled with one great trouble, her mind rose superior over lesser trials. The sight of tears in Florence Badenock's eyes, however, roused her up.

"Lio has written. He is down with fever. I warned him against sailing for England in mid-winter. Mamma too is in a dying state. My sister Jane writes from Glasgow that she is calling for me, poor old soul, day and night. She says she cannot die until she sees my face." And, resting her head on the fragile shoulder of the other, the consoler sobbed aloud, – "the three I most love in all the world – what shall I do?" she added.

"Do not fret over much, Flor, dear, about me. Go you must. Duty calls you. If I am to live I shall live," said the invalid bravely.

"Do you promise, dear, to take care of yourself while I am away? Will you do all I advise you, and send me your photo regularly every other mail, that I may with the aid of lenses examine your looks?"

"Yes, dear," said the invalid, "I shall do as you wish," her eyes swimming the while.

"O, dear, O, dear, what a cruel change!" cried Florence Badenock. "Papa does his best to avoid me. He gives curt answers and charges Edith with whatever he wants done," she added.

"He loved you for my sake," said Gwendoline. "He loves me no longer now."

"O, dear, O, dear," cried Florence Badenock.

"Dearest Flor, do not distress yourself so. A boat goes across to New York to-morrow. Do not wait for the English mail.† You should be brave and cheerful. The inevitable we must accept. Be satisfied to know I am content with what you have done. Do not worry over what you say you have left undone."

They sat up late into the night, while Edith knelt packing up. On the morrow, when mist clouded the hills, Gwendoline Serle stood waving tremblingly to her departing friend. Thus came to an end the first stay of Florence Badenock in Iere.† Her sojourn marked an epoch in more than one life. The greatest grief to the lady doctor was her not seeing Mr. Serle. She sought him at the club in vain. He was not at the store. She left kind adieus for him. She saw him never more.

Edith accompanied Miss Badenock on board. The steam launch was placed at her disposal, but Pierre stood up in his fine comfortable boat.

Edith beckoned to him. In no time their luggage was got in; he helped them in and away.

Miss Badenock would sail by a direct line and cross from New York to Liverpool. The liner was anchored far out. Already steam was being got up. There was no time to lose. Soon they stood on deck.

"Edith," she said kindly, in a hurried whisper, placing both hands on the maid's shoulders, "care Miss Gwendoline† till I come back, and behave yourself."

Edith could not answer.

"Thanks, François," Miss Badenock said, offering Pierre money.

"E . . . . eef ah-ah-take money ah-ah-insult meself," said Pierre, declining the handsome tip.

"You must not fetch so much liquor up to the house, François, or when I return Mr. Serle will be dead," she said.

"Where you b-bung you m-mus' obey,"† he answered, as he helped Edith down into the boat.

The anchor was being weighed. There is a fascination in departure, no matter how sad the farewell, particularly when leaving love to go to love. Pierre turned his boat's bow shorewards. The Scotch passenger lingered on deck. The sun was fast rising behind the eastern hills.

At the foot of the Lady of Laventille,† looking down upon the city, the hillside teemed with roofs of galvanized iron. Domes, steeples, towers, trees, nestled below. Port-of-Spain is a pretty town, but not as seen from the sea. The customs buildings are about the chief ornament of the otherwise indifferent looking quay. The houses at Woodbrook faced the sea as far as Mucurapo Point.† On the right the Naparimas slumbered, hardly distinguishable from clouds. The steamer had stood out to sea, leading a trail of smoke.

"M-Miss E-Edith," said Pierre, resting on his oars, "long t-time ah had dat to axe you. Ah, ah ent a marridin' man, b-but ah make up me mind to marrid wi-wid you."†

"Don't talk such sinful things on the sea, Mr. Pierre. The boat are capsizing," said Edith, as the gig† danced on the sunlit waters. "Please rows me back to land. Dr. Johnson wrote in the days of King George the Third that the sea is detrimental."

"W-well, say you love me fus'," stipulated Pierre.

"I can't say that on sea, Mr. Pierre. I was brought up in religion. I am in peril on the sea.† Do, take me to the jetty; Miss Gwendoline must be dying," said Edith, much concerned.

Pierre sat silently gazing into her full, dreamy eyes.

"Mr. Pierre, you are shipwrecking me," cried Edith. "Miss Gwendoline will have to know I was shipwrecked," she added uneasily.

"Well, s-say I love you then," said the wily oarsman.

The boat drifted. François Pierre must have an answer. The negro maid sat in the stern with her broad straw on her lap. Her soft, glossy plaits were disposed thick and full and parted over the brow. Her handsome lips wore a tinge of cherry. Her teeth were like ivory, and she laughed often. Her ebony skin looked silky, unspoiled by rouge or powder. In her eyes reposed a depth of passion. Leaning back she looked the queen of those waters – a swarthy empress of some kingly harem.

"S-say I love you," said Pierre.

"Say I love you," the coy maid repeated, gazing behind at the trail of smoke the steamer was leaving behind. The boat shot home like an arrow. That night two lovers sat under the bamboo clump beside the fishing basin. This time there was no disparity of class, or colour; no let to their romance. Romeo and Juliet were both black.

The afternoon following, Mr. Serle and his daughter met in circumstances not the most pleasant. During his absence she used sometimes to sit in her father's study, where he entered and met her. His indulgence in drink had soured him down to moroseness. Bad news from the junior partner had kept him at the bottle all day. At first he was unaware of the presence of anyone. She had two minds. Her first thought was to sit still and escape when he turned out. A second thought told her that that meant cowardice and a painful prolongation of the suspense of a first meeting. This consideration nerved her.

"Papa," she cried, timidly, "can you forgive me and let us be as before?"

Mr. Serle started backward. He hesitated. His head was swimming with the fumes of spirit. His posture was unsteady. He looked a wreck of his former self.

His daughter rose to her feet trembling pitifully. Her heart smote her at his miserable condition. She knew his weakness for drink was artificial. Her father, she thought, could never be a causeless drunkard. His present hesitation was her chance, she felt.

"Remember, papa, I am your own. You are punishing me above my offence. Why please the world by sacrificing your child? Why lacerate your own feelings and bite your nails in secret? I have done no great crime. Is loving a crime? O, papa, think of mamma's last words, you used to repeat always ———"

He motioned her with an outward gesture as if thrusting away something. His haggard face was purple. It became pale at the mention of the dead.

She persisted. "Let your better nature plead for me, papa," she said weeping, her emaciated frame trembling too violently to allow of her standing any longer. "Remember, I am an orphan – a motherless, lonely creature. Papa, for God's sake do not make me an outcast – you are killing me by slow degrees. You are committing suicide over the bottle. Let us return to the old life."

Her last nettled him – suicide at the bottle. She saw the effect too late. He became sober at once. That dazed, stolid expression fled from his face. His thin lips pressed each other. He drew himself together with a dash of the old dignity in his pose:

"What!" he cried, "after heaping disgrace upon me through an infernal scoundrel, a thousand times my inferior – after making me the butt of ridicule, of shaking of heads – after raising up enemies who had never seen my face, you come now under that apparently harmless guise seeking an impossible reconciliation! Leave my presence at once, please, hypocrite – go, seek comfort from him who led you astray. Death and only death shall atone."

"Papa, papa, do you mean to drive – "

"Go, actress – go, and never return – never let me see your face again!" yelled her father with a loud stamp, every vein in neck and forehead swelling.

"Very well, papa," she said, crying bitterly, "I leave all in the hands of God. I shall indeed go and never return."

Her father left the house immediately. That night he slept at the club. Next day he went to San Fernando and was there for a month.

Gwendoline wrote to Rupert Gray that she felt her end approaching.

One night he stole across the grounds and was ushered into her presence by Edith, who guarded the open door like an amazon on sentinel.

The beautiful invalid reclined in an arm-chair beside which her lover knelt. "O, Rupert, dear," she said, stretching out her wasted hand, "how good of you to come."

Gently his arm stole around her as he kissed her upturned face. Tenderly he stroked the tresses back from off her marble brow. Gallant and true he looked as he bent and pressed his lips against the hand lying in his.

"Kiss my hand, dear," she whispered. "Soon there will be no more Gwendoline whose hand you will kiss. Ah, Rupert, see what women get for loving. But I am content. I have spoken to you once more – I shall die in peace."

"Do not talk of death, sweetheart. My heart is already broken. A dagger pierces it through. I feel its blood trickling. Refrain from wringing it further. Let us look on the bright side – let us hope to meet again."

"Meet again, yes, but not as lovers. On the resurrection morning they neither marry nor are given in marriage,"† she murmured, with a world of expression in her eyes.

Kneeling there, he soothed her with sweetest words of love; convinced her of his undying loyalty, and consoled her with tender caresses.

"O, love, my love, farewell!" she cried at parting. "After I am gone when another fills my place in the years that are to come, you will then found out how much Gwendoline cared – how much she truly loved."

One kiss more – another, and then another – one squeeze of the hand – one last lingering look – and Rupert Gray was gone.

On the very day Mr. Serle intended leaving San Fernando, he received a telegram – three words only: "Daughter is dead." He never drank as he drank then. On reaching home the cabman helped him out. He staggered into the first apartment he came to, where he lay, poor man, helplessly drunk, unable even to hold up,† much less to find the chamber of death, to look upon the face he was never more to see.

The death of Gwendoline Serle was universally regretted. Many wept for the generous, faithful heart that at last had ceased to throb. If she had sinned in not loving a white man, many felt she had suffered in expiation. The majority of those who had shunned her in life now flocked to pay their tribute of respect.

Strange world this: scrambling for the shell when the kernel is out. So, too, in by-gone times, kings and princes deluged Palestine with blood, fighting for an empty tomb. Higher up in history:

"Seven Roman cities strove for Homer dead
Thro' which the living Homer begged his bread."†

"She died and was buried,"† might with truth be said of Gwendoline Serle. Wreaths and pall-bearers, plumes and pricked horses, and an endless cavalcade of shining vehicles, headed by that of the Governor, lent pomp and circumstance to the terrors of death as pointed out by Erasmus of Rotterdam.† Edith was chief mourner.

There was one peculiarity about it all. Nobody was allowed to see her face – none but Edith entered the chamber of death. It was her last and only request. It was to the negro maid an imperative trust which she faithfully performed.

"Death, what art thou
To whom all bow
From sceptred King to slave?
The last best friend,
Our cares to end,
Thine empire's in the grave.

When all have fled,
Thou giv'st a bed
Wherein we calmly sleep:
The wounds all heal'd,
The dim eyes seal'd,
That long did wake and weep."†

CHAPTER XVI

Fiat Justitia, Ruat Coelum

The bereaved lover had walked in the procession. His pathetic figure was the cynosure of eyes as he stood far off uncovering to the bier. Sorrow such as his was too deep for tears. Give me the grief that is silent. He felt a change of scene would help him. Before long he sailed for England. He must do something before his slender means went.

He arrived in Britain. At last, at last! The dream of boyhood realised – an ambition capped – hope crowned. Every black man in the West Indies expects to see England some day.

He took train from Southampton. A single passenger was in the same saloon – a short gentleman, with a big head who, throughout the journey, sat reading a newspaper. As the train thundered within sight of London, in a gush of enthusiasm, hat in hand, the negro exclaimed: – "Hail, murky sky, canopy of industry; hail, twentieth century Rome – roaring metropolis of empire."†

His fellow passenger looked up in surprise. "Excuse me, stranger, from what part of the world are you?"

"The West Indies," said Rupert Gray, looking round.

"Great Scott, what a likeness!" cried the Englishman, looking from Gray's face to the newspaper several times. "Where about in the West Indies do you hail from?"

"Trinidad."

"You should know these faces, then," said the other, folding the paper and holding it up before the stranger.

There was no mistaking. There was the likeness of Rupert Gray and of Gwendoline Serle, a report of whose death and tragic love-story filled the columns. The ex-accountant started back in surprise.

"Just arrived in England to find yourself famous," observed the white man.

"To find myself notorious," said the negro, partly recovering from his first surprise.

The headlines were meant to be sensational. They read as under:–

"ROMANCE IN THE CARIBBEES.

A TALE OF BLACK AND WHITE.

MERCHANT PRINCE'S DAUGHTER IN LOVE WITH BLACK BOOK-KEEPER.

A BAPTISM OF FIRE – BLOOD – AND WATER.

DEATH OF THE CREOLE DESDEMONA[†] WHO WAS WELL-KNOWN IN

ENGLISH SOCIETY.

A MODERN NARCISSUS." [†]

The whole story in all its naked truth was carefully narrated. No detail of any value was omitted.

"Thank you but I cannot read it now," said the swarthy hero, handing back the paper. The enthusiasm in his face had died out.

"You should not let it affect you so. Are you not glad truth has come to light? You can say with Caesar: 'I came, I saw, I conquered,' "[†] said the white man, kindly.

"Rather, I am forced to parody Caesar's boast: 'I came, I saw, I suffered;' " said Rupert Gray, sadly, as his journey came to an end.

"Will you accept my hospitality?" asked the gentleman.

"Who does me that honour? may I enquire."

"You are speaking, sir, to Sir Askingall Clubbock, President of the Linnaean Society. This story exonerates you from the base calumnies your election drew forth. Would that her ladyship were alive. You are in time to see her statue unveiled. This way, Neville," called Sir Askingall, as his phaeton[†] drove up.

"I do accept your courteous invitation, Sir Askingall. I rejoice to meet you. I have but little time, though, to spare. I come to the Inns of Court,"[†] said the West Indian.

"You, a born naturalist, going in for law? Never. The Countess would have said 'No!' " protested Sir Askingall. "We shall restore the thousand guineas and restore your name to the list. Let justice be done, though the heavens should fall,"† said the leader of the Linnaeans.

"A man may be born several things, but he is pre-eminently born one thing. The law I want, and the law I shall have. I have already begged to decline all moneys, Sir Askingall," said his black companion in silvern whispers, as they drove through crowded streets.

Lady Askingall was deeply interested. "How mysteriously Providence moves," she said. "Mr. Gray's vindication has come without effort on his part."

"Mummy," said Sir Askingall's young son and heir, who was with her then, "the gentleman's black all over." The sturdy youngster did not forget to kick and struggle as his nurse lifted him away. "Want see the true, true Yankee, mummy, dear, want play with the darkie what's black all over."

The stranger spent some weeks, during which he came into touch with a good many personages. The English are said to be a grand race at home. Invitations poured in. The negro was feted. The "Sunflower Manse Romance," the thousand guineas story, the man's own personality, his conversational powers, won him friends.

The Princess of Wales wrote an autograph, from White Lodge, to the Rothberry Memorial Committee, regretting her inability to attend the unveiling in consequence of the serious indisposition of the Prince.† The committee at once decided to invite the West Indian, whose patroness the dead Countess had been, to be a substitute in the stead of Her Royal Highness.

"We trust you will see your way to furthering on our arrangements by stepping into the breach. Your doing so will lend uniqueness to the occasion, since you belong to a race she strenuously laboured to help."

So wrote the Secretary of the Memorial Committee to Rupert Gray.

"In deciding to comply with the request of your committee," the ex-accountant wrote in answer, "I do so with a deal of doubt as to my fitness for the responsibility. Gratitude, however, impels me to set aside personal considerations and identify myself with the national endeavour to preserve the memory of good Lady Rothberry."

The unveiling ceremony took place in splendid weather. Nobility, fashion, science, art, letters, assembled in the spacious courtyard of the Home for Stranded Natives.† The statue, a bronze one in *mezzo-rilievo,* was the work of Champney.† Opposite was a fine park where the large concourse of spectators gathered.

All being ready, the negro stood and addressed. He was in excellent voice. What excitement! A black man unveiling a statue – a negro, with bold, forward chest, from the land where the trees bear sugar,† addressing the English people! At the pedestal of marble stood the new Earl of Rothberry, a youth in his teens – nephew to the late Countess. The black speaker waxed taller as he plunged into *medias res.*†

Who says the English blood is sluggish? Flushed faces, handkerchiefs of every hue, silk hats, straw, felt, parasols, umbrellas, sticks, pipes held in air, responded to every period. Projecting his voice till it curled round the borders of the crowd, the orator came to his peroration.

"You can but faintly realise," he said, "the thrill of emotion I feel, standing, as I am at the pedestal of this memorial to the virtue of a good woman. England is rich in resources – men, money, ships, – rich in the blue blood of her aristocracy and the brain-power of her leaders; but the priceless gem of all is the purity of her womanhood as it blossoms and bears fruit in lives such as that of Laura, Countess of Rothberry, daughter of a house of empire-builders – herself an empire-builder – a peaceful welder of nations – an iconoclast of racial barriers. It is in the fitness of things, that I, a representative of those for whose welfare she toiled, should pronounce her praises; should be a palpable proof of the possibilities of her efforts; a living sample of what the negro can become. I speak it here to you – you a most enlightened people – Ethiopia self-uplifted† is destined to advance with hands outstretched to heaven. I conjure you to conduce to it. I call on you to emulate your dead country-woman in drawing aside prejudice and disability – as now I do these curtains from round her monument. Then you will have found true imperialism the best earnest of the immortality of empire† – the first empire with an out and out christian soul – a soul whose breadth of view ought to exclude inequality among the races which comprise the body it keeps alive. You, descendants of the sea-kings, accord the sons of Africa fair field and no favour. Have no upper storey and lower storey of chances and preferment. Looming down the avenue of years to come, see a multitude of dusky peoples, under the banner of the arts of peace, pressing forward in loyal phalanx to encircle altar and throne. Hear each unit mingle, as I do now, in the federated boast, drowning the voices of your enemies – *Civis Romanus sum.*"[†]

He concluded. What followed beggars description. The young Earl embraced him. The negro became the lion of the season. "Have you met the negro?" was the fashionable mode of salutation for a month. He was commanded to the castle where he basked in the presence of royalty.

The young Earl of Rothberry who entered the inns at the same time prevailed upon Rupert Gray to select the Inner Temple. In due course he passed his final and was called to the bar. He came off with the degree of LL.B., and was Roman prizeman.[†]

The Earl of Rothberry took him on a grand tour.[†] First they scoured the British Isles. They visited Enniskillen; enjoyed the beauty of Giant's Causeway; stood where the stalactites hung in Fingal's Cave; drank inspiration in the Lake District; traversed highland and lowland; ancient ruins and battlefields; inspected Haddon, still haunted by the memory of Dorothy Vernon; Binabola, "Norham's castled steep"; "Newark's stately tower"; Gilnockie; Wye Bridge, the glory of Hereford; Canwick; Stonebyres; Silver Strand; Glen Tilt and romantic Braemar smacking ever of the memory of the rival of the Guelphs; Oriel, Magdalen and Lime Walk, Oxford, that nursery of divines; Trinity Avenue, Gate of Honour, Jesus' College, Cambridge; Devils' Bridge, Aberglaslyn, Penrhyn Quarries; Glencoe and Culloden, famed "in song and story": Ballachulish and its wonders: Anstis Cove, Berry Pomeroy and Dartmoor in Devonshire, which last gave to Virginia a breed of sturdy colonisers under the Virgin Queen: Derwentwater, Yewdale, Stockghyl and Stye; Devils' Chimney: Tintern Nave: St. Gowans: Ilfracombe's frowning rocks, historic Carisbrook and sunny Bonchurch in the Isle of Wight. Then turning from nature they walked in Westminster upon the ashes of the great and good. The negro paid his tribute of respect at the Mausoleum of Wilberforce; they explored the British Museum: asked a hundred questions in the Tower of London; saw the Commons in session; saw the Anglo Saxon race working at home – miners, fishermen, labourers, artisans; passed through factory and warehouse, docks, theatres, picture-galleries and churches;

stood on the deck of the *Victory* where Nelson fell; went up Eddystone; crossed Gibraltar and overland through France; sailed on "placid Leman," floated down the Rhine; walked the saltmines of Germany, beheld the Fata Morgana with its cities and vineyards floating in air; entered Italy among "vine-clad ruins where the voice of Cicero is succeeded by the voices of shepherds calling to their fellows"; peeped down the crater of Vesuvius, feasted their eyes upon the frescoes in Great St. Peter's; for Virgil's sake visited Mantua; Florence for Dante's. Stood in Pisa at the base of the leaning tower; floated down in ornate gondolas the waterways of Venice. Then on to the "city of the violet crown," in the classic land of Greece – the home of epic and of the gods, they glided over the "phosphorescent sea" towards the land of the Pharaohs; looked up at the pyramids. Then away to Holy Ground; they dipped in Jordan, stood by Gennesaret; walked Gethsemane; viewed Salem from Olivet. On shipboard again they drifted eastward, under "spice-laden gales from Araby the Blest" – on to other climes among nations with bizarre worship and fierce blood and battle cries. They entered Juggernaut, went underground before the rude idols of the Destroyer; supped with Maharajas from plates of gold; watched the snow-capped Himalays from the vantage-ground of Simla; then down the mighty Ganges and across to the tea-gardens of the world at the gateway of the Orient amidst mandarin mansions and national institutions older than the deluge, through Behring Strait and by Pacific Railway, to hear the voice of God in great Niagara; they crossed the forty-ninth parallel into Uncle Sam's country – the land of skyscrapers and of the dollar – of national energy and progress. They were banqueted in the black belt of the South by the following of Booker Washington – black professors, judges, capitalists and authors. Then New York at last; he was better educated, had seen men and manners in the biggest centres of the hemispheres.

"Gray," said the young Earl on parting, "in deciding to live in the West Indies, you are committing a gross error of judgment. Come out to Europe, there you will carve out for yourself undying fame. We will get you into the House of Commons. You are a man capable. You can be anything you wish to be."

"Thanks – a thousand thanks, 'Lord Bill,' " as he called the Earl, "for both the offer and the compliment, but England is already made. Trinidad needs her sons to make her."

The run over was short. On his return to Trinidad Pierre was the first to greet him.

"Ah-ah-glad to c-c-see you b-boss," he said, leaping on deck. "Ah-ah-hear 'bout you in England. Ah-ah-hear you been in Jer-Jer-Jeloosaram and Nah-Nah-Nazarus."

Hearty were the greetings.

The first bit of news Pierre gave the ex-accountant as he rowed him to the jetty, was that at two o'clock that day Jacob Canaan Clarke would be married.

Rupert Gray lost no time. He longed to see Gwendoline's grave. Within two hours of his landing he stood beside it. It is a consolation to look at the place where the loved one lies. "Interment or cremation" – debating clubs have a care.

It was midday. How lonely *and* sad the young man was. The world was to him a desert now. There was a void in his heart. What did life hold for him? Ambition, and nothing more.

Talk of any man of action – warrior, statesman, poet, philosopher, explorer, inventor – whither does his ambition lead consciously or unconsciously? What underlies his activity, but the hope of possessing one of the best of women – of sunning himself in her smiles, of reading hero-worship in her eyes? Alas, Gwendoline had gone – good, warm-hearted suffering Gwendoline. Who could love him as she? Hold such a high opinion of him? Endure torture for his sake? Run the whole gamut and still refuse to give him up? None.

A wild bee buzzed around. It might be her spirit whispering consolation. Even in death she loved him. She had gone to God with all that great love perfuming her soul as the jessamines and geraniums were the air around.

> "Love may come and love may go,
> And fly like a bird from tree to tree;
> But I will love no more – no more
> Till Ellen Adair come back to me."†

What a pity, poor child. Alas for one so young, so beautiful, gifted.

Had she not a right to live? To breathe God's air and enjoy His sunshine like everyone else? She never harmed a fly. Can there be death before one's time?

Whether there can or not – one thing was certain – she had been done to death by the traitor Clarke. She fell a victim to espionage; sold, slandered, contemned, her pure soul took wing to a more congenial clime: "Where the wicked cease from troubling and the weary are at rest."[†]

And the traitor! To-day, his hands, stained with the blood of the Serles – father and daughter – would clasp in holy wedlock that of his betrothed. What a burning shame! Should this be? Never. Gwendoline must be avenged. The traitor having "sown the whirlwind" should be made to "reap the storm."[†]

Plucking a wild geranium-leaf for a buttonhole, Rupert Gray strode away. Dignity and solemn determination marked his mien, as with bowed head he walked towards a cab, muttering under breath: *Fiat justitia, ruat coelum.*[†]

CHAPTER XVII

"Your Day of Reckoning Shall Come"

As was hinted in the last chapter, Mr. Serle was dead. He died over the bottle. By his will, strange to say, Jacob Clarke came in for a legacy of fifty thousand dollars. His nuptials were to be solemnized at Holy Trinity Cathedral.† The guests were already fast arriving. A crowd filled Brunswick Square.† Around the gates of the sacred edifice, Hart and Abercromby Streets† were well-nigh impassable. A congregation of pretty girls sat in the cathedral. The rolling of carriage wheels, the flourish of hunters† adorned with ribbons, the dust, the false alarms of the advent of the bride, all told of the grand display in progress.

Presently a carriage and pair came tearing down Abercromby Street from the direction of the Audit Office.

"That's the bridegroom's carriage," said a bystander. "I know the coachman. He told me last night he had the bridegroom."

A black gentleman in frock coat and silk hat stepped from the Brigade Station† out into the street. The brigadesmen were at their athletic sports on the Savannah. The stranger moved up to meet the carriage. He looked like one of the wedding party. Standing in the centre of the street, he motioned Jehu to pull up. The powerful bays came to a standstill a good distance from the church gate. Restively they champed their bits.

Both the occupants of the vehicle rose from their seats and looked from behind the coachman's box. One was Jacob Canaan Clarke; the other his bestman. They looked at Rupert Gray.

"What do you mean?" asked the bridegroom-elect.

"War to the knife," muttered the obstructionist in a confidential gutteral.

"Man, stand out of the way," shouted Clarke. "Move, I say, you low-life vagabond," he added, as he leaped out.

In the act of alighting, his bell-topper,† getting knocked off, rolled under the wheel. Clarke stooped to take it, all crushed, as the vehicle was drawn a yard or two by the spirited animals.

Quick as thought Rupert Gray carried on. Drawing the enormous frock-coat over the head of the stooping bridegroom, he commenced to flog him with a short, thick hunter he carried.

Clarke darted up, but his head was wholly concealed beneath the broad-cloth hood. Like lightning his assailant's hunter played all over his anatomy. The crowd closed in. People ran from every direction. The bestman stood bewildered.

Cries of "the bride – the bride" arose. The great crowd surged. The hubbub was deafening. The hunter moved like a threshing-flail.

Up drove the bride – a comely black girl with a fine head of hair. Her arrival unnerved Clarke. With a desperate tug he got his arms out of his coat-sleeves and with a shambling hip-walk, made for the Brigade Station in bare waistcoat, leaving his marriage-vestment in the hand of his chastiser who tossed it over to the bestman.

A sergeant of police came doubling up, followed by two of his men. It was Sergeant Jolliman whom Miss Badenock had entertained at "Sunflower Manse." He had been promoted to Head-quarters.

"Arrest that man," shouted the bride's father.

"I did not witness the assault," said the officer; "your son-in-law will have to complain him. It is not my fault that the honey-moon is spoilt," and he went about clearing the crowd.

The wedding could not take place. The disappointed guests filed out of Church. As the bride's carriage wheeled round she sank into her father's arms.

To the crest-fallen bridegroom, as he rode home, came the words of the junior partner: "Your day of reckoning shall come."

.　.　.　.　.

Rupert McKinley Gray stood charged with that he did on the ——— day of ——— assault and beat one Jacob Canaan Clarke. The names of the parties were first called.

"Jacob Canaan Clarke," shouted the clerk.

"Shake up, Canaan Clarke," shouted the constable at the inner door, not hearing well the name.

"Wake up, Canaan Clarke," bellowed the constable below stairs.

"No appearance," opined that functionary.

"No appearance," re-echoed him of the inner door.

Meanwhile the complainant was being sworn. Defendant admitted having given him a sound thrashing and was duly fined.

. . . . .

Rupert McKinley Gray, barrister-at-law,† sat in his chambers. "Come in," he said, in answer to a gentle rap, and in walked Mr. and Mrs. Murchison, the latter *née* Florence Badenock, looking the picture of good health. Just the day before, they had arrived from Scotland where they had been married now over three years. Her daughter's presence had proved a wonderful tonic to old Mrs. Badenock; had brought her back to life.

Cordial indeed were the greetings: then there was a pause – somebody was missing to complete the circle "of Auld Lang Syne."

"Have you had a case yet?" asked Mr. Murchison, breaking the silence at last.

"Not yet," he returned.

"Then we're in time to give you your first brief," said Mrs. Murchison, delighted, as the lawyer led husband and wife into his innermost chambers where they remained closeted for the rest of the day. The consultation ended, the lawyer looking pale and perturbed, accompanied his clients to the door.

"Mind you come this evening, Mr. Gray," said Mrs. Murchison.

"Yes," was his only answer, as half-a-dozen shades of feeling chased one another from his face.

"O, I shall come myself to fetch you, you unbelieving Thomas,"† promised Mr. Murchison, as they walked away.

CHAPTER XVIII

A Cause Celebre

The "Heirs of Serle *versus* Jacob Clarke and others" was the only case down on the list. Rupert McKinley Gray, Esq., Barrister-at-Law, appeared for the plaintiffs.

For the defence were arrayed three gladiators of the Trinidad Bar. First, the Hon. Hay Russia, K.C.,† was there – a canary bird at the bar – whose persuasiveness and brilliant diction will captivate a jury. Next him, sat joking sonorously in patois French,† the living digest, that apostle of case-law, Man-you-well Africanus Polbutter.† Third in the row, smiling, sat the Hon. Papyrus Wiseman Jonathan, K.C.† – a master at welding law and logic – an advocate with a subtle analytical mind. The combination meant address, precedent and cross-examination. They were instructed by Mr. San Fernando Mango,† the doyen, and Mr. Voice-in-the-Wilderness Buyier,† another prince of the lower branch.† Mr. He Murambo Salagar,† late of "spurs and big guns" fame,† instructed Mr. Gray.

"Court!" the usher called.

All rose. The Judge bowed, took his seat, and the contest opened. The plaintiffs' case was that the will of the late Primrose Ebenezer Serle be set aside.

Lionel Mordaunt Murchison† propounded a rival will, bearing earlier date, and of which he was sole trustee and executor. Probate was duly proved of the will under which the defendants took. In the pleadings, counsel or the plaintiffs set up undue influence against the defendant Clarke. The other co-defendants were darkies.

All day the battle raged. Africanus Polbutter thundered like a titan against the cases adduced by the other side, overwhelming them with a host of counter-authorities and distinguishing as he went along.† A line of witnesses – clerks, customers, porters, servants of the deceased, filed past. Objection after objection was either allowed or over-ruled.

On the second day Dr. Lamaralle gave evidence that the deceased was a victim to *delirium tremens.* Wiseman Jonathan tortured the doctor half the day over Taylor's Medical Jurisprudence.† In the end the defence rebutted completely the allegation of undue influence, Africanus establishing clearly that of all the cases relied on not one "was in the same street" with the one at issue. The importunity of the defendant Clarke was all that could be proved; and even that was not done till François Pierre gave his evidence. Wiseman Jonathan rose to cross-examine:

"You say your name is François Pierre?"

"Ah-ah-en s-say so. D-d-dat is me name c-c-since ah-ah born."

"Do you know the defendant, Jacob Clarke?"

"Em-eef ah-ah-know 'im. Ah could make out 'e two lef' foots, ah-ah-mile off."†

"You say you saw him around the store often, what do you mean by often?"

"Au-au-always."

"How many times a week or a month?"

"Au-au-always, ah-ah tell you. You don' know English?"

"You said in your examination-in-chief he was a bore to the deceased, what do you mean?"

"Ah-ah-mean ah weary tell 'im b-bring b-bedding an pli-pillah to sleep in d-de-wharf."†

"Sleep where?"

"*Domi assu chay,*"† shouted Pierre, feeling more secure in patois.

"That's not it – did he bother out Mr. Serle?"

"De-de ole m-man weary booce 'im."†

"What you ever overheard him telling the old man?"

"He always t-talk easy when 'e see me com-comin."

"You never overheard any conversation between them?"

"Mr. Wiseman O, who you tink ah-ah be? Man don' listen and d-den b-bring come and carry go. Me is Trin-Trin-Trinidadian *oui.* Ah-ah-tell you d-de man live in de place like fly 'pon molasses. Wha' mo' you want."[†]

"What fetched him there?"

"He foot."

"I mean what he went there for?"

"Wuk. He m-make d-de boss loss 'e wuk."[†]

"Who is the boss, Mr. Serle, or who?"

"Ah chien, how you want d-de man make Mr. Serle loss 'e wuk. You self too. Is Mr. S-Serle store."[†]

"Who then is the boss?"

"Mr. Gray, nuh! You don' know Mr. Gray? Look 'e day wi-wid d-de lead p-pencil i'-in 'e teet."[†]

"That will do," said counsel.

"Ah-ah-tink so meself," muttered Pierre, as he walked back to his seat. "You en axe me nutten yet. *Z-zut pacah jamais trouver yun lut Maxwell, jamais.*"[†]

The case for the plaintiffs looked ugly.

On the third day Mr. Gray fell back upon another position. He drew the attention of the Court to this peculiarity in the drafting of the disputed will, viz.: that a motive was assigned for each bequest. "*Because the said my beloved child, Gwendoline Serle, departed this life, etc., etc., I give and bequeath, etc., etc.*"

"If we can prove," he said, "that Gwendoline Serle did not depart this life, the gifts to all the defendants must fail; and we are prepared to prove it." The three lawyers on the other side laughed aloud.

At once they put in a certificate of the death of Gwendoline Serle. The keeper of the cemetery who had been served with a writ *Ad duces tecum*[†] was there to produce his books in proof of interment.

This, Mr. Gray stated, would be displaced by primary evidence. The defence contended that the evidence was conclusive. Mr. Gray held on for dear life.

As a preliminary, one Edith Ollivierre was called into the box. This witness swore that she had been maid to Miss Gwendoline Serle, who was alive at the date of the will in dispute. Wiseman Jonathan tackled her. Each time she was cornered, back she fell upon the dominant reply:

"*I can't remember.*"

"Her body was not put into the coffin, you say?"

"No, it wasn't."

"Then, where was it?"

"I can't remember."

"Weren't you there?"

"Yes."

"And can't remember where your mistress's body was?"

"No."

"Have you seen her since?"

"I can't remember ever seeing her since."

"Is it not inconvenient to have such a bad memory?"

"Yes, sir," said the witness. "Dr. Johnson wrote in the days of King George the Third, that that is detrimental."

Then came a bombshell. After a short conference with Murambo Salagar, Mr. Gray fixed his band, settled his wig, rose and said: "We suggest the viewing of the locus – we move that the body be exhumed."

"That," said Hay Russia, "would not be primary evidence."

"It would be leading up to it," explained Mr. Gray.

.   .   .   .   .

Five o'clock in the afternoon of the fourth day was the hour fixed for the exhumation of the body. All the necessary formalities were quickly gone through, thanks to the courtesy and despatch of the Town Clerk.

The Judge, who believed that the "pomp and circumstance"[†] of the dread majesty of the law would work a salutary effect on the vulgar mind, insisted on the practitioners not removing their robes.

"It is not customary," explained Hay Russia.

"True," said His Honour, "but it would lend solemnity to the occasion."

Cabs waited outside. At ten minutes to five Bench and Bar[†] set out for Lapeyrouse Cemetery.[†] A temporary platform had been erected near the grave round which stood fifty constables with fixed bayonets.

The Registrar led the Judge to a seat placed for him on the dais on the platform. His Honour was a powerfully built son of nemesis, with a venerable look, and he wore a scarlet robe. On either side were ranged opposing counsel all robed. The three solicitors wore full dress. Six doctors were in attendance. Two being M.D.'s, appeared in their robes.

The grave was near the wall facing Tragarete Road. Two grave-diggers with pick-axes stood ready. It was now five o'clock. A vast concourse – a countless multitude thronged God's acre. Every tombstone, every vault, was made a coign of vantage. The walls, the trees around, the roofs of houses at Woodbrook, were covered with on-lookers. The afternoon was fine.

The sun was sinking into the Gulf of Paria – a ball of gold. Crimson clouds, as of glory – flamed in the west. The silent spectators seemed a resurrected multitude waiting for judgment – quickened by the awful blare of the "last trump"[†] – looking for the appearance of the Son of Man.[†] The keeper of the cemetery stood at the head-stone.

"Do you recognise the grave of Gwendoline Serle?" the Registrar asked, solemnly.

"I do," said the keeper, touching the head-stone.

A grave-digger then cleared away the wild geraniums about it. The Registrar read the inscription aloud:

"GWENDOLINE ELOISE SERLE,

AGED 22.

SHE IS NOT DEAD, BUT SLEEPETH."[†]

The work of digging commenced.

> "Such murmur fill'd
> Th' assembly, as when hollow rocks retain
> The sound of blustering winds."[†]

At length the coffin was reached. The casket enclosed lead. The men had great difficulty in hoisting it. Placing it beside the open grave, they went to work to remove the lid. Free use was made of disinfectants. Standing three on a side, the doctors bent over. The shroud was opened. The doctors all started back and looked towards the judge. The grave-diggers lifted up from the coffin the effigy of a woman in plaster-of-Paris.

As they bore it to the platform the Judge stood up in amazement, his scarlet robe contrasting with the creamy white of the image. The lawyers crowded together. Rupert Gray, a pace in advance, stood with folded arms. The thing was raised aloft. It was a complete likeness of Gwendoline Serle, in graveclothes.

The police shouldered their rifles. The people nearest the clearance fell back in affright. Some screamed. Some groaned. Some kneeling, crossed themselves. Some ran away. Others with clasped hands turned up their bewildered eyes to heaven. Sobs were heard. Small boys slid down from their elevation and whistled through their fingers.

Six o'clock sounded from the belfry of the Church of the Sacred Heart.† The exhumation was over. Night settled like a dusky pall upon the city. Noisy crowds forced their way through the gates. Within an hour silence reigned in the city of dead.

.   .   .   .   .

The morning broke over a feverish and excited city. Long before 10.30 a.m. every avenue leading to the Red House† was blocked. The police were kept busy. Counsel for the defence came prepared for war.

Difficulties only nerve some men and bring out their latent genius. No use trying to oppose them. You spend your ammunition in vain. You may delay; you may even thwart for a time, but defeat them you never can. They were born under a superior planet.

Hay Russia rose to the occasion. "The other side has proved," he said, "that the grave visited was not that of Gwendoline Serle. That only neutralises the effect of the entry in the Cemetery Books as to place of burial, but the certificate of death still stands. The information the Registrar of Deaths received was given by the deceased's own maid who swears she has not seen her mistress since. We say she is dead. Upon whom falls the *onus* of locating the grave? Surely not upon us. We are in under the will. They seek to defeat our legacies. They allege she is not dead, they must prove it. *Prima facie*† we have proved our contention. There is no equity to compel us to point out where her body lies. The Court cannot go trotting all over the country peeping into graves. We submit that evidence of death as proved by the Registrar's certificate is conclusive. Let them produce the deceased since they allege she is alive. You cannot rely on the weakness of our title. You can only hope to succeed upon the strength of your own. That is a correct statement of the law of England as I understand it, and I submit that I do understand it." Hay Russia resumed his seat.

Would counsel for the plaintiffs take up this formidable gauntlet of defiance? A stillness as of death, broken only by the whir of the electric fan, pervaded the hall of justice.

"Expectation held them mute."[†]

Mr. Gray, Murambo Salagar and Mr. Murchison were seen to be in consultation. The tension was fearful. Presently counsel rose:

"I shall call one more witness," he said, as a woman in deep black, thickly veiled, stepped into the box. The witness was sworn. In the excitement nobody observed she kissed the book underneath her veil.

"What is your name?" asked Mr. Rupert Gray, in a silvern tremor.

"Gwendoline Eloise Serle," said the witness, throwing back her veil.

"O, God!" shouted the spectators, springing to their feet, like one man, as the beautiful face of the heroine of "Sunflower Manse" was revealed.

A loud buzzing filled the hall. White-helmeted constables motioned for order.

"Silence in Court!" the Registrar stood and cried, as he raised to his lips, with trembling hand, a glass of iced water.

The three lawyers for the defence sat bolt upright. Rupert Gray, trying to be calm, gazed at the motionless vision in the witness box. Confusion reigned. The Judge whispered to the Registrar.

"This case stands adjourned for a week," cried the latter.

. . . . .

Public interest never flagged. At the resumption, Gwendoline Serle went into the box. Her beauty charmed. The rest of the case was smooth sailing. In her examination-in-chief, witness told a pathetic story.

"I happened to have incurred my father's displeasure. A misunderstanding followed. In a fit of anger he forbade me to enter his presence again. My death he swore could alone wipe out his disgrace. It grieved me to see how unhappy he was, and how he was ruining his health. I had a great temptation to end my life, but I had something to live for. Moreover, I shrank from ushering myself into the presence-chamber of

God before I was wanted. It was always my conviction that such souls are made to stand aside till the effluxion of their alloted span. I prayed to God. I was anxious to save my father's life – to make any atonement. I began to feel that my own end was approaching. My friend in Scotland wrote to tell me that my photographs were not satisfactory enough to admit of a diagnosis with any certainty. She requested me to send her my bust done in plaster-of-Paris. While Mr. Bocaccio, the Venezuelan sculptor,[†] was etching the preliminary, a thought struck me. Instead of a bust, I paid him handsomely for the exhumed effigy. My father was at San Fernando. Nobody used to visit me. Muriel Faithful was at Barbados. I disguised myself in widow's weeds and lay out the image for burial. None but my trusty maid had access to the room. The report of my death was no surprise, as it was known my health was impaired. I watched my supposed funeral from a window. Next day, I visited my grave while someone was there. I took lodging in a hotel, was careful not to be recognised, and sailed for Europe by the very next mail. I sought out my friend Miss Badenock and explained the whole affair. Change of air, of scene and diet, moderate calisthenics, and the hope that my death would satisfy my father, brought me strong again. I attended Miss Badenock's wedding. I went with the Murchisons to Canada, where we lived with his relatives all the time. While there my poor father died. Mr. Murchison came out to look after his affairs."

The Court listened with interest. Counsel refrained from cross-examining. There were no addresses.

After luncheon, His Honour Mr. Justice Duck[†] summed up as follows: – "This is a suit brought by the heirs of the late Mr. Primrose Serle, to have his will set aside on the ground – as I conceive – of mistake. Mr. Lionel Mordaunt Murchison[†] propounds a will of earlier date – namely, that of the 27th March, ——— 18——, whereby deceased devised and bequeathed all his real estate and personal property to his only child, Gwendoline Serle. The defendants claim under the will in dispute, dated the ——— of ——— 19——. What appears strange is that while the earlier will is evidently the work of a lawyer, there are internal traces of a layman's hand in this disputed will. Counsel's attempt at setting up the doctrine of undue influence seems to have been only tentative. We sympathise with his vain endeavour to keep the young lady out of Court. The case substantively commences when he challenges for unreality, the motive upon which the respective legacies purport to have been based. That is to say, the testator believed, at the date of this will, he would be without heir or next of kin; whereas his daughter was not dead. Here is a clear instance of mistake. In the earlier will she is sole beneficiary. In the last will her death is recited as a preamble to each bequest. I cannot go along with the defence in seeking to minimize the importance of the exhumation. The fact of having found an empty coffin goes a great way towards confirming the identity of the young lady who claims to be Gwendoline Serle – an identity the defence has left unchallenged. In the interpretation of wills the Court is guided by the intention of the testator. Reading both wills together we get this result: – "I give away to third parties all I own because my child is not alive." The Court finds that the child is in fact alive. Here the maxim must apply – *ignorantia facti excusat.*† Equity cannot therefore suffer her to be excluded. We see clearly what the testator's intention was. That intention must be effectuated. To hold otherwise would be tantamount to disherison.† The legatees shall have to be disappointed. The will under which they claim is accordingly set aside. Judgment goes for the plaintiffs with costs. Counsel is to be complimented for the marked ability displayed on the occasion of his first appearance at the bar. It gives the Court pleasure in saying we are favourably impressed with the way in which he conducted his case."

The Court then rose. The great fight was over – the battle lost and won. The immense wealth of Mr. Primrose Serle reached its natural destination. It fell to his only child, Gwendoline Serle. Upon the advice of her lawyer a reasonable portion was allotted to each of the charities.

CHAPTER XIX

Riding to the Resurrection

We must now return to the day when Mr. and Mrs. Murchison first entered the chambers of Mr. Rupert Gray, to entrust him with his first case so fraught with interest to the public.

His chambers comprised three apartments – an outer occupied by the clerks, a middle where he ordinarily would see clients, and an inner for important consultations. It was into this last he had led the pair. Mrs. Murchison sat on a couch on the right of the elaborately designed desk, while her husband occupied a seat beside the lawyer's left. The past revived at sight of these visitors; every association memory held stalked by. Self-control was hard to maintain.

When at length silence was broken, they pursued topic after topic. Their own marriage, their two fine children, their return to Trinidad, Mr. Serle's death, Mr. Murchison's business prospects, the success of the English accountant who had been in charge all the time, the young lawyer's own experiences abroad, his resolve never to marry, his collision with Jacob Clarke, all came in for attention.

Then passing on to business, Mr. Murchison explained that the object of their coming was to retain him to see after the will of Mr. Serle. He placed before the lawyer copies of both wills. They watched him peruse them slowly with due professional solemnity.

Then wheeling round his large chair to face the lady, he asked: "Had Mr. Serle left any relatives alive?"

"Yes," answered Mrs. Murchison.

"Where are they?"

"Here in Trinidad."

"Who?"

She hesitated. Husband and wife exchanged glances. "A near kinsman – kinswoman I mean – a relative – a blood relation," she stammered.

The lawyer marvelled at her embarrassment. Surely he thought marriage had altered Florence Badenock.

"Is the person you speak of a relative of Mr. Serle or that of his wife?" he asked encouragingly.

"A near relative of both," said Mrs. Murchison, seriously turning pale; as, rising, she stood before the desk. "Mr. Gray," she continued, "you are a man of courage – you can endure – Mr. Serle left a daughter."

"A daughter!" cried the advocate, in a puzzled incredulous tone, rising also from his chair: then, addressing the husband rather, he asked: "How many daughters had he?"

"One," answered the Murchisons, simultaneously.

All three were standing now. The advocate was tilting back his chair with both hands.

"I do not understand you," he said, looking from one to the other several times.

"One daughter, we mean," said Mrs. Murchison, feeling that the chance had come, "one child living and looking – one sole heiress – she is alive – she is at our house – she longs to see you – O, Mr. Gray, be prepared for this news – it is Gwendoline herself."

The chair fell to the floor. Rupert Gray kept backing till impeded by the wall. "Who?" he gasped, swallowing hard.

"Gwendoline – Gwendoline is alive," said Mr. Murchison, "and you shall see her."

"See her at doomsday," said the lawyer, laughing the laugh of a person about to lose his reason.

Husband and wife feared to proceed. His looks were reproachful. Distrust showed in his whole manner. He seemed to resent what he deemed an outrageous practical joke. He was leaning his back to the wall. One leg was drawn up, the footsole resting against the wall. He looked anxious to bring the interview to a close. Husband and wife went nearer to him. Placing one hand on his shoulder, Mr. Murchison said in the familiar voice of old: "Gray, you know me. You know I would not lie to you or to any man. I tell you before God, Miss Gwendoline Serle is alive."

"Risen from the dead," said the lawyer, struck, however, by the earnestness of Lionel Murchison.

His unbelief seemed to waver for a while. The possibility dawned upon him. He was a lawyer – a man of the world – no stranger to the uncertain vicissitudes of life. He paced the room, expressing his thoughts aloud. They stood mute, watching the great struggle sorrow makes before it can be ousted from the human soul into which it has once settled. He was utterly unmindful of their presence.

"Gwendoline alive – I saw her corpse, with my own eyes – conveyed from her father's house – I was in the cortege. I saw her buried. I visited her grave. I do so daily since my return. A mystery – a mockery – a cruel joke. O, Mrs. Murchison, is this your love for her? She would not see such pain inflicted. I had looked to you for consolation."

"You refuse the consolation I offer," she said.

He came up to the couple. "Mr. Murchison, what do you tell me?"

"I tell you," said the latter, "I swear to you in all good faith – your af – Miss – the dead you mourn – Gwendoline lives."

"I know she lives," answered Rupert Gray. "Your words, like those of the oracle at Delphi,† will bear a dual construction. She lives on another plane, beyond time, where it is all work, all usefulness, without the drawbacks of mortality – where constant activity is constant rest. Yes, there she lives."

"Mr. Gray," said the wife, wiping her eyes, "will you call this evening? Nothing but seeing will convince you."

"I will not be persuaded," he said, "though one rose from the dead."†

It has fallen to the lot of no man for his sweetheart to die and be buried and then rise again after the third year. It fell to the lot of Rupert Gray.

That night, as he took his seat beside Mr. Murchison in the cab that came to fetch him, he remarked in a half-mystified way: "I am riding to the resurrection." The popping of champagne corks – the chiming of table silver – the noiseless gliding of trained waiters – the constant irritation of the telephone – laughter and merriment – piano and song – all amidst a blaze of electricity, beneath the roof of the hotel facing the Grand Savannah,† proclaimed it the palace of Oberon.†

A cab has just stopped. Cabs come and go always. Two gentlemen are entering at the north central gate – a black and a white. The former is no stranger to the place, though he has not been there since the days of Mrs. Kathleen Hill.

A negro maid greets them. It is Edith, showing her pearly teeth. She had disappeared the very evening of the funeral. It nearly broke François's heart. Guess his joy when Edith wrote from Scotland to say she had become maid to Miss Badenock, who had sent for her. She accorded Mr. Gray a kind reception, and led the way upstairs.

"Show Mr. Gray in, Edith," said Mr. Murchison, as he walked to his own apartments.

Rupert Gray was ushered into the self-same room where he used to enjoy the society of Mrs. Kathleen Hill. He seated himself near a window, but could not remain in that posture. He felt that by standing all would be over quicker.

In that beautiful recess, amidst Japanese furniture and quaint aesthetic ornaments and pictures stood the black man with bowed head, waiting for the appearance of his bride – waiting for her resurrection from the dead. Every second seemed a lifetime. Anxiety almost displaced his doubts. Suppose it was not she – it might be her sister – but would Lionel Murchison lie – what does she look like now – is she grown lovelier – she is grown older. Could she love me still? – If she loved me why did she die? – "she has been dead or rather absent too long," he finally soliloquized.

"Absence makes the heart grow fonder,"† said a rich, familiar voice.

Rupert Gray looked up. There, standing at the door between the snow-white drapery, in all the bloom of luscious womanhood, smiled Gwendoline Serle.

"Gwendoline! Gwen-do-line!" he cried in wide-eyed amazement; as with pleated brow and clenched fist he backed slowly. "My God – it – is – Gwen – do – line!"

He tried to speak, but could not. His lips moved. He thought he was speaking, as with outstretched arms he made to advance. He was powerless to move. The sound of chanting floated across from All Saints' Church,† overflowing with the triumphant swell of the organ. Below yawned the Savannah like a vacuum of gloom encircled by the lights in the dwellings of the upper classes. In the distance the belt cars,[†] hidden all to their ridges, trailed like enormous glow-worms around the borderline forever. The form did not seem to breathe as it stood with one hand lifted as if in the act of parting the drapery; he tried to stand but failed.

"It is an angel – it is Gwendoline," he heard himself say. He looked around to make sure it was his own voice.

The form amidst the drapery began showing signs of pity. The snow-white bosom rose and fell; crimson dyed the cheeks; the kind eyes glistened. His self-possession returned.

Rupert Gray rose up and advanced with outstretched arms, murmuring: "My own – my long lost Gwendoline – new-risen from the dead."

Let the curtain fall over a scene too sacred for unhallowed eyes. Here, indeed, were human love and fidelity that had survived the test of time and the tomb – that waded through blood, fire and water – that had torn down the partition of race – that laughed public scorn to scorn – that had trodden the winepress of disappointment and despair – aye, run the whole gamut of humiliation faithful to the end.

· · · · ·

The celebration of Jacob Clarke's nuptials had been put off, pending the result of the case. This unfortunate marriage never took place. Before a day could be fixed the bridegroom-elect found himself in the toils.

Sergeant Jolliman swore out a warrant for the arrest of Jacob Canaan Clarke for that he did on the ——— day of ———, forge, sign, counterfeit and publish falsely a paper-writing purporting to be a will – to wit the last will and testament of one Primrose Serle, late of "Sunflower Manse," in the Ward of ——— in the island of Trinidad.

· · · · ·

The marriage of François Pierre and Edith Ollivierre took place without a hitch. Mr. Murchison gave away the bride, while Mr. Rupert Gray acted as bestman.

While driving home from church the bride said to the bridegroom: "François, people says stammering men has bad tempers, and is not kind and gentle. I hope it are not so with you. Dr. Johnson wrote in the days of King George the Third that that is detrimental."

"Ooman is a nation," said the bridegroom, "way well bodderation.† Ah-ah don' get vex quick, b-b-but when ah-ah vex, ah vex."

. . . . .

Mr. and Mrs. Gray live in the splendour of loneliness at "Sunflower Manse," along whose stately corridors patter tiny feet, and within whose walls re-echo childish laughter.

Mrs. François Pierre, who, since her marriage, seems to have become left-handed, is no longer in their service. "Her infant son," she says, "is to be an agricultree and botanner; for Dr. Johnson wrote in the days of King George the Third that too many frock coats and beaver hats are detrimental." Her ambition is due to the proposed erection of a Negro-Industrial Institute in the West Indies.†

Here a day in each week will be set aside for negro literature exclusively. The staff will consist entirely of black professors. Two exhibitions for primary school candidates of both sexes will, under certain conditions, be awarded yearly. After a six years' course, students will graduate; top-man and top-woman receiving a prize of £300 to be laid out, under the guidance of a committee, in the purchase of free-hold farms in any of the Antilles.

The immense funds for the founding of the proposed institution were collected in Great Britain by the admirers of Rupert Gray. The Duke of Westminster,† Baron de Rothschild,† Baroness Burdett-Coutts† and Mr. Cecil Rhodes,† each endowed liberally. The Earl of Rothberry undertook to maintain a chair for the Professor of Rhetoric. There is to be a picture-gallery of eminent negroes. A statue of Wilberforce† will occupy the centre of the Quadrangle.

All the blacks in England, chiefly from the inns of court and the medical centres, attended the preliminary meeting held in London to devise ways and means. The Duke of Devonshire was in the chair. "Joe Chamberlain," with his William Pitt's face, represented the Colonial Office.†

In a practical address, punctuated with applause, a black bishop from the West Coast† told his compatriots: "Miscegenation would soon oblit-

erate the strongest traits of race. West Indian negroes, be proud to per-
petuate your seed unmixed. Fraternize and hold your heads up. Variety
is a law of nature. You represent one of the four ruling colours in
mankind. Nature brought you, nature bred you. 'Nature does nothing in
vain.' Why vex your souls when called negro? Which white man, or yellow man, or red man does that? Turn to this scripture and 'smoke your
pipes' over it: 'I am black but comely, O ye daughter of Jerusalem. – As
the tents of Kedar as the curtains of Solomon.'† So long as you fret and
chafe and disrespect your own because 'the sun hath looked upon you,
your own vineyard never shall you keep.' "†

.   .   .   .   .

The curtain falls over a prominent native who lives for the good of his
people, entering without fear of contamination into their every phase of
social life; identifying himself with their sorrows and their joys, over a
brilliant jurist whose lofty eloquence adorns the bar; over a local statesman whose deep wise counsel is almost indispensable in the Senate; over
the rising hope of Trinidad and the West Indies – over Rupert Gray.

THE END

ANNOTATIONS

Rupert Gray

Epigraph

† **Secundus dubiisque rectus. / – DEBRETT's:** The phrase is legal Latin meaning
  "the second in line and in cases of doubt the right or direct heir". Debrett's
  Peerage, first published in 1802 by John Debrett, is a reference work giving
  information about royal, noble and titled families and individuals in England.
  There have been numerous editions up to the present day, and it is therefore
  difficult to know exactly where this phrase comes from. The general idea
  seems to be that Rupert is a worthy heir to the wealth and position Mr Serle
  holds at the beginning of the story.

p. 7

† **coolies:** "Coolie" was the name given by Europeans in India and China to a
  native hired labourer or burden-carrier. In Trinidad, "coolie" was widely used
  to designate any person of East Indian descent, but eventually came to be generally considered highly derogatory.

† **tram car:** From 1895 to 1950, Port of Spain, Trinidad's capital city, was served
  by electric trams, a popular means of getting around the city and its nearby
  suburbs.

† **hucksters:** Vendors, especially of food and drinks, operating on street pavements
  or in markets, mainly African-Trinidadian women; at the time, more commonly called "marchandes".

† **the last down-train to San Fernando:** The Trinidad Government Railway operated trains throughout Trinidad; the Port of Spain–San Fernando line opened
  in 1882. There was no night service; the last train from the capital to San
  Fernando, Trinidad's second city situated in the south of the island, left at
  four o'clock in the afternoon.

p. 9

† **saloon:** The saloon car, or saloon carriage, is a railway carriage without com-
  partments, furnished more or less luxuriously; see also p. 98.

† **The Serles were a proud old family, without a trace of intermixture:** That is, the
family had no non-white ancestors; it was a "pure white" family of English
descent.

p. 10

† **by this mail:** The Royal Mail Steam Packet Company operated a steamship passenger service between the West Indies and England, sailing fortnightly. It was
contracted to carry the mail, and its service was therefore known as "the
mail".

† **cocoa planters of the Naparimas:** The Naparimas was the district around San
Fernando in the south of the island. Better known as a sugar district, cocoa
was also important there in 1907, when the cocoa industry was prosperous
and expanding.

† **Gran Couva:** A village in Central Trinidad, in a district that had flourishing
cocoa estates in the early 1900s.

† **Manzanilla's coconut palms suck moisture from the spongy beach:** The long
lower portion of the eastern coast of Trinidad, where Manzanilla is situated,
was famous for its coconut plantations, and was called "The Cocal" as a
result (from the Spanish for a place planted with many coconuts).

† **"Nigga too black . . . set down close bakra gul, tink heself big guvanah.":** "That
Negro is too black. He sits down close to a white woman, and thinks himself
a big governor [boss]."

p. 12

† **Neptune's yawning troughs:** A rather fanciful term for the hollows between the
waves of the sea. Neptune, the Roman god of the sea, was conventionally
invoked in poetic maritime references, but by the time of *Rupert Gray* this
would have seemed a poetic cliché. Cobham may be alluding to a line in
William Falconer's "The Shipwreck" (1762): "Still in the yawning trough the
vessel reels" (canto 2, line 904).

† **the land of the Humming Bird:** The island of Trinidad, apparently from "Iëre"
or "Iere", an Amerindian term said to mean "land of the hummingbird",
from the local abundance of these birds.

p. 13

† **"Ef me was marchant nevah keep black book-keepah.":** "If I was a merchant I
would never keep a black book-keeper."

† **"Dat fellah Ubut Gray, way he know? P'raps self de gal go keep de books. Old
fahdah sen way Gray. Serve he right. Have fo' haul molasses fo' a livin'
now.":** "That fellow Rupert Gray, what does he know? Perhaps the woman
herself will keep the books. The old father sent Gray away. Serves him right.
Has to haul molasses for a living now."

† **"N-n-no. D-d-dat en fair. D-d-de boyo know 'e wuk. Is because he black. Au-au-
all you nigga cuss. Bet you white dog never eat white dog. Who way don' like**

it g-g-jump.": "No, that isn't fair. The boy knows his work. It's because he is black. All of you Negroes are cursed. I bet you that a white dog never eats a white dog. Those who don't like it, jump."

† **thinking discretion the better part:** An echo of a famous phrase from Sir John Falstaff in Shakespeare's *I Henry IV* (*c.*1596–97). Falstaff, having played dead in battle, justifies himself by claiming that "the better part of valour is discretion, in the which better part I have sav'd my life" (5.5).

p. 14

† **ship chandlery:** The business of, or goods dealt in by, a ship-chandler, who supplies ships with necessary stores.

† **cocoa store:** Warehouse of cocoa beans ready to be shipped.

† **They came the biggest consignees in the colony:** That is, they became the largest business in selling Trinidad-grown sugar, and providing estates with imported supplies.

p. 15

† **"Workpeople's Advance Loans":** Presumably the firm gave employees advances on their salaries as a form of loan.

† **Gulf of Paria:** The area of water between western and southern Trinidad and Venezuela.

† **schooner:** A small seagoing vessel, fore- and aft-rigged, that is, with triangular sails set parallel to the length of the vessel.

† **"touch of human nature which makes the whole world kin":** Though often quoted out of context, this phrase is from Shakespeare's *Troilus and Cressida* (*c.*1601–2). Ulysses, trying to persuade Achilles to stop sulking and fight, tells him that his fame is eroding because he has not been seen in battle, and because human beings tend to value shiny novelties rather than remember real but invisible worth: "One touch of nature makes the whole world kin, / That all with one consent praise new-born gauds" (3.3).

p. 16

† **"B-b-b-but, Mr. Gray, O, an you s-say you done help you cullah, c-c-c-since d-d-dat last f-fellah p-p-put you in.":** "But Mr Gray, and you said you were finished helping your coloured people, since that last fellow did you in." The vocative "O", said after someone's name, is an African form of address.

p. 17

† **shylock – a miserable exacter of his pound of flesh:** Shylock, the titular character of Shakespeare's *The Merchant of Venice* (*c.*1596–97), is famous for lending his enemy Antonio money, asking only a pound of Antonio's flesh as collateral. When Antonio's financial reverses force him to default on the loan, Shylock prepares to extract his collateral from Antonio's body.

† **shades of Crusoe's man:** In Daniel Defoe's *Robinson Crusoe* (1719), Crusoe
saves a Carib's life, renames him "Friday" and makes him his servant, or his
"man Friday". The character has often been used to suggest a subservient
relationship, especially in colonial contexts: Friday signals his "thankful dis-
position" and willingness to serve by putting Crusoe's foot on his head.

† **Dawson:** Peter Dawson, a brand of blended Scotch whisky.

p. 18

† **puncheons:** Large casks for holding liquids and other commodities, varying from
72 to 120 gallons.

† **red-spittled Madrassees:** "Madrassi" in Trinidad designates a person descended
from Indian immigrants who came through the south Indian port of Madras,
usually Tamil-speaking. The red spittle referred to here is a result of the habit
of eating betel nut.

† **the recipe Sir John McAdam gave to the world:** John Loudon McAdam
(1756–1836) invented a kind of roadway, called "macadam", made of successive layers of stone broken into pieces of nearly uniform size, each layer being
allowed to consolidate under the pressure of ordinary traffic before the next is
laid.

† **Bimshire wives:** Women from Barbados; "Bim" or "Bimshire" was a traditional
term for Barbadians/Barbados, of uncertain derivation. Many Barbadians
lived in Trinidad during this period, generally residing in the towns; vending
food and working as cooks were typical occupations of the women.

† **Flatmen slowly hoist or reef sails:** Flatmen navigate broad flat-bottomed boats
or "flats". To "reef" a sail is to pull it in so as to reduce its area.

† **Phoebus Apollo:** The Greek god Apollo in his role as the god of light: the epithet
"Phoebus" means "the bright". Because of his association with light, Apollo
is often (as here) seen as the sun god, although in classical contexts he is usually not specifically connected to the sun.

p. 19

† **Cascades:** "The Cascade" usually refers to a waterfall in the Northern Range of
Trinidad, emptying into the Blue Basin in the Diego Martin valley, at that
time a picturesque location. It also refers to the Maracas waterfall in the St
Joseph–Maracas valley.

† **Sunflower Manse:** Though "manse" once meant "house" or "manor", by the
early twentieth century the word was obsolete except as used for an ecclesias-
tical residence (especially that of a Presbyterian minister). Cobham's use of it
in the older and more general sense thus has a touch of archaism. Compare
this creole garden to that of the Romelia family in *Adolphus* (Anon., 1853
[volume 2, this series]); particularly notable here is the combination of
European flowers with African folk magical practice.

Annotations

p. 20

† **stephanotis:** *Stephanotis floribunda,* a tropical climbing shrub having fragrant white flowers.

† **sunflowers:** "Sunflower" refers to any of the *Helianthus,* mostly native to North America, having conspicuous yellow flower-heads with a large seed disk and bright yellow-rayed petals suggesting the sun; the flower turns so as to follow the course of the sun during the day.

† **myrtle:** The common (European) myrtle, *Myrtus communis,* is a shrub with shiny evergreen leaves and white sweet-scented flowers; the myrtle was held sacred to Venus and used as an emblem of love.

† **enclosed by upturned bottles, blue, green, and colourless:** Bottles, especially blue ones, were "mounted" with obeah and put on sticks to protect houses, and especially gardens, from theft. "Obeah" is a folk system of magic and using supernatural forces to bring about effects ranging from success in love or business to harming an enemy, based primarily on West African rituals but incorporating Christian and other practices.

† **"thing of beauty":** A quotation from the opening line of John Keats's *Endymion* (1818): "A thing of beauty is a joy forever." Since it recounts the love between a mortal man and a goddess, the poem has an obvious relevance to the plot of *Rupert Gray,* but the first line is often quoted out of context and has become nearly proverbial.

† **"a ministering angel":** Cobham could be quoting from one of two sources here. In Shakespeare's *Hamlet* (*c.*1600–1601), Laertes berates the priest for not giving his sister Ophelia full Christian burial, telling him, "A ministr'ing angel shall my sister be / When thou liest howling" (5.1). In Walter Scott's *Marmion* (see note to p. 36), Constance is compared to "a ministering angel" as she tends the dying Marmion (canto 6).

† **"The touch of a vanish'd hand / And the sound of a voice that is still.":** A quotation from Alfred Lord Tennyson's "Break, Break, Break" (1842), one of several mourning poems for his dead friend Arthur Henry Hallam. The speaker contrasts the movement and voices of the living with the dead; here, after describing "stately ships" coming into harbour, he exclaims "But O for the touch of a vanish'd hand, / And the sound of a voice that is still!" (lines 11–12).

† **shorthand and typewriting exercise:** Someone of Gwendoline's station would not usually take up shorthand and typing, but apart from giving Cobham a way to put Rupert and Gwendoline together, this plot detail may suggest her egalitarian spirit and desire for a useful occupation: "the girls" she associates with probably see this as an eccentricity in her. It is worth noting that office jobs (especially the more prestigious ones) were still largely the domain of men in the first decade of the twentieth century; perhaps Cobham intends to present Gwendoline as breaking gender barriers in addition to racial ones.

p. 21

† **Othello:** See note to p. 99.

† **as strong as Sandow:** Eugen Sandow (1867–1925) was a Russo-German exponent of physical culture and exercise, held to be the perfect type of a strong
man.

† **fixtures:** meetings, appointments.

† **landeau:** A four-wheeled carriage, the top of which, being made in two parts,
may be closed or thrown open. When open, the rear part is folded back and
the front part entirely removed. Usually spelled "landau".

p. 22

† **Portuguese:** A person of (Madeiran) Portuguese origin or descent; in Trinidad,
typically owners of dry-goods shops, groceries and rumshops, but also often
employed as gardeners by wealthy householders.

† **the least of the apostles:** a quotation from one of St Paul's Epistles to the
Corinthians (1 Corinthians 15:9). Paul calls himself "the least of the apostles", not fit to be called one, because he persecuted the Christian church
before his conversion.

† **"Dr. Johnson wrote in the days of King George the Third that that is detrimental.":** Samuel Johnson (1709–84), was famous for his pithy remarks, both in
writing and in conversations recorded by his friends. Since, however, Edith
always refers to Dr Johnson with her trademark "that is detrimental" line, it
seems likely that she is invoking Johnson as a learned authority to bolster her
own opinions rather than using actual Johnsonian sayings. Johnson's dates do
overlap with those of George III, who reigned from 1760 to 1820.

† **script type:** A typeface intended to imitate handwriting, and so appropriate for a
silver-keyed typewriter that seems designed more as a lady's plaything than as
an office machine.

† **theatricals:** Performance of a play in a private house by amateurs, with admission by invitation only. This was a common form of elite socializing and
entertainment in Britain and the British Caribbean. Generally admission
would be free to the invitees, unless tickets were sold to raise funds for a char-
itable purpose, as here, to raise funds for an impoverished playwright.

p. 24

† **bishop's sleeves, short only to her elbow:** A "bishop's sleeve" in a woman's dress
is soft and full, gathered in at the wrist like the sleeves worn by Anglican
bishop robe. They are usually full-length rather than elbow-length, and were
fashionable in the first decade of the twentieth century.

† **"form divine":** A quotation from William Blake's poem "The Divine Image".
Blake wrote two poems by that name and containing the phrase Cobham
quotes here; the first appeared in his *Songs of Innocence* (1789) and both
appear in some copies of *Songs of Innocence and of Experience* (1794). The

"Innocence" poem celebrates "Mercy, Pity, Peace, and Love" as reflections of human "virtues of delight"; Love has "the human form divine" (line 11) and "every man of every clime / That prays in his distress, / Prays to the human form divine" (lines 13–15). The darker "Experience" poem identifies the "Human Form Divine" rather with "Terror". That one is more obscure than the "Innocence" poem, however; in most copies of his (hand-made) books Blake used "The Human Abstract", a subtler "Experience" companion to the "Divine Image" of "Innocence". Clearly the "Innocence" poem is more directly relevant to Gwendoline, though one might argue that other "human forms divine" in the book (her father, for example, or Clarke) suggest humanity's potential for evil. Cobham may also have had Homer's *Odyssey* in mind. Alexander Pope's translation (1725–26) has the following line (at the point where Circe turns Ulysses' men into pigs): "No more was seen the human form divine" (10:278).

p. 25

† **St. Clair car:** The electric tram ran to St Clair, an upper-class suburb of Port of Spain near the Queen's Park Savannah.

† **"not gods, men, nor columns":** An altered quotation from the satirical poem "Mr Jesse's Song" (1830), probably by William Maginn, the butt of which is the minor reviewer and man of letters Cyrus Redding. The "Song" is part of "The Election of Editor", a spoof that appeared in the May and June numbers of the brash *Fraser's Magazine* (largely edited by Maginn). "Mr Jesse" is probably John Henaege Jesse, a contributor to the magazine who may have helped write the "Election". *Fraser's* had attacked the Literary Union, of which Redding was secretary, and he had retaliated by banning the magazine from the club's reading room. According to the poem, "silly Cyrus" determines, despite his lack of brains, to be a writer: "So he began to scribble trash, / Nor gods, nor men, nor columns dreading" (lines 30–31).

p. 27

† **C.M.G.:** Companion of (the Order of) of St Michael and St George, a British honour frequently given to colonial officials and military men.

† **in the days when sugar was king:** Sugar was the major export of Trinidad for nearly all of the nineteenth century, and certainly in the 1860s to 1870s when Mr Serle probably began his career. By 1907 cocoa had overtaken sugar as Trinidad's most valuable export crop, though sugar was still vital to its economy.

p. 29

† **through the tube:** A speaking tube, used for communication within a large building.

† **fingle:** Pass the fingers on, along or around an object, touching absent-mindedly or feeling its shape, without skill or politeness.

† **nasal twang:** "Yankee" English (of the United States) was often characterized and presented by others as "nasal" in the nineteenth and early twentieth centuries.

p. 31

† **Uncle Sam negro:** The American black; "Uncle Sam" is a traditional character used as a shorthand representative for the United States (replacing the older "Brother Jonathan").

† **Esau Clarke:** The New Yorker either has a bad memory for names or is suggesting that Clarke, despite his name, plays Esau (who sells his birthright to his brother Jacob for a mess of pottage) to Rupert's Jacob, the man who, despite many reverses, is renamed "Israel" by God and becomes the progenitor of "a nation and a company of nations" (Genesis 25:29–34 and 35:11).

† **blooming noisy haw-haw style:** "Haw-haw" can refer both to boisterous loud laughter and to affected upper-class speech; in the latter a drawled "haw-haw" expresses hesitation. "Noisy" suggests that the former is what the New Yorker has in mind, but given Clarke's desire to rise by any fair or unfair means, he may also be imitating fashionable speech: perhaps some such habit has earned him his school nickname of "Starch Nose" (p. 16).

p. 32

† **They live too much in the present, preferring fine clothes to Crown lands; large rental to small freehold:** This was a traditional stereotype of West Indian working-class blacks, held by whites, but also by many educated black and mixed-race West Indians: they were seen as improvident, extravagant, loving fancy clothes, neglecting to buy lands and houses with which to build a solid future. "Crown lands" were lands owned by the state, which could be purchased in small lots at fairly low prices during this period.

† **the late Bishop Hayes:** John T. Hayes, Anglican bishop of Trinidad and Tobago, 1889–1904; Hayes Court, the Anglican bishop's residence opposite the Queen's Park Savannah in Port of Spain, is named for him.

p. 33

† **"weighed in the balance a thousand times and never found wanting.":** A biblical reference to the handwriting on the wall that Daniel interprets for the Babylonian King Belshazzar (Daniel 5:27): "Thou art weighed in the balances, and art found wanting." The message warns of the Persians' impending invasion of Babylon.

p. 34

† **The play was written by a native; none of his people therefore cared to read it, and the books lay unsold at the booksellers:** The play performed at the Serle house is probably based on one written by a Trinidadian, George Hubert Wilson, a friend of Cobham's (see note to p. 35). The bitter comment about

unsold books might reflect Cobham's knowledge of Wilson's experiences, or those of others known to him.

† **song from the head of Abbotsford:** Sir Walter Scott is often identified with the elaborate country house he built at Abbotsford (Scotland). The song in question is from his *Marmion* (see note to p. 36).

p. 35

† **Ethelred Wencelas:** Probably "Wenceslas"; we have not been able to identify the model for this character, if he is based on a real person or literary character, nor the possible significance of the names, those of two early British kings.

† **Irving:** Sir Henry Irving (1838–1905), born John Henry Brodribb, was a famous English actor and theatre manager, knighted in 1895 for services to the stage.

† **inimitable Johannes Warbattleton:** We have not been able to identify the model for this character, if he is based on a real person.

† **Port-of-Spain Theatrical Club:** Port of Spain had a long tradition of amateur drama performances, going back at least to the 1820s and 1830s, when E.L. Joseph put on several productions, some written by himself. Around the time of this novel's publication, there was both a Port-of-Spain Theatrical Club, and an Amateur Dramatic Club; Edgar Maresse-Smith, a man greatly admired by Cobham, was at one time (he died in 1905) president of both (see note to p. 58). We have not been able to identify the characters – presumably based on real persons – referred to by Rupert Gray in this passage. Rupert's rather flowery commentary sounds like a contemporary newspaper review and may be intended to imitate or spoof one.

† **St. Maryite:** Student or "old boy" of St Mary's College (also known as the College of the Immaculate Conception), Trinidad's leading Catholic boys' secondary school, established in 1863.

† **That Arima star, named after the hero of Barra:** Arima, in east Trinidad, is a borough dating back to the eighteenth century. Barra may refer to one of the Outer Hebrides, remote islands off the Scottish coast, but we have been unable to identify the "hero of Barra".

† **Mr. George Hubert, the author:** This probably refers to George Hubert Wilson, a Trinidadian author who died in 1901 at the age of forty-two. He belonged to the same Roman Catholic Friendly Society as Cobham, and was probably a friend of his (Cobham attended his funeral). At the time of his death, he was described as a "playwright, novelist and poet"; his works were said to have included *Violet of Icacos*, *The Storm* and *Recorded Reflections*. We have not yet been able to see any works by Wilson, which were probably published locally (see note to p. 35).

p. 36

† **verses of a threnody found in Walter Scott:** This threnody (lament) is found in canto 3 of Scott's *Marmion* (see following note).

† **words were those of the self-same roundelay Fitz Eustace sang to beguile the tedious hours of Lord Marmion after his all-day ride across "the heights of Lammermoor"**: In canto 3 of Sir Walter Scott's *Marmion* (1808), Lord Marmion's party have completed their first day's journey on a diplomatic mission to Edinburgh, taking a difficult mountain path across "the height of Lammermoor" to avoid a marauders' ambush on the easier path. As they rest at an inn, Marmion asks the squire Fitz-Eustace for a song. The love-lament chosen, however, disturbs Marmion more than it beguiles: it was a favourite of his former page "Constant" (that is, his disguised mistress Constance, a nun who leaves her convent for love of him, and is then discarded when he decides to marry a wealthy woman). The narrator's description of the play's situation echoes the opening lines of the song: "Where shall the lover rest, / Whom the fates sever / From his true maiden's breast, / Parted for ever?"

† **"Eleu loro, Eleu loro, / Never, O never."**: A refrain line from the song discussed in the preceding note. The "Never, O never" refrain occurs in two places in the song. In the first it refers to the faithful lover, parted from his beloved only by fate and death; though he is "never again to wake", he rests peacefully. In the second it underlines the traitrous lover's dishonour. He, too, is dead, but his grave is shameful: "Blessing shall hallow it,– / Never, O never!" (Not long afterwards, as he lies dying, Marmion deliriously recalls the section about the traitor.) "Eleu loro" is a conventional sound-phrase, without specific meaning; such devices are common in Celtic poetry.

† **"As it were, / Nerves . . . all chained up in alabaster, / As Daphne was. / Rootbound that fled Apollo."**: An altered quotation from John Milton's masque *Comus* (1637; published as *A Maske*). The enchanter Comus warns his prisoner, known simply as "the Lady", not to try to rise from the enchanted chair where he has placed her: "Nay, lady, sit; if I but wave this wand, / Your nerves are all chained up in alablaster [*sic*], / And you a statue, or as Daphne was / Root-bound, that fled Apollo" (lines 659–62). Comus alludes here to the Greek myth of Daphne and Apollo. Wishing to remain a virgin but pursued by the god Apollo, Daphne begs her father, the river-god Peneus, to help her by destroying her beauty. Peneus accordingly turns her into a tree (a laurel, which from that time becomes Apollo's tree).

† **Not Vishnu, with the flame flashing out from finger tips, could have rained more magnetism around upon his Brahman votaries**: A reference to one of the principal Hindu deities, regarded as the preserver of the world; Brahmans are the highest and priestly Hindu caste.

† **Lord Byron sings that – "Women, like moths, are caught by glare."**: Loosely quoted from canto 1, stanza 9, of Byron's *Childe Harold's Pilgrimage* (1812–18). Byron is introducing Childe Harold, his brooding hero and alter-ego. This stanza comments on Harold's failure to find love among his followers and parasites; the women who appear to love him are fascinated only by his wealth and station: "Maidens, like moths, are ever caught by glare." The

line seems inappropriate to Gwendoline, who is fascinated with Rupert's
"voice and presence" and risks losing her station altogether by loving him.

p. 38

† **"The Violet of Oropuche"**: Oropuche is the name of a village and a river in
north-east Trinidad. The title is probably based on the work, *Violet of Icacos,*
by Cobham's friend, George Hubert Wilson (see note to p. 21). Icacos is a
village in south-west Trinidad.

† **Government House**: The residence of the governor (now President's House),
opposite the Queen's Park Savannah.

p. 39

† **"Old, unhappy, far off things, / And battles long ago."**: From William
Wordsworth, "The Solitary Reaper" (1807). Though attracted by the song of
a "Highland Lass", the speaker is unable to understand her (Gaelic) words,
and can only speculate about the subject of her song: "Perhaps the plaintive
numbers flow / For old, unhappy, far-off things, / And battles long ago" (lines
18–20).

† **whirl of terpsichore**: Terpsichore was the ancient Greek muse of dance.

† **white bachelor's button**: *Gomphrena globosa,* a plant with rounded flower-
heads, usually magenta, sometimes mauve, rarely white, from
bachelor's/bachelors' button, several flowers with double-petalled, round or
button-like shapes. In England, this name usually refers to *Centaurea cyanus,*
and in the language of flowers stands for "hope in solitude"; it was also said
that a woman who placed a flower under her apron could have her pick of
bachelors.

p. 40

† **"Woman is the lower man, and all her passions matched with mine, / Are as
moonlight unto sunlight and as water unto wine."**: A slightly altered quotation from Tennyson's "Locksley Hall" (1842). In the poem, "lower" is
"lesser" and "her passions" are "thy passions" (line 151); the speaker is
addressing Amy, his cousin and former lover, who has given in to the
demands of her family and married a wealthier man. The quotation seems
oddly inapt since Gwendoline, unlike Amy, has refused to marry all her eligible suitors and remains loyal to Rupert, but its bitter misogyny does accord
with the preceding paragraphs on women's "instinct of Eve".

pp. 41–42

† **"George Withers thought so, and sings it, too: 'If she love me, this believe, / I
shall die ere she shall grieve. / But if she slight me when I woo, / I can scorn
and let her go, For if she be not for me – What care I for whom she be!' "**:
From "Shall I wasting in despair", a sonnet by George Wither (note correct

spelling). First issued at the end of his elegy *Fidelia* (1615), this poem is a light-hearted song declaring the poet's refusal to "Die because a woman's fair" (line 2).

p. 42

† **love-vine:** *Cuscuta americana*, "dodder", a leafless twining plant with smooth slender yellow or orange stems, found spreading over grass, shrubs, trees, rocks and poles. Cobham may not have been aware when using this simile that the plant is parasitic.

p. 43

† **"glassy wave" Sabrina:** A reference to Milton's *Comus* (see note to p. 36). Comus has been defeated, but the Lady's rescuers cannot free her from the enchanted chair, and so call on Sabrina (the nymph associated with the river Severn) to help them: "Sabrina fair, / Listen where thou art sitting / Under the glassy, cool, translucent wave" (lines 859–61).

† **matin gear:** Informal morning attire.

† **Japanese sleeves:** Probably wide kimono-style sleeves.

p. 44

† **I am a modern Joseph:** The biblical Joseph, imprisoned in Egypt, interprets a dream for Pharaoh that warns of a coming famine (Genesis 41).

† **collaret of ruching:** A collaret was a small collar, usually made of a material that contrasted with the rest of the dress it formed part of. "Ruching" is a pleated or gathered trim made of thin, fine material such as lace or net.

p. 45

† *via media*: A naturalized Latin phrase meaning "a middle way" between two extremes.

† **Byron: "Here's a sigh for those who love me, / And a smile for those who hate, / And whate'er sky's above me, / Here's a heart for any fate.":** An altered quotation from Byron's "To Thomas Moore": "Here's a sigh to those who love me, / And a smile to those who hate; / And, whatever sky's above me, / Here's a heart for every fate" (lines 5–8). Associated with Byron's final departure from England in 1816, in the wake of marital scandal and separation, the poem takes the form of a toast to those left behind, with special reference to his friend and fellow-poet Thomas Moore, to whom Byron sent the poem in 1817.

p. 47

† **Cherche la femme:** Properly "Cherchez la femme", or "look for the woman" at the heart of significant (and especially negative) events.

† **"When you spread cocoa in the sun look out for rain":** A traditional proverb

indicating that caution must be taken when you have something in a vulnerable position. From the practice of spreading fresh cocoa seeds, removed from pods and enclosing pulp, to dry in the sun; they must be quickly covered by a sliding roof or other protection when rain falls, or they will spoil.

† **"Abel's blood for vengeance"**: From a hymn, "Glory Be to Jesus", translated into English by Edward Caswell (1857) from an eighteenth-century Italian original: "Abel's blood for vengeance / Pleaded to the skies; / But the blood of Jesus / For our pardon cries" (stanza 4). The biblical root of the phrase lies in the story of Cain and Abel, the sons of Adam and Eve. Cain, jealous that God looks more favourably on Abel's sacrifice than on his, kills his brother and so becomes the first murderer. God then tells Cain, "the voice of thy brother's blood crieth unto me from the ground" (Genesis 4:10), and marks Cain out for divine vengeance.

p. 48

† **"envy, hatred and malice, and all uncharitableness"**: From the Church of England Litany, a set form of prayer involving petitions and responses. This petition is for deliverance "from all blindness of heart; from pride, vainglory and hypocrisy; from envy, hatred, and malice, and all uncharitableness".

p. 49

† **Conspire with the assiduity of Guy Fawkes and his crew**: Guy Fawkes (1570–1606), a Roman Catholic, attempted to blow up the English Houses of Parliament on 5 November 1605. The day is celebrated in England as Guy Fawkes Day, with fireworks, bonfires and the like.

p. 50

† **red ochre wash**: A paint containing ochre, iron-rich clays varying in colour from light yellow to deep orange or brown, and used extensively as pigments. In original, *okre*; see editorial note at the end of the introduction.

p. 51

† **Botanic Gardens**: Established in 1818, these are situated just opposite the Queen's Park Savannah, close to the governor's residence.

† **Governor's palace**: The governor's residence, now President's House, built in 1876.

† *hoi polloi*: A semi-naturalized Greek phrase meaning "the many" or the masses, the majority of ordinary people. (Since "hoi" actually means "the", "the hoi polloi" is redundant, though commonly heard.)

† **"See Naples and then die," runs the Italian proverb. "Play in England and live," dreams the average Trinidad batsman**: Cricket was immensely popular in Trinidad and local players would aspire to play for the West Indies on one of the tours made to England. The first took place in 1900, and the team

included the famous black Trinidadian player Lebrun Constantine, father of the great cricketer Learie Constantine.

† **savannah:** The Queen's Park Savannah, a large open savannah (a naturally flat area covered with low or sparse vegetation), about two hundred acres in area, at the northern end of the city of Port of Spain. Originally part of the Paradise sugar estate, it was purchased from the Peschier family by Governor Sir Ralph Woodford as a public park in 1816.

† **snow-white turban, fluttering from her broad-brimmed straw:** The lady is evidently wearing a hat rather than a turban, but she seems to have wound or "turbaned" a scarf around it, leaving the ends to flutter in the breeze.

† **Queen's Park Hotel:** Situated just opposite the south side of the Queen's Park Savannah, this was Trinidad's leading hotel from the 1890s, particularly renowned for its fine cuisine.

† **Hyde Park:** London's largest park, Hyde Park was often used for military reviews.

† **Viceroy's palace:** The British often held large military reviews, parades and the like during their imperial rule of India; the one referred to here seems to have been outside the vice-regal palace in Calcutta (the capital of British India from 1772 to 1912).

p. 52

† **from Maraval to the Naparimas . . . Mucurapo and Diego Martin:** Maraval is a valley in the Northern Range, the mountains close to Port of Spain; the Naparimas are around San Fernando in the south; Mucurapo, then a coastal village to the west of Port of Spain, is now a suburb; Diego Martin is a valley at the westernmost end of the Northern Range, just north of Port of Spain.

† **"Hog Plum" tree:** The "hog plum", a bit further on identified as *Spondias graveolens,* now *Spondias mombin,* is a large native tree; the fruit is small, oblong, yellow, aromatic and juicy, with a small amount of highly acidic translucent yellow pulp and a large hard fibrous pit. The fruit is often used to make wine and jam. The wood is soft, light and not very durable, sometimes used to make coffins.

† **Bushes' tombstone:** In the middle of the Botanic Gardens there is a small cemetery where senior colonial officials and their relatives were buried. J. Scott Bushe was colonial secretary of Trinidad, 1861–87. Charles Warner (see note to p. 54) is also buried there.

p. 52–53

† **rope-like lianes . . . *Tanaecium jaroba*:** A climbing shrub native to South America and the Caribbean, though not Trinidad.

p. 53

† ***Wellingtonia gigantia*:** The huge coniferous sequoia tree, native to California.

† **Mr. Froude is right. Nature in the tropics is always grand.:** "Let man be what he

will, nature in the tropics is always grand" is found in J.A. Froude's *The English in the West Indies* (1888, 69). Kingsley described the Botanic Gardens in *At Last* (1871, 101–5); Froude acknowledges there that it was Kingsley's account that had piqued his interest in tropical nature, but that he had not credited its beauty and luxuriance until seeing it with his own eyes. Froude is as glowing in his description of the Botanic Gardens and the vegetation in general as he is critical of the island's mosquitoes, and scornful of the "election virus" he finds (62–67). However, neither Kingsley's nor Froude's description of the Botanic Gardens seems to have provided a basis for Cobham's, that being doubtless based on his own personal experience.

† cloves . . . *Caryophyllus aromaticus*: The dried flower-buds of this tree provide the pungent aromatic spice, native to the Moluccas but cultivated throughout the tropics, though not in Trinidad on any noticeable scale.

† **cinnamon specimens – a fine sample of *Cinnamomum zeylanicum*:** There are about 250 species of *Cinnamomum* (mistakenly "*Cinnamonum*" in the original text) native to East and Southeast Asia and Australia. Widely cultivated in tropical areas, *C. zeylanicum* is the source of bark used as a commercial spice.

† *Coffea arabica* . . . No, *Coffea liberica*: *Coffea arabica* is "Arabian", "Arabica" or "Creole" coffee, whereas *C. liberica* is "Congo", "Excelsa" or "Liberian" coffee.

† **Linnaean Society:** Founded in 1788, the Linnaean Society is the oldest extant biological society. It is named for the Swedish naturalist Carl Linnaeus (1707–78), who developed the scientific method of binomial nomenclature (genus and species) and organized the world's plants and animals into a standard classification system. See the section "Gardens of Empire" in the introduction.

† **coffee leaf fungus, the *Hemeliae vastatrix*:** *Hemileia vastatrix*, a rust fungus that attacks coffee trees.

† **kodak:** The proprietary name of a number of popular cameras produced by Eastman Kodak, beginning in the 1880s; at the turn of the twentieth century, the term was often use to refer to any camera, regardless of the brand.

† **poui-tree, whose eastertide blossoms flared out yellow:** *Tabebuia serratifolia*, the yellow poui, a tall deciduous tree, with showy masses of yellow flowers at intervals during the dry season. A single tree stands out from the surrounding vegetation and can be seen from a long distance off.

p. 54

† **some lonely passerine:** One of the order of perching birds, often indicating a small bird.

† **"cigale's" endless monotone, silvern or graterlike:** "Cigale" refers to several species of cicada, large brown insects with transparent lacy wings. The calls of the adults, heard especially during the dry season in early morning and late evening, are usually loud and high-pitched, with a droning or sawing quality.

† **Semp, acravat and picoplat:** These are all small songbirds, highly prized as cage-birds. The adult male "semp" (*Euphonia violacea*) is black glossed blue above, with forehead and underparts golden yellow. The "acravat" (*Euphonia trinitatis*) is bluish-black above and bright yellow below, with a black throat; known more commonly as "cravat". The male "picoplat" (*Sporophila intermedia*) head and upperparts are dark grey and lower underparts white; the bill is pink or pinkish yellow, giving a silvery appearance.

† **spice tree:** Although "spice" locally usually refers to the cinnamon tree (see above), this probably refers to the allspice or pimento, the dried berry of *Eugenia pimenta*.

† **blue-birds:** The "bluebird", *Thraupis episcopus,* is bright greyish-blue, with a patch of vivid violet blue on the wings. Also known locally as "blue jay" and "blue jean".

† **Kiss-ke-dees:** The "kiskadee" (*Pitangus sulphuratus trinitatis*) is a conspicuous and aggressive bird often found near houses. Its usual call is a raucous three-part phrase which sounds like "qu'est-ce-qu'il-dit" (French, "what did he say"). Usually now spelled "keskidee" or "kiskidee".

† **"king-page" butterflies:** The "king page" (*Papilio thoas*) is a large butterfly, black with two broken vertical yellow bands, with tails on the lower wing-tips. Note: "page" is pronounced as in French.

† **yellow-winged "zabuecoes":** The "abricot" or "zabrico", *Phoebis argante,* is a medium-sized butterfly, apricot orange with black spots on the margins.

† **Charles Warner's grave:** Charles Warner (1806–87) was an influential attorney-general of Trinidad, 1844–70, and the main leader of the "anglicization" campaign of those decades. He was a creole from a prominent local family of English descent (like the Serles).

† **daughter of the Teutons:** That is, her descent from Germanic tribes can supposedly be seen in her features. The implication seems to be that her line includes both Norman French and Anglo-Saxon blood.

pp. 54–55

† **Coeur de Lion . . . kopje and veldt:** The general point in these two paragraphs is that the countess's ancient and noble line is courageous, and at the heart of the action whenever England is at war. The events and campaigns mentioned are among the most famous in English history, including the Crusades under Richard I ("Coeur de Lion" or Lionheart, 1157–99, reigned 1189–99), in what is now the Middle East ("the Moslem's bristling centre"); the battle of Crécy (1346), and the battle of Agincourt (1415) under Henry V ("Harry of Monmouth"). The "Field of Cloth of Gold" (1520) was not a battle but a royal festival in which Henry VIII met Francis I, King of France; the meeting derives its name from the great amount of costly cloth of gold used for the participants' clothing and accoutrements. " 'Grand' and 'Petit' sergeantry" (or sergeanty) refers to the various kinds of service nobles and landowners owed

to the king; though precise definition of the distinction is elusive, "Grand sergeantry" usually involved more major contributions, such as raising armies. Henry VIII did not in fact hold the title of *Fidei Defensor,* or Defender of the Faith, in 1520; Pope Leo X conferred it on him in 1521, in recognition of a book Henry had written opposing the reformer Martin Luther. "The cause of the fated Stuart" refers to the various struggles of the Stuart royal house between 1642 and 1745 as they tried to retain and then regain their hold on the British Crown. These include the Civil Wars (1642–48), the execution of Charles I (1649), the restoration of Charles II (1660), the "Glorious Revolution", which deposed James II (1688), and unsuccessful uprisings in support of the exiled Stuart heirs in 1715 and 1745. The battle of Malplaquet (1709) was an especially bloody one; the battle of Waterloo (1815), which ended the Napoleonic Wars, was preceded by the Duchess of Richmond's famous ball in Brussels. During the battle of Waterloo, the main body of English troops was positioned on a ridge covering the road to Brussels; Plancenoit, however, where the troops engaged against the French were largely Prussian, is some distance away. The disastrous charge of the Light Brigade (1854) took place at Balaklava in the Crimean War. In 1857, during the "Indian Mutiny", Sir Henry Lawrence and the European inhabitants of Lucknow were besieged for several months. The British defeated the Egyptians at Tel-el-Kebir (1882), and so occupied Egypt, but then had to deal with the uprising by the followers of the "Mahdi", Muhammad Ahmad, already underway in Egyptian Sudan. In 1884, General Gordon was besieged by the Mahdists in Khartoum; the British commander sent a force to relieve him. After fighting the battle of Abu Klea (January 1885) against another group of Mahdists, that force embarked at Metemneh for Khartoum, but arrived to find the city fallen and Gordon and the garrison dead. During the Boer War (1899–1902), the British captured Pretoria, capital of the Republic of the Transvaal, in June 1900; in 1902, at the close of the war, the Transvaal became a British colony. "Tremendous cheering" may be a quotation from the extensive British newspaper coverage of the Boer War, coverage which encouraged the public celebration of war victories and made such Afrikaans terms as "kopje" (small hill) and "veldt" (semi-arid plain) household words in Britain.

† **Maoris:** the aboriginal inhabitants of the then British colony of New Zealand; they were considered a particularly war-like group by colonial administrators.

† **"I heard a story about your Carnival . . . pretty mulatto girls.":** It was illegal to parade publicly after midnight on Carnival Tuesday (Shrove Tuesday), which marked the end of the two-day Carnival celebrations. This "story" partly refers to the 1903 Water Riots, a serious affair during which the Red House (the main government building in downtown Port of Spain) was destroyed by fire, and sixteen persons, including women, were killed (shot or bayoneted) by police and troops. The riots were not connected to the Carnival.

† **We had three days' Carnival in honour of the relief of Ladysmith:** During the Boer War, a celebrated event was the relief by British forces of the South African town of Ladysmith, which had been besieged by the Boers. It took place in February 1900, just before that year's Carnival celebrations.

p. 56

† **"stars of earth":** "Earth stars" commonly refers to small rosette-leaved ornamental plants such as *Cryptanthus,* though these are not scented. Another possibility is *Nicotiana,* which has a star-like flower part, and is fragrant later in the day.

† **pagoda pines:** Most likely *Araucaria bidwillii,* usually known as "bunya-bunya pine", which grows in a formal conical shape. (The "pagoda tree" is *Plumeria,* which is common and noticeable, but nothing like a pine.)

† **dusky cicerone:** "Dusky" was often applied to people of colour, usually with pejorative or patronizing overtones, as when a woman is called a "dusky charmer". Cobham is doubtless using the adjective ironically. A "cicerone" is a knowledgeable guide, especially one who introduces strangers to local antiquities or curiosities.

† **Bentham:** George Bentham (1800–1884), botanist, associate of Hooker (see following note) and author of several books, including the still-standard *Handbook of British Flora* (first edition 1858). See discussion in the section "Garden and Empire" of the introduction.

† **Hooker:** Sir William Jackson Hooker (1785–1865), botanist, first director of the Royal Botanic Gardens at Kew (London) and author of many important books on British flora, especially ferns, mosses and fungi.

† **Leguminosae and Rosaceae:** The botanical family Leguminosae comprises plants with seeds borne in pods (legumes); these include peas and beans, and trees such as tamarind, *Cassia, Bauhinia,* acacias and mimosas. The rose family, genus *Rosa,* including wild and cultivated species, is the basis of the Rosaceae, which also includes herbs, shrubs and trees with many kinds of edible fruit, for example, strawberries, raspberries, blackberries, apples, cherries, pears, peaches and plums.

† **St. Clair:** See note to p. 25.

p. 57

† **Sir Humourous Southfold:** This probably refers to Sir Ernest Northcote, the chief justice of Trinidad and Tobago at the time of the novel's publication (first appointed in 1903).

p. 58

† **wear the ermine:** Ermine (the winter fur of the stoat, white with black tips) is traditionally worn only by royalty, judges, peers and others of high rank.

† **Booker T. Washington:** Booker T. Washington (1856–1915) was a famous

African-American educator and social reformer, who believed blacks in the
United States should work for advances in education, employment and business, not for social or political equality with whites. Under his leadership, the
Tuskegee Institute, established in Alabama in 1881, became a world centre for
the higher education of black people. By 1907, he was probably the most
famous black person in the Anglo-American world.

† **Mr. Maresse-Smith**: Edgar Maresse-Smith (1861–1905) was a mixed-race solicitor. He was strongly race conscious, agitating for a high-profile celebration in
Trinidad of the jubilee of emancipation in 1888, and was a key leader in the
short-lived local branch of the Pan-African Association (1901–2). He was a
prominent leader in the agitation that led up to the Water Riots in 1903 (see
note to p. 55), and was charged for incitement to riot – and acquitted.
Cobham admired him, and a poem by him on the occasion of Maresse-
Smith's death was published in the *Mirror* (31 January 1905, reprinted on
p. xviii of the introduction). (See also note to p. 35.)

† **the best study of mankind was womankind**: Both Maresse-Smith's comment and
Florence Badenock's echo Alexander Pope's *Essay on Man* (1733), which
counsels the reader, "Know then thyself; presume not God to scan; / The
proper study of Mankind is Man" (1.1–2).

† **race of Ham**: The story of Ham, the second son of Noah, has often been co-
opted for racist ends. The idea is that the descendents of the biblical Ham are
cursed because Ham sees his father naked (Genesis 9:22–27). Though the biblical passage mentions only Ham's son Canaan, who is to become "a servant
of servants . . . unto his brethren", the curse is usually assumed to include all
of Ham's and Canaan's descendents, linked to Africa and Africans in many
racist ideologies.

p. 59

† **Toussaint L'Ouverture the brilliant slave of Breda**: Toussaint L'Ouverture was
the main leader of the Haitian Revolution up to 1802, when he was betrayed
by the French general Leclerc and sent into exile in France on Napoleon's
orders, dying in 1803 in a remote prison in the Jura mountains. "Breda" was
the name of the plantation on which he had been a slave.

† **Jean Francois**: Jean-François was a former slave in Ste Domingue (Haiti) who
became the main leader of a band of insurgent slaves who fought for Spain
(the island of Hispaniola was divided between French Ste Domingue and
Spanish Santo Domingo) between 1793 and 1795, in exchange for promises
of freedom and land. He and his men were notorious for their ferocity against
French colonists in the slave rebellion and civil war of those years. When
Spain and France made peace in 1795, Jean-François and some of his men
were settled in Spain; he died there in 1805.

† **Biassou**: Georges Biassou was a prominent ex-slave leader of the insurgent soldiers who fought for Spain in Hispaniola in 1793–95 (see note above). After

1795, he and some of his men settled in Florida, then a Spanish colony; he died there in 1801.

† **King Christophe:** Henri Christophe (1767–1820) was born enslaved in Grenada or St Kitts and taken later to Ste Domingue (Haiti). He joined the great slave rebellion in 1791 and became a key leader under Toussaint and later under Dessalines. After the latter's assassination, he became the ruler of the northern part of independent Haiti in 1806, proclaiming himself Henri I, King of Haiti, in 1811. A strongly authoritarian ruler, he built the famous Citadel, and his great palace (Sans Souci) at Cap-Haitien. He founded schools and issued the Code Henri, Haiti's first code of laws. Facing revolts and illness, he committed suicide in 1820.

† **Dessalines:** Jean-Jacques Dessalines (1758–1806) was born a slave in Ste Domingue (Haiti) and became a leading general in the Haitian Revolution from 1791. He led the resistance in 1802–3 to Napoleon's attempt to re-establish slavery and regain control over the colony, and was known for his ruthlessness. After a fierce campaign marked by atrocities on both sides, the French forces were defeated; on 1 January 1804, Dessalines proclaimed the independence of Haiti. He ordered the annihilation of all Frenchmen still on the island. He proclaimed himself emperor later in 1804, but was assassinated in 1806.

† **Edward Wilmot Blyden:** Edward Wilmot Blyden (1832–1912) was born in St Thomas, one of the Danish (later US) Virgin Islands in 1832, but emigrated to Liberia in 1851 and lived in West Africa for most of the rest of his life. An educator, writer, diplomat (Liberian ambassador to Britain, or the "Court of St James", as the British court is known in diplomatic language) and statesman, he became a famous spokesman for the interests of people of African descent everywhere, and a champion of Africans against racism and colonialism. He was a strong advocate of race pride and African cultural nationalism, and by the 1870s was one of the best-known spokesmen for black people in the Anglo-American world.

† **Sir Conrad Reeves:** Conrad Reeves (*d.* 1902) was a mixed-race Barbadian lawyer. The son of a slave woman and a white man, Reeves rose from humble origins to achieve high posts in his native colony. Appointed solicitor-general in 1874, he resigned in 1876 over the attempt to link Barbados to the Windward Islands and abolish its independent elected assembly. He helped persuade London to drop these plans, and as attorney-general (1882–86) he played a major role in reforming the Barbadian system of government and widening the franchise. He was appointed chief justice of Barbados in 1886 – the first non-white to hold such a post in the British Caribbean, possibly in the British Empire – and was knighted in 1888. Reeves was a source of great pride to Barbadians in Trinidad and in general to black and brown West Indians.

† **Little England:** Barbados was called "Little England" for its loyalty to England,

and its supposedly strong English culture; it had been under continuous British rule from 1627.

† **Michel Maxwell Philip:** Michel (or Michael) Maxwell Philip (1829–88) was a mixed-race barrister. He was active in the 1850s and 1860s in movements for political reform and struggles against the anti-Catholic policies of the colonial government of the day. He was the first non-white mayor of Port of Spain (1867–70). Philip served as solicitor-general and official member of the Legislative Council from 1871 to his death in 1888. He published in 1854 one of the first novels by a native of Trinidad, *Emmanuel Appadocca*. Philip was a famous orator, multilingual and very much a star in the courtroom.

† **demosthenic:** Resembling in speaking style the great Athenian orator Demosthenes (384–322 BC).

† **John Jacob Thomas:** John Jacob Thomas (*c.*1840–89) was an African-Trinidadian educator and self-taught scholar and writer. He taught in primary schools in Trinidad after training at the Normal School in Port of Spain, and became a civil servant in 1870; he was the first African-Trinidadian to be appointed to the magistracy (1874), albeit only briefly in an acting position. Thomas was a self-taught linguist and philologist who published *Creole Grammar* (1869), the first serious study of the French Creole which was then the majority language of Trinidad (see note to p. 109). In 1889, at the end of his life, he published *Froudacity*, a brilliant polemic refuting J.A. Froude's strictures against West Indians in his well-known book, *The English in the West Indies* (1888) (see note to p. 53). Thomas was strongly race conscious, and an early pan-Africanist thinker, like Blyden.

† **Vincent Brown:** Vincent Brown (1855–1904) was a mixed-race barrister. He was mayor of Port of Spain (1889–90) and a leader of the movement to reform Trinidad's Crown Colony constitution in 1892–95. He was appointed solicitor-general in 1893 and attorney-general in 1903, the first non-white attorney-general of Trinidad.

† **Crown Colony:** Crown Colony government implied direct rule by the Crown, through a Legislative Council which was wholly nominated (officials, and nominated "unofficials" chosen by the governor). Trinidad had had this form of government since 1831, and had never had an elected legislature. Reformers agitated for the inclusion of elected members in the council, but were unsuccessful until 1924–25.

† **"arises like a giant refreshed with wine":** Psalm 78:66. The translation quoted is not that of the Authorized Version (the "King James" Bible), but rather that of the Coverdale Psalter, used in the Church of England's *Book of Common Prayer*: "So the Lord awaked as one out of sleep: and like a giant refreshed with wine." (The corresponding verse in the Authorized Version is 65.) Psalm 78 is a long account of the history of Israel, leading up to the point where David becomes King.

† **Bocas:** The "bocas" – from Spanish *boca* "mouth" – are sea channels between a

number of small islands in the Gulf of Paria, between the island of Trinidad and the Paria peninsula of Venezuela.

† **what Canute said to the waves: "Thus far and no farther.":** According to a famous legend, King Canute "the Great" of England (994?–1035) became annoyed at his courtiers' repeated assurances that he was omnipotent. To teach them to moderate their flattery, he told them to carry him in a chair to the water's edge as the tide was coming in, and then commanded the waves not to come any farther. When the tide came in and began to surround Canute and his chair, he used the occasion to emphasize that only God can force the waves to obey (cf. Job 38:11). Mr Serle appears to forget that Canute's command to the waves was inevitably futile.

p. 60

† **The Working Men's Association stands out the one exception – thanks to the unostentatious public spirit of a gentleman of Chinese extraction:** The Trinidad Workingmen's Association was formed in 1896 or 1897. After a period of dormancy, it was revived in 1906 under the leadership of Alfred Richards (*c*.1862–1947), a pharmacist of mixed African-Chinese ancestry. Under Richards, in 1907 the Trinidad Workingmen's Association established an informal linkage with the British Labour Party; a Labour member of parliament would ask questions in the House of Commons on Trinidad affairs as the "Member for Trinidad". The Trinidad Workingmen's Association was active between 1906 and 1914, but achieved its greatest influence after World War I.

† **the plantain men in the street:** The ordinary labourers who ate working-class creole food such as plantains, a starchy, not very sweet, banana-like fruit.

† **Creole born and English bred – my entire stock is English:** Born in Trinidad – or elsewhere in the Caribbean – but of "pure" English ancestry.

p. 61

† **Santa Rosa Races:** A horse-racing meeting traditionally held at the Arima Savannah on Santa Rosa Day, at the end of August.

† **Arima:** Arima is a borough to the east of Port of Spain, dating back to Spanish times, and the centre of a prosperous cocoa district in the early 1900s.

p. 65

† **immortelle trees:** *Erythrina poeppigiana,* a tall tree reaching twenty-five metres (eighty feet), with stout branches and a tall spiny trunk, and bright orange-scarlet flowers; widely used to provide shade to crops, especially young cocoa and coffee trees.

† **under the cocoa:** With "the cocoa", "the coffee" and so on, "under" refers to the cleared area beneath these trees planted on an estate; generally considered a pleasant environment, especially for walking.

p. 68

† **Debé and La Civa:** Debe and La Seiva (the more usual spellings) are villages in
    the Maraval valley to the north-west of Port of Spain. (There is also a village
    called Debe in south-central Trinidad.)

p. 69

† **dilated like lynx's:** The original text has "dilated lynx" and this correction has
    been made as most plausible.

p. 70

† **"The bleak winds of March, Made her tremble and shiver, / But not the dark
    arch, / Nor the black flowing river. / Mad from life's history, / Glad to
    death's mystery. / Swift to be hurl'd, / Anywhere, Anywhere, / Out of the
    world.":** From Thomas Hood, "The Bridge of Sighs" (1844, lines 63–71).
    Hood's poem is a melodramatic account of a despairing "fallen" woman who
    commits suicide by jumping off a bridge. (The original has "bleak wind" and
    "Or" rather than "Nor".)

p. 71

† **"from battle and murder and sudden death, good Lord deliver us":** Edith is
    repeating one of the petitions from the Litany (see note to p. 47).

p. 75

† *clair-audient*: having the ability to hear sounds beyond the range of physical
    hearing – in this case, the physically inaudible voice of God, heard only by the
    spiritual ear.

† **"This do in remembrance of me.":** An echo of a phrase ("Do this in remem-
    brance of me" in the Church of England *Book of Common Prayer*) from the
    Prayer of Consecration in the Communion service or Mass, the point at which
    the bread and wine are blessed. This prayer recalls the blessing of the bread
    and wine by Jesus the day before the crucifixion (Luke 22:19); "this" refers to
    the blessing, breaking and sharing out of the bread among the disciples.

† **"which passeth all understanding":** A phrase from the blessing which ends many
    Christian worship services. At the end of the Church of England Communion
    service, for instance, the blessing begins: "The peace of God, which passeth all
    understanding, keep your hearts and minds in the knowledge and love of
    God, and of his Son Jesus Christ our Lord."

† **mammon:** Wealth regarded as a devil, idol or evil influence; usually "Mammon".

p. 76

† *Port-of-Spain Gazette*: Founded in 1825, this was Trinidad's leading daily news-
    paper in 1907.

† **"The best laid schemes of mice and men gang aft agley.":** From Robert Burns,

"To a Mouse" (1786); Burns has "o' mice an' men". These famous lines (39–40) from Burns's poem have become nearly proverbial; in context they comment on the parallel between the mouse, whose carefully prepared nest is destroyed by the speaker's plough, and human beings, who discover that "foresight may be vain" (line 38).

p. 77

† **Sir Askingall Clubbock:** The name is doubtless derived from Algernon Aspinall, secretary of the West India Committee in London for many years and the author of popular books about the West Indies; and Sir Nevile Lubbock, sugar magnate and long-serving chairman of the West India Committee (see note to p. 88). Both men held these respective offices in 1907.

p. 78

† **Mutual Friendly Society:** A friendly society provided benefits during illness and burial grants in return for small regular payments by members. These societies were important institutions in Trinidad at this time, especially for black artisans and lower-middle-class families. There was a Trinidad Mutual Friendly Society in Port of Spain in the early 1900s.

† **"Black, and that was all . . . but comely.":** An echo of the biblical Song of Songs, or Song of Solomon: "I am black, but comely, O ye daughters of Jerusalem" (Song 1:5). Even though the biblical phrase refers to a dark complexion rather than to specifically African descent, it was inevitably a key passage for race-conscious blacks at the turn of the century. (See also note to p. 124, and the note on "Ethiopia self-uplifted" to p. 101.)

p. 80

† **"Howe'er it be, / It seems to me, / 'Tis only noble to be good, / Kind hearts are more than coronets, / And simpler faith than Norman blood.":** From Tennyson's "Lady Clara Vere de Vere" (1842, lines 53–56; "simpler" is "simple" in the original, and "Howe)'er it be, it seems to me," is all on one line). The speaker criticizes Lady Clara, "The daughter of a hundred Earls" (line 7), for wooing men whom she has no intention of marrying, and so breaking their hearts, driving some even to suicide. In this passage, he asserts that nobility would be better expressed through acts of kindness.

p. 81

† **peeler:** A nickname (originally Irish) for a policeman, based on the role that Sir Robert Peel (1788–1850) had in founding the professional police forces, first in Ireland and later in England.

† **"morbey":** A bitter liquid, sweetened for drinking, made from boiling pieces of the dried bark of *Colubrina arborescens*, a small tree. Usually spelled *mauby*.

Annotations

p. 82

† **granulation:** The formation of grain-like prominences on sores.

† **"Laugh, and the world laughs with you. / Weep, and you weep alone.":** Ella Wheeler Wilcox, "Solitude" (1883). The most famous poem by this popular American poet, "Solitude" incorporates what might be called platitudes or homely wisdom; these opening lines in particular have been widely quoted since the poem first appeared.

† **sullied her escutcheon:** that is, tainted her reputation. Because an escutcheon is the shield or shield-like device on which a coat of arms is displayed, this expression implies that the family's honour as well as the individual's has been stained.

† **Like the miserable lepers in Jewry, ostracised to camp out in the wilderness for a lazaretto, crying "tame – tame," she was deemed unclean:** Because leprosy (now called Hansen's disease) was believed to be highly contagious and was widely feared, lepers in many parts of the world have traditionally been ostracized, housed in isolated leper colonies or lazarettos (shelters for the sick and destitute), and made to ring a bell or cry out that they were "unclean" to warn others away. The biblical verse Cobham probably has in mind is Leviticus 13:45, from a chapter that deals with the laws concerning leprosy; the leper is to "put a covering upon his upper lip, and shall cry, 'Unclean, unclean' ". ("Tame", pronounced "ta-may", is a Hebrew word for "unclean or ritually impure".)

† **link-man:** A person serving as a liaison between groups of people or institutions.

† **plunged through her fair name "coach and four":** That is, drove through her reputation and left it in tatters. A coach drawn by four horses is large, and would do a lot of damage if driven through anything.

p. 83

† **"And to be wroth with those we love / Doth work like madness in the brain.":** From Samuel Taylor Coleridge's "Christabel" (1816). These lines (412–13) occur at the point in this fragmentary poem where Sir Leoline, Christabel's father, remembers Sir Roland, his long-estranged friend and the enchantress Geraldine's father. Christabel initially pities Geraldine and brings her home, only to be horrified by the nameless mark that Geraldine calls "this mark of my shame, this seal of my sorrow" (270). Lines 412–13 are prophetic as well as retrospective, because Sir Leoline, bewitched by Geraldine, ends up turning against his own daughter when she pleads with him to send Christabel away.

† **"For blood than water is yet more thick.":** From Alfred Austin's "The Old Land and the Young Land" (1899). Written during the period of the Boer War in South Africa (see note to pp. 54–55) and the Spanish-American War of 1898, the poem sees both wars as fought in "Freedom's Cause" (line 37); at this point Spain is seen as turning to Britain and asking her to curb the "overweening growth" of the brash "young" United States; Britain (the "Old

Land") brushes Spain aside, saying, "And blood than water is yet more thick, / And this Young Land is my child. / I am proud, not jealous, to watch it grow" (lines 23–25).

† "B-b-boss, O! . . . when d-d-de m-man sh-shoot you, why you en s-s-sen fo' me? T-t-tonnier, crazay, moi gad, *c-c-c-se moi ta la.* E- - - -eef ah – ah was d-day": "Boss, o! . . . When the man shot you, why didn't you send for me? Thunder, craziness, I see, it was I who was there. I was there."

† "Doc-Doctor . . . ah-ah is a pure Trin-Trin-Trinidadian b-bred and b-born. Me fahdah is b-bajan, me muddah yarabah. Ah-ah is man to stan fo' me cullah. Exvantage is a bad have it. Feah play is a jewel.": "Doctor . . . I am a pure Trinidadian bred and born. My father is Barbadian, my mother Yoruba. I am a man to stand up for my colour [race]. Advantage is a bad habit. Fair play is a jewel." The author here is undoubtedly poking fun at the habit of Trinidadians to claim special status as Trinidadian "by birth", as opposed to immigrants, Trinidadian "by boat", despite the high proportion of the latter in virtually all local families. "Advantage" is "to take advantage of"

p. 86

† "monarch minstrel" of old, weeping for him who drove him from his throne at Salem: The "monarch minstrel" is King David, weeping for Absalom (see note below), and "Salem" is a shortened form of "Jerusalem". "Monarch minstrel" is a quotation from "The Harp the Monarch Minstrel Swept" in Byron's *Hebrew Melodies* (1815), a collection of poems written for and set to music by Isaac Nathan. Byron is here echoing the most famous of Thomas Moore's *Irish Melodies* (1807–34), "The Harp That Once through Tara's Halls".

† "O, Absalom, my son, my son.": From King David's lament for his son Absalom, who rebels against and yet is loved by his father. When news reaches David that Absalom is killed and the rebellion quashed, David mourns instead of rejoicing: "O my son Absalom, my son, my son Absalom! would God I had died for thee, O Absalom, my son, my son!" (2 Samuel 18:33).

† "He liv'd for life may long be borne / Ere sorrow breaks its chain. / Why comes not death to those who mourn? / He never smil'd again.": From Felicia Hemans's, "He Never Smiled Again" (1825), a poem about King Henry I of England, said never to have smiled again after the drowning of his son and heir, Prince William, in 1120. Hemans' poem describes the king surrounded by "proud forms" and by "the stately and the brave" (lines 9–10), but neither they nor "England's glorious crown" (line 3) can make up for the loss of the Prince.

p. 87

† "Défin Tammas ta led, mai de bwes, neg la ta savant": "Although Thomas was ugly, but . . . that black man was very wise."

† **Maxwell Philip. "Avocah fama mon ami"**: "That lawyer is my friend."

p. 88

† **Stooping to conquer:** A reference to the title of Oliver Goldsmith's play, *She Stoops to Conquer* (1773). The heroine of the play wins the excruciatingly shy hero by pretending to be a servant so that he will not be terrified of talking to her. The phrase seems to be used here without specific reference to the play's plot.

† **"Prompt to ire":** From Scott's *Marmion* (see note to p. 36), this phrase is part of the initial description of Lord Marmion: "His eyebrow dark, and eye of fire, / Showed spirit proud, and prompt to ire" (1.5).

† **West India Committee:** A committee of prominent businessmen based in London, who had property and commercial interests in the British Caribbean. First established in the eighteenth century, by 1907 it spoke mainly for British sugar interests. It frequently lobbied the Colonial Office and Caribbean governors, and exerted a strong influence on policy making for the West Indian colonies.

† **"The Junius of the West":** The "Letters" of Junius comprised a series of essays on British politics published under this pseudonym in a London newspaper in 1769–72. They became a model for subsequent polemical writings. "The West" here means the Western Hemisphere.

p. 89

† **yellow and black water fevers:** Yellow fever is an infectious fever of tropical areas, characterized by vomiting, constipation, jaundice and so on. Blackwater fever is a tropical fever to which mostly white people are subject, characterized by a brown or blue-black colour of the urine.

† **pitch lake at La Brea:** The "Pitch Lake" is a large natural asphalt deposit, located in La Brea in south-western Trinidad.

† **oil wells at Guayaguayare:** Guayaguayare, on the south-eastern coast of Trinidad, was an early site for oil drilling. The first successful well in this area was drilled by Randolph Rust in 1902 and development proceeded rapidly in the following years.

† **"cascaladoo":** The "cascadura" or "cascadu", *Hoplosternum littorale,* is an armoured catfish, to twenty-three centimetres (nine inches) long; the sides of the body are covered by two rows of bony plates. It lives in muddy free-flowing streams, canals, drainage ditches and swamps, and is an important food fish. According to legend, those who eat this fish are bound to return to or actually die in Trinidad. Also "cascadoo", "cascadoux", "cascaladoo" and "cascaradura".

p. 90

† **fashion-plated grecian girls:** The "Grecian bend" was a fashionable female affected carriage of the body, in which it is bent forward from the hips.

† **"The East Indians are victims to yaws. Their cutlasses do not spare spouse nor estate managers. They monopolise the milk trade and cleanse their vessels in gutter water.":** Yaws is an infectious skin disease, still common in the Caribbean at that time. Persons of African descent were just as prone to it as the Indians; it was essentially a disease of poverty and poor sanitation. Indian men had a reputation for attacking unfaithful or troublesome wives with their cutlasses (machetes), and many Indian women met their deaths in this way during the indenture period (1845–1917). Violent attacks by Indians on estate staff were, however, quite rare in Trinidad. Cobham may have been recalling (or "foretelling") an incident in March 1907 when an overseer, W.H. McKenzie, was beaten to death by Indian estate labourers. Indian women monopolized the vending of milk in the island, and were often prosecuted for diluting their milk with water and for unsanitary practices.

† **The Chinese are gambling kings in whé-whé palaces:** Whe-whe is a gambling game of Chinese origin, in which the organizer or banker chooses one number or "mark" from a set of numbers and seals it in an envelope; people then bet on what number it is, traditionally according to dreams. Also spelled "we-we", "whay-whay" and "whey whey".

† **ochroes:** The ochro (*Abelmoschus esculentus*), English "okra", is a plant with edible green pods, pointed at one end, and sides slightly ridged; it is slimy when cooked.

† **the legal eunuch whose forte is monkeyism:** Since a eunuch has been castrated, Clarke might be using "legal eunuch" to point to a powerless lawyer, or perhaps to a weak man who gains power only through being a lawyer. "Monkeyism", or monkey-like behaviour, involves such things as imitation, chattering, mischief and so on; in the nineteenth century, the British often called the behaviour of the French "monkeyism".

† **beet root bounties:** In the 1880s and 1890s, European governments, including Germany, France and Austria, gave a stimulus to their beet sugar growers by bounties (subsidies) for each ton exported. This seriously damaged the cane sugar producers of the West Indies, as it caused a glut on the British sugar market and a drastic fall in prices. By international agreement, the bounty system for European beet sugar was terminated in 1903.

† **thirty per cent differential:** This refers to the 30 per cent tariff imposed by the Venezuelan government at this time on imports from Trinidad. Of course, this was a major grievance to the mercantile community of the island.

p. 91

† **wait till the clouds roll by:** Florence is quoting the title and refrain line of a popular ballad (*c.*1881) by J.T. Wood, in which the speaker, who is leaving his "own true loved one", exhorts her to be faithful and wait for his return.

† **Shakespeare is right. Troubles do come in battalions.:** A reference to Shakespeare's *Hamlet* (4.5). After watching Ophelia, who has gone mad,

apparently as a result of Hamlet's strange behaviour and his murder of her father, the usurper Claudius laments that sorrows "come not single spies, / But in battalions".

p. 92

† **English mail:** See note to p. 10.

† **Iere:** See note to p. 12.

† **care Miss Gwendoline:** that is, care for Miss Gwendoline.

p. 93

† **"Where you b-bung you m-mus' obey":** "Where you are bound, you must obey."

† **Lady of Laventille:** The Roman Catholic Church, dedicated to the Virgin Mary, in Laventille, an area just south of Port of Spain.

† **Woodbrook faced the sea as far as Mucurapo Point:** Woodbrook is a middle-class suburb of Port of Spain, new in 1907, which stretched to the west of the city as far as Mucurapo (now also suburban), close to St James (see note to p. 52).

† **"M-Miss E-Edith . . . long t-time ah had dat to axe you. Ah, ah ent a marridin' man, b-but ah make up me mind to marrid wi-wid you.":** "Miss Edith . . . for a long time I have had that to ask you. I, I'm not a marrying man, but I've made up my mind to marry you."

† **gig:** A light narrow ship's boat whose external planks overlap downwards, fastened with clinched copper nails; it can be adapted for rowing or sailing.

p. 94

† **in peril on the sea:** From the refrain of William Whiting's hymn, "Eternal Father, Strong to Save" (1860): each verse until the last ends "Oh hear us when we cry to thee / For those in peril on the sea".

p. 96

† **on the resurrection morning they neither marry nor are given in marriage:** This echoes Christ's answer to those who challenge him about a woman who has been married to seven brothers in succession. Asked whose wife she would be at the resurrection, Christ answers that "in the resurrection they neither marry, nor are given in marriage, but are as the angels of God in heaven" (Matthew 22:30; see also Mark 12:25 and Luke 20:35).

p. 97

† **"Seven Roman cities strove for Homer dead / Thro' which the living Homer begged his bread.":** An altered quotation from "Poetry Its Cure", fable 13 of *Æsop at Tunbridge, or a Few Select Fables in Verse* (1698) by "No person of

quality", a poem in which a "youth of pregnant Parts and Wit" thinks of taking up poetry to win fame. To dissuade him, his father sends him the following couplet: "Seven wealthy Towns contend for Homer Dead, / Through which the Living Homer beg'd." (It is difficult to see why Cobham's version identifies the towns as Roman, since Homer was Greek.)

† **"She died and was buried":** A biblical phrase which appears in several places. The one echoed here is probably Genesis 35:19, where Rachel, Jacob's wife, dies bearing their last son, Benjamin: "And Rachel died, and was buried in the way to Ephrath."

† **Erasmus of Rotterdam:** The humanist scholar Desiderius Erasmus was born in Rotterdam. No exact match for "the terrors of death" has been found in his works, but there is a section on this subject in Seneca's *Epistle IV,* which Erasmus translated, and which he frequently echoes in his *In Praise of Folly* (1511).

† **"Death, what art thou / To whom all bow / From sceptred King to slave? / The last best friend, / Our cares to end, / Thine empire's in the grave. / When all have fled, / Thou giv'st a bed / Wherein we calmly sleep: The wounds all heal'd, / The dim eyes seal'd, / That long did wake and weep.":** No source has been yet found for this quotation; it may be from Cobham's own poetry. The first line is a common formula in funeral/memorial poetry, and the phrase "last best friend" has been used by several poets, notably by Robert Southey in *Carmen Nuptiale* (1816), where it is spoken by an allegorical figure of death: "My name is DEATH, the last best friend am I" (line 642).

p. 98

† **"Hail, murky sky, canopy of industry; hail, twentieth century Rome – roaring metropolis of empire.":** This seems to be Rupert's own invention rather than a quotation. On the Roman reference, see note to p. 102 below.

p. 99

† **creole desdemona:** This reference to Shakespeare's *Othello* (*c.*1604) picks up on Gwendoline's earlier parallel between Rupert and Othello (p. 21). Desdemona is the white Venetian lady wooed, married and finally killed by the Moorish general Othello. Gwendoline clearly parallels – and differs from – Desdemona in many ways, just as Rupert does Othello. (See discussion in the section "Race and Gender" in the introduction.)

† **a modern narcissus:** Narcissus, a youth in Greek mythology, is much loved by many nymphs, but he always shuns them as soon as he has made them love him. They are avenged when the goddess Nemesis makes him fall in love with his own reflection; Narcissus pines away with unrequited love and dies. Unless the newspaper reporter supposes that Rupert has pushed Gwendoline away (unlikely if the story has been told "in all its naked truth"), it is hard to see the relevance of the Narcissus reference. Perhaps the point is that Rupert,

as a modern Narcissus, falls in love with someone who in racial terms is his opposite rather than his likeness.

† **Caesar: "I came, I saw, I conquered":** The original is in Latin, "Veni, vidi, vici", Julius Caesar's proverbial account of his victory over Pharnaces, King of Pontus, in 47 BC. Caesar displayed a placard with these words in his triumphal procession (Plutarch, *Life of Julius Caesar,* 50:3, and Suetonius, *The Deified Julius,* 37).

† **phaeton:** A light, four-wheeled open carriage, usually pulled by a pair of horses, and with one or two seats facing forward.

† **Inns of Court:** There were four Inns of Court in London – Lincoln's Inn, Gray's Inn, Inner Temple and Middle Temple – ancient societies of English advocates which trained barristers, set standards for the profession, administered examinations through which one could qualify to be called to the Bar (admitted to practise as a barrister in England and the colonies), and disciplined practising barristers. A member (student) attended lectures and courses organized by his Inn, sat the various examinations, and "kept terms", which meant dining in his Inn a certain number of times per term. The Inns did not grant degrees, and one could be admitted to the Bar without a degree, though many did obtain a Bachelor of Laws degree from one of the English universities before entering an Inn of Court. Around this time the Inner Temple enjoyed especially close links with Oxford and Cambridge and many of its members had earned Bachelor of Laws degrees from one of the two ancient English universities. It was considered the most prestigious of the four Inns, the natural choice for an aristocrat such as the Earl of Rothberry, who persuades Rupert Gray to select it.

p. 100

† **"Let justice be done, though the heavens should fall.":** See note to *Fiat justicia,* p. 105.

† **The Princess of Wales wrote an autograph, from White Lodge, to the Rothberry Memorial Committee, regretting her inability to attend the unveiling in consequence of the serious indisposition of the Prince:** The Princess of Wales in 1907 was Victoria Mary, wife of the future George V. An "autograph" is a personal letter, handwritten or at least hand-signed by the sender herself; in either case the princess' autograph would be a mark of great favour. The note could hardly have been written from White Lodge, however, unless the novel is set farther back in time than it appears to be. As the residence of her parents (the Duke and Duchess of Teck), White Lodge at Richmond Park had been the princess's home, but in the first decade of the twentieth century it was in other hands.

p. 101

† **Home for Stranded Natives:** This name is almost certainly fictional. However,

the Trinidad *Mirror* reported in 1907 on a League of Universal Brotherhood and Native Races Association, based in London, which (among other things) lobbied for native Africans in Britain; Henry Sylvester Williams, whom Cobham knew and admired (see discussion in the introduction), was linked to this organization.

† **The statue, a bronze one in *mezzo-rilievo*, was the work of Champney:** There does not appear to have been a sculptor called Champney, though several members of the American Champney family were artists (for example, Benjamin Champney, painter, 1817–1907; James Wells Champney, painter, 1843–1903). Cobham may have invented a fictional member of the family who works in bronze. *Mezzo-rilievo,* or "half-relief", is a style of sculpture in which the figures project half their true proportions from the surface on which they are carved or moulded.

† **from the land where the trees bear sugar:** This satirizes British ignorance about the West Indies (the sugar cane is a grass).

† ***medias res*:** "the middle of things" (Latin). The phrase most commonly refers to the convention that an epic poem starts in the middle of events – *in medias res* – not at the beginning, and then doubles back later on to fill in the initial stages of the action.

† **Ethiopia self-uplifted:** Ethiopia was often used as a metaphor for Africa or for those of African descent at this period. The phrase "Princes shall come out of Egypt; Ethiopia shall soon stretch out her hands unto God" (Psalms 68:31) became an important symbol. Ethiopia itself, as an ancient independent African kingdom ruled by a dynasty claiming descent from Solomon and Sheba, was a source of great pride to the race-conscious blacks of the Americas; in 1896 the Ethiopians had defeated an invading Italian army and "to fight as an Abyssinian" was an admiring comment. "Ethiopianism" developed as a movement for the upliftment of those of African descent everywhere.

† **true imperialism the best earnest of the immortality of empire:** This articulates the trusteeship doctrine of empire: the British Empire was a great force for good in the world, selflessly working for the advance of the "subject races" through its civilizing mission. This altruistic mission would ensure that the empire would endure, as a partnership with the progressively more civilized subjects of the king world-wide. The view articulated here was quite typical of the early 1900s, the zenith of the British Empire, and was held by many educated non-white colonials such as Rupert Gray.

p. 102

† ***Civis Romanus sum*:** "I am a Roman citizen" – the proud boast of the citizen of the ancient Roman Empire – was often used metaphorically of the British Empire, in the sense that the subject of the British Crown, whatever his ethnicity and wherever he lived, could (theoretically) claim the same rights as the

British-born. There may be an echo of St Paul here: as a Roman citizen, he had particular rights despite his ethnic identity as a Jew, and he used the citizenship claim strategically (see, for example, Acts 22).

† **Inner Temple . . . LL.B. . . . Roman prizeman:** The Inner Temple was one of the four Inns of Court (see note to p. 99). The Bachelor of Laws degree (LL.B.) was not awarded by the Inns, but by one of the English universities, from one of which Gray has presumably graduated before entering the Inner Temple. At the Temple, he wins top honours in the courses on Roman law and jurisprudence, a compulsory part of the programme organized by the Inns.

† **grand tour:** Many men from well-off British families took a Continental "grand tour" at the threshold of their careers or their adult lives, and by the early twentieth century, a round-the-world tour was becoming more common for the wealthy in Great Britain and America. As a first-time visitor, Rupert naturally starts with England, Scotland, Wales and Ireland; he and the earl seem to visit some places for the sake of their interesting topography or buildings: Stonebyres Linn, Fingal's Cave in Scotland; Canwick, Wye Bridge (Hereford), Stye Heath, Ilfracombe and Anstis Cove in England; Devils' Bridge, Aberglaslyn and St Gowans Head in Wales; and the Giant's Causeway, Silver Strand, in Ireland. Others have literary and historical associations, explained in the following notes.

† **Enniskillen:** The siege of Enniskillen Castle (1594) began the Nine Years' War in Ireland between Irish rebels and the English.

† **Lake District:** The Lake District of Westmoreland and Cumberland counties is known for its scenery, but also for its association with the Romantic poets, particularly Wordsworth, who grew up there and later lived there with his wife and sister. Derwentwater is one of the lakes, and Yewdale and Stockghyl are both in the Lake District.

† **Haddon, still haunted by the memory of Dorothy Vernon:** As legend has it, in the mid-sixteenth century, Dorothy Vernon of Haddon Hall in Derbyshire loved John Manners, but the match was opposed by her father, Sir George Vernon. As newly rich Protestants, the Manners were upstarts to the Catholic Sir George, and their recent acquisition of a title failed to impress him, so Dorothy had to elope with John. The truth seems to be that the match was welcomed by both families, but there have been popular renditions of the legend, notably Sir Arthur Sullivan's light opera *Haddon Hall* (1892, libretto by Sydney Grundy).

† **Binabola, "Norham's castled steep":** This has tentatively been identified as an Irish location, on the basis of a passage in William Thackeray's *Irish Sketch Book* (1842), chapter 18, which refers briefly to a walk at Roundstone, in Connemara. Thackeray mentions having a view of the Atlantic on one side and "the Binabola" on the other; most likely "Binabola" is an anglicized version of "Na Beanna Beola", the Gaelic name for the "Twelve Bens" or "Twelve Pins", a line of mountains visible from Roundstone.

† **"Norham's castled steep"**: A quotation from canto 1 of Scott's *Marmion* (see note to p. 36): "Day set on Norham's castled steep, / And Tweed's fair river, broad and deep."

† **"Newark's stately tower"**: A quotation from the introductory section of Scott's *Lay of the Last Minstrel* (1805). The tower is that of Newark Castle in the Border area of Scotland, where the aged minstrel finds shelter with Anne, Duchess of Buccleuch and Monmouth, and widow of the Duke of Monmouth (executed in 1685 after leading an unsuccessful rebellion against James II).

† **Gilnockie:** Gilnockie Tower, near Dumfries in Scotland, was the home of the Borders outlaw hero Johnnie Armstrong, the subject of many ballads. Armstrong was killed with his men by James V of Scotland in 1530, after they accepted what seemed to be the king's gracious invitation to wait on him.

† **Glen Tilt:** In Perthshire, Scotland. Famous as one of the sites the geologist James Hutton used to prove his "Plutonism" theory, that heat from beneath the earth's crust had lifted rocks from under the sea onto the land.

† **romantic Braemar smacking ever of the memory of the rival of the Guelphs:** The Hanoverian royal house of England, from George I to Victoria, bore the family name of "Guelph". Their "rivals" were the exiled Stuarts (see note to pp. 54–55); the rebel standard was raised at Braemar in Scotland to begin the first Jacobite rebellion in 1715. ("Jacobite" was the name given to the supporters of the Stuarts, "Jacobus" being the Latin version of "James".)

† **Oriel, Magdalen and Lime Walk, Oxford, that nursery of divines; Trinity Avenue, Gate of Honour, Jesus' College, Cambridge:** These are various colleges and sites in Oxford and Cambridge; each university could in fact be seen as a "nursery of divines", since Church of England clergy took degrees at Oxford or Cambridge as a prelude to ordination. Cobham, almost certainly a Roman Catholic, was probably sympathetic to the High or Catholic wing of the Anglican Church, which would be why he singles out Oxford, where the High Anglican "Oxford Movement" was born in the 1830s.

† **Penrhyn Quarries:** Reputedly the largest slate quarry in the world, Penrhyn, in Wales, had been much in the news during the decade before *Rupert Gray* was published as the site of two major and bitter strikes (1896–97 and 1900–1903).

† **Glencoe and Culloden, famed "in song and story":** Historic sites in Scotland. Nearly forty members of the Clan MacDonald of Glencoe were massacred at Glencoe in 1692, in the wake of the "Glorious Revolution" of 1688, when William and Mary took the throne and displaced James II, the last Stuart king. The MacDonalds had been labelled as Jacobites and miscreants because they had not sworn an oath of loyalty to King William within the allotted time; accounts vary widely, but it seems clear that the MacDonalds were singled out as an example. At the Battle of Culloden (1746), the second Jacobite rebellion was decisively quelled by British forces loyal to the Hanoverian King George II. "Famed in song and story" is a common poetic formula.

† **Ballachulish and its wonders:** The village of Ballachulish in Glencoe is known
for its slate quarries, and made a great impression on Queen Victoria during a
royal visit, but it is not clear what "wonders" Cobham refers to here.

† **Berry Pomeroy and Dartmoor in Devonshire, which last gave to Virginia a breed
of sturdy colonisers under the Virgin Queen:** Berry Pomeroy is a castle in
Devon, famous for ghost sightings, and Dartmoor is the site of a prison –
hence the joke about its provision of "sturdy colonisers" (transported felons)
to Virginia. (In fact, however, these particular transportations ceased nearly
two centuries before a prison was established at Dartmoor in 1850.)

† **Tintern Nave:** Tintern Abbey is the ruined abbey in Monmouthsire, Wales, that
inspired Wordsworth's poem "Tintern Abbey" (in full, "Lines composed a
few miles above Tintern Abbey, on revisiting the banks of the Wye during a
tour. July 13, 1798"). There is no special reason for referring to the nave (the
main part of the abbey's chapel), though it is unusually well preserved, with
most of its columns still standing.

† **historic Carisbrook:** Charles I was imprisoned in Carisbrooke Castle on the Isle
of Wight before his execution in 1649.

† **sunny Bonchurch in the Isle of Wight:** Bonchurch was one of the earliest settlements in the Isle of Wight; the island as a whole is noted for its climate, con-
sistently warmer and sunnier than that of the mainland, and even capable in
places of supporting tropical vegetation. There is a rock cleft called the Devil's
Chimney near Bonchurch, though there is also a more famous rock formation
(possibly man-made) of the same name near Cheltenham in Gloucestershire.

† **Westminster upon the ashes of the great and good . . . Mausoleum of
Wilberforce . . . British Museum . . . Tower of London . . . the Commons in
session:** Westminster Abbey, the British Museum, the Tower and the House of
Commons are among the principal sights of London. William Wilberforce
(1759–1833), the most prominent British leader in the campaigns in Britain
against the slave trade and slavery in the British Empire, is one of the "great
and good" buried and memorialized in Westminster Abbey.

p. 103

† **the *Victory* where Nelson fell:** Admiral Nelson's flagship, the *Victory,* on which
he died during the Battle of Trafalgar (1805), was and is moored at
Portsmouth. At the time of *Rupert Gray,* it had been dismasted and was in
use as a stationary flagship.

† **Eddystone:** A famous lighthouse near Plymouth which warns boats off the dan-
gerous Eddystone Rocks. The fifth lighthouse, built in 1882 by Sir James
Douglass and still standing, would be the one mentioned here.

† **sailed on "placid Leman":** In Byron's *Childe Harold* (see note to p. 36), the poet
contrasts "Clear, placid Leman" (Lake Leman in Switzerland) with "the wild
world", saying that he learns from the lake's stillness "to forsake / Earth's
troubled waters for a purer spring" (canto 3, stanza 85).

† **Fata Morgana:** This Latin name of the Arthurian enchantress Morgan le Fay is also given to a particular sort of mirage – the illusion of a castle half in the air and half on the sea or land. It is created by alternating layers of warm and cold air near the surface of the ground or water.

† **Italy among "vine-clad ruins where the voice of Cicero is succeeded by the voices of shepherds calling to their fellows":** This quotation has not yet been identified.

† **Vesuvius:** A volcano in Italy, the one which buried the city of Pompei.

† **the frescoes in Great St. Peter's:** St Peter's Basilica in Rome, the seat of the Pope.

† **for Virgil's sake visited Mantua; Florence for Dante's:** The Roman poet Virgil is said to have been born in Mantua; the Italian poet Dante was born in Florence.

† **"city of the violet crown," in the classic land of Greece:** Athens: the epithet is found in Aristophanes (*Knights* 1323, 1329 and *Acharnians* 637).

† **"phosphorescent sea":** The Mediterranean; "the phosphorescent sea" is the title of three sections (22–24) of William Sharp's long poem *The Human Inheritance* (1882).

† **Gennesaret:** A fertile plain northwest of the Sea of Galilee, mentioned in the Bible (for example, Luke 5).

† **Gethsemane:** The garden of Gethsemane in Jerusalem, sacred to Christians as the place where Jesus was arrested prior to being tried and crucified.

† **viewed Salem from Olivet:** That is, viewed Jerusalem from the nearby Mount Olivet.

† **"spice-laden gales from Araby the Blest":** An inexact quotation from book 4 of Milton's *Paradise Lost*. Milton has a long epic simile describing the wonderful smell of Paradise as Satan perceives it on his way to tempt mankind: it is like those that sailors encounter sailing up the East African coast, when "northeast winds blow, / Sabaean odours from the spicy shore / Of Araby the Blest" (lines 161–63).

† **Juggernaut:** The English word "Juggernaut" derives from "Jagannatha", the form in which the Hindu god Krishna is worshipped at Puri, in India. The Festival of Rathayatra, held in Puri, involves an image of the god pulled on a wagon so heavy that hundreds of devotees are needed to pull it, and thousands take part over several days. Here presumably the reference is to the temple, since the two men enter it.

† **went underground before the rude idols of the Destroyer:** Most likely they went into the caves at Ellora in India. The "Destroyer" is a reference to the Hindu god Shiva, a complex divinity who is both destroyer and restorer.

† **watched the snow-capped Himalays from the vantage-ground of Simla:** Simla, in northwestern India, is located on the edge of the Himalayan Mountains; it was a favourite summering spot of the civil servants and military personnel of the British Raj.

† **forty-ninth parallel into Uncle Sam's country – the land of skyscrapers and of the

dollar – of national energy and progress: The United States was often seen as a land of progress and material wealth. (West of the Great Lakes, the forty-ninth parallel of latitude divides Canada from the United States.) Interestingly, Rupert Gray and the earl go to the Southern states first, presumably focusing on Alabama and Booker T. Washington's Tuskegee Institute (see note to p. 58). Only then do they go to New York, the more typical starting point of an American tour.

p. 104

† **"Love may come and love may go, / And fly like a bird from tree to tree; / But I will love no more – no more / Till Ellen Adair come back to me.":** From Tennyson's short ballad "Edward Gray" (1842). Edward's mourning for Ellen, unlike Rupert's for Gwendoline, is tinged with guilt. Edward has deserted her, mistaking her shyness for coldness and fickleness, and so contributed to her death.

p. 105

† **"Where the wicked cease from troubling and the weary are at rest.":** From Job 3:17; this verse is part of Job's curse. Chapter 3 begins, "Let the day perish wherein I was born"; in this section Job contemplates the rest he would have had with the dead had he died at birth: "There the wicked cease from troubling, and there the weary be at rest."

† **"sown the whirlwind" should be made to "reap the storm":** Altered quotations from Hosea 8:7, predicting vengeance on Israel ("For they have sown the wind, and they shall reap the whirlwind").

† *Fiat justitia, ruat coelum:* The Latin version of Isaiah 45:8 ("Drop down, ye heavens, from above, and let the skies pour down righteousness"), part of a series of prophecies involving Cyrus, King of Persia and his role as an instrument of God who will "subdue nations before him" (45:1). The phrase is often used in legal contexts to emphasize the impartial workings of justice and its inexorability, no matter the consequences. (See also Sir Askingall Clubbock's paraphrase on p. 100.)

p. 106

† **Holy Trinity Cathedral:** The main Anglican church in downtown Port of Spain, built in the 1820s, this became a cathedral in 1872.

† **Brunswick Square:** The main square in downtown Port of Spain, named by the British after a military division, involved in the 1797 British conquest of the island, whose soldiers were from Brunswick in Germany. It was renamed Woodford Square in 1917 during World War I.

† **Hart and Abercromby Streets:** Two streets forming two of the four sides of Brunswick Square; Hart Street faces the Cathedral.

† **flourish of hunters adorned with ribbons:** "Hunter" here and just below seems to mean a type of riding crop (a short, thick whip, usually without a lash).

† **Brigade Station:** The tram stop and transfer point next to the headquarters of
the city Fire Brigade, close to the Anglican cathedral.

p. 107

† **bell-topper:** A top-hat, especially one of the then old-fashioned type with a bell-
shaped crown.

p. 108

† **Barrister-at-Law:** A person called to the Bar, entitled to practise as an advocate
in all the higher courts. Only persons who had studied and "kept terms" (see
note to p. 99) at one of the Inns of Court in London could be so called; anyone who had been called to the English Bar was automatically eligible for
admission to the Bar of any British colony.

† **you unbelieving Thomas:** A reference to the biblical story of the disciple
Thomas, who at first refuses to believe Jesus has risen from the dead unless he
can put his "finger into the print of the nails" and his "hand into his side"
(John 20:25). The more common phrase is "Doubting Thomas".

p. 109

† **Hon. Hay Russia, K.C.:** This probably refers to Henry Albert – invariably abbre-
viated as H.A., hence "Hay" – Alcazar (1860–1930). Alcazar, a mixed-race
barrister, was a famous orator and enjoyed a large practice; he was perhaps
the leading lawyer practising in Trinidad in the early 1900s. ("K.C." stands
for King's Counsel, an honour reserved for very senior barristers.) He had
been active in anti-Crown Colony politics in the 1890s and was a mayor of
Port of Spain for four terms during that decade. The title "honourable" was
bestowed on members of council; Alcazar was an Unofficial Member of the
Legislative Council (1894–99 and 1903–30).

† **patois French:** The French Creole language; a creole language with mostly
French-derived vocabulary, but with grammar and phonology also derived
partly from African and other languages. Varieties of this language have been
or are spoken in numerous Caribbean territories (as well as elsewhere), with
different dialects or varieties spoken in different areas, for example, St Lucia,
French Guiana and Haiti. This was the most widely used language in Trinidad
from the late eighteenth to early twentieth centuries, usually known in
Trinidad as "Patois" (formerly also "broken French" or "Negro French", and
"Patwa", "Creole" or "Kwéyol" elsewhere). "Creole French" usually referred
to the Creole-influenced French spoken by local creoles of European descent.

† **Man-you-well Africanus Polbutter:** This probably refers to Emmanuel Scipio-
Pollard, a mixed-race barrister active in the late nineteenth and early twentieth centuries (cf. Scipio Africanus, the Roman general famous for his defeat of
Hannibal at Zama in 202 BC). Scipio-Pollard (the names were usually, but not
always, hyphenated) was a successful lawyer with a busy practice. He was

also race conscious, and active in movements in the early 1900s to restore the elected Port of Spain Borough Council (abolished in 1899) and to win elected members in the Legislative Council.

† **Hon. Papyrus Wiseman Jonathan, K.C.:** This probably refers to Cyrus Prudhomme David (1867–1923), an African-Trinidadian barrister. A protégé of J.J. Thomas and Vincent Brown (see notes to p. 59), he was one of the main leaders of the unsuccessful campaign for constitutional reform in 1892–95 and was an opponent of Crown Colony government. He was nominated as an Unofficial Member of the Legislative Council in 1904, the first African-Trinidadian to be a member of the council.

† **Mr. San Fernando Mango:** This probably refers to Ferdinand Joseph Maingot, a practising solicitor since 1878. A senior member of the profession, in 1907 he was chairman of the Solicitors' Committee and a member of the Council of the Incorporated Law Society of Trinidad and Tobago (the solicitors' body).

† **Mr. Voice-in-the-Wilderness Buyier:** This probably refers to John Baptiste Sellier, a solicitor since 1882. Like Maingot, a senior member of the profession, in 1907 he was a member of the Solicitors' Committee and treasurer of the Incorporated Law Society.

† **another prince of the lower branch:** While barristers could argue cases before the judges in the highest courts, solicitors could not; they "instructed" barristers (did the research and prepared them for court) but could only actually argue cases in the magistrates' courts. Hence, their branch of the legal profession was considered the "lower" one in comparison to the "higher" branch of the barristers. In Trinidad, it had been possible since 1871 to qualify locally as a solicitor (see the introduction), while to be called to the Bar, one had to attend one of the Inns of Court in London. As a result, the "lower branch" was attractive to mixed-race and black Trinidadians who had obtained some level of education but lacked the means to study in London.

† **Mr. He Murambo Salagar:** This probably refers to Emmanuel M'zumbo Lazare (1864–1929), an African-Trinidadian solicitor – the first African-Trinidadian to pass the local examinations and be admitted to practise as a solicitor, in 1895. He was strongly race conscious, taking an African middle name, and was the leader of the Trinidad branch of the Pan-African Association 1901–2. Lazare was a key agitator behind the events which culminated in the 1903 Water Riots (see note to p. 55) and (with Maresse-Smith; see note to p. 58) was tried and acquitted for incitement to riot. He was a nominated member of the Legislative Council 1920–24.

† **"spurs and big guns" fame:** E.M. Lazare was a lieutenant in the Trinidad Light Infantry Volunteers (in which capacity he represented Trinidad and Tobago at Queen Victoria's diamond jubilee celebrations in London in 1897 and met the queen) and helped to form the Trinidad Artillery Volunteers.

† **Lionel Mordaunt Murchison:** This first appearance of Murchison's middle name may be a respectful nod to Lionel Mordaunt Fraser, an English colonial

official who served in Trinidad in the Police and Prison Services and as court registrar. He also wrote the two-volume *History of Trinidad* (volume 1, 1783–1813, published in 1891, and volume 2, 1814–39, published in 1896).

p. 110

† **distinguishing as he went along:** "Distinguishing" is the technique of countering precedents presented by the opponent in a case as not being applicable, by differentiating the current case from that of the precedent on the basis of facts.

† **Taylor's Medical Jurisprudence:** Alfred Swayne Taylor (1806–80) was recognized as a world authority on the law as it relates to the practice of medicine. He wrote, among other works, *Principles and Practice of Medical Jurisprudence, Elements of Medical Jurisprudence, Cases and Observations in Medical Jurisprudence* and *Manual of Medical Jurisprudence,* going through many editions. The early-twentieth-century fictional detective Lord Peter Wimsey referred to Taylor's *Medical Jurisprudence* as "that canon of uncanonical practice and Baedeker of the back doors to death" (Sayers 1937, 223).

† **"Em-eef ah-ah-know 'im. Ah could make out 'e two lef' foots, ah-ah-mile off.":** "Him, if I know him [of course I know him!]. I could make out his two left feet, a mile off."

† **"Ah-ah-mean ah weary tell 'im b-bring b-bedding an pli-pillah to sleep in d-de-wharf.":** "I'm tired of telling him to bring bedding and a pillow to sleep on the wharf."

† **"*Domi assu chay*":** "Sleep under the house", that is, under the floor of a house built upon pillars.

† **"De-de ole m-man weary booce 'im.":** "The old man is tired of boosting [that is, assisting, encouraging] him."

pp. 110–111

† **"Mr. Wiseman O, who you tink ah-ah be? Man don' listen and d-den b-bring come and carry go. Me is Trin-Trin-Trinidadian *oui*. Ah-ah-tell you d-de man live in de place like fly 'pon molasses. Wha' mo' you want.":** "Mr Wiseman, who do you think I am? The man doesn't listen, and then spreads gossip. I am a Trinidadian, yes. I tell you the man lives in the place like a fly on molasses. What more do you want?"

p. 111

† **"Wuk. He m-make d-de boss loss 'e wuk.":** "Job. He made the boss lose his job."

† **"Ah chien, how you want d-de man make Mr. Serle loss 'e wuk. You self too. Is Mr. S-Serle store.":** "Ah, you dog, why do you want the man to make Mr Serle lose his job. Yourself too. It's Mr Serle's store."

† **"Mr. Gray, nuh! You don' know Mr. Gray? Look 'e day wi-wid d-de lead p-pen-**

cil i'-in 'e teet.": "Mr Gray! You don't know Mr Gray? Look at him there
with the lead pencil in his teeth."

† **"You en axe me nutten yet. *Z-zut pacah jamais trouver yun lut Maxwell,
jamais."***: "You haven't asked me anything yet. They will never find another
Maxwell, never."

† *Ad duces tecum*: Properly, a *subpoena duces tecum,* that is, a subpoena which
constrains the recipient to bring to court or to a deposition whatever
documents relevant to the lawsuit at hand may be under his or her control.

p. 112

† **"pomp and circumstance"**: The phrase has become virtually proverbial, but it
occurs in *Othello* 3.3 (see note to p. 99). It is from Othello's farewell to the
"tranquil mind" as he enters the toils of jealous rage: among the things he
sees himself losing is his military career, along with the "Pride, pomp, and
circumstance of glorious war". The phrase had recently received new currency
thanks to Sir Edward Elgar's popular *Pomp and Circumstance Marches*
(1901–30).

† **Bench and Bar**: The "Bench" is the judge or judges (who sat on a "bench" or
raised dais in court); the "Bar" refers to the barristers.

† **Lapeyrouse Cemetery**: The main cemetery of Port of Spain. One side of the
cemetery faces Tragarete Road, which leads out of Port of Spain proper to the
western suburbs.

p. 113

† **"The silent . . . Son of Man"**: The Last Judgement (see following entry) is also to
be the second coming of Jesus, or the "Son of Man", who will "reward every
man according to his works" (Matthew 16:27).

† **"last trump"**: Perhaps because it is so often a part of Christian funeral services,
this phrase has become virtually proverbial, but it comes from 1 Corinthians
15:52, where it refers to the beginning of the Last Judgement, when the living
and the dead are to undergo a sudden change "In a moment, in the twinkling
of an eye, at the last trump".

† **she is not dead, but sleepeth**: The phrase comes from the biblical story of Jairus,
who asks Jesus to heal his daughter. The girl appears to have died by the time
Jesus arrives, but he tells the sceptical people of the house that "the damsel is
not dead, but sleepeth" (Mark 5:39). The story and the phrase also occur in
Matthew (9:24) and Luke (8:52).

† **"Such murmur fill'd, / Th' assembly, as when hollow rocks retain, / The sound
of blustering winds."**: Milton, *Paradise Lost,* book 2, 284–86. This "murmur" is the applause for Mammon's speech at the fallen angels' council in
Hell. Mammon has counselled against renewing the war against God in
Heaven, advising his fellows to make the best of their new abode in Hell
instead.

p. 114

† **Church of the Sacred Heart:** A Catholic church, located on the northeast corner of Richmond and Sackville Streets in Port of Spain.

† **Red House:** A large building on Brunswick (later Woodford) Square, constructed from 1844 to 1848, painted red in honour of Queen Victoria's Diamond Jubilee of 1897, which housed in 1907 the governor's office, the Legislative Council and most major government offices. It was burnt down in the 1903 Water Riots and had only recently been rebuilt in 1907.

† *Prima facie*: Latin for "at first sight", or on first consideration, a common legal phrase.

p. 115

† **"Expectation held them mute.":** A Miltonic echo. In book 1 of *Paradise Lost*, Satan is about to address the fallen angels, who have just gathered themselves together after leaving the lake of fire where they land after their fall from Heaven: "their doubl'd ranks they bend / From wing to wing, and half enclose him round / With all his Peers: attention held them mute" (lines 616–18).

p. 116

† **Mr. Bocaccio, the Venezuelan sculptor:** We have not yet been able to identify this person, if based on a real artist.

† **His Honour Mr. Justice Duck:** This probably refers to R.A. Swan, a British puisne judge serving in Trinidad between 1903 and 1913.

p. 117

† *ignorantia facti excusat*: The whole of this legal Latin saying is *Ignorantia facti excusat, ignorantia juris non excusat*, "Ignorance of fact excuses, while ignorance of the law does not". The idea here is that Mr Serle's ignorance of his daughter's continued existence makes the later will in favour of Clarke void.

† **disherison:** Disinheritance; the cutting off of an heir.

p. 120

† **oracle at Delphi:** The oracle of the Greek god Apollo at Delphi was famous for the ambiguous wording of its prophecies.

† **I will not be persuaded . . . though one rose from the dead:** A biblical echo from the story of Lazarus, the beggar. The rich man at whose gate Lazarus used to lie ends up in hell, but Lazarus goes to lie in Abraham's bosom in Heaven. When the rich man asks if Lazarus can be sent back to warn his five brothers, so that they can avoid the same fate, Abraham tells him that even the testimony of the dead would not convince them: "If they hear not Moses and the prophets, neither will they be persuaded, though one rose from the dead" (Luke 16:31).

p. 121

† **the hotel facing the Grand Savannah:** The Queen's Park Hotel (see note to p. 51).

Annotations

† **palace of Oberon:** In Ben Jonson's masque *Oberon, The Faery Prince* (first performed in 1611), the opening set shows a single large rock in the moonlight.
It opens some time after the action begins, as if by magic, to reveal Oberon's
"bright and glorious Palace".

† **"Absence makes the heart grow fonder":** Originally from a line of an anonymous song in Francis Davidson's collection *Poetical Rhapsody* (1602), but
popularized and made virtually proverbial after it appeared in Nathaniel
Thomas Haynes Bayly's song "Isle of Beauty" (*c*.1825): "Absence makes the
heart grow fonder: / Isle of Beauty, fare thee well." These lines appear in the
third stanza of the song, however, which may not have been written by Bayly
at all. The version first published in his *Songs to Rosa* has no third stanza,
and neither does that published in the posthumous *Songs, Ballads, and Other
Poems* (1844, edited by Bayly's widow).

† **All Saints Church:** An Anglican church facing Queen's Park West at Marli Street.

p. 122

† **belt cars:** The electric tram line which ran around the Queen's Park Savannah,
opened in 1903, was called the Belt Line.

p. 123

† **"Ooman is a nation," said the bridegroom, "way well bodderation.":** "Women
are a nation . . . which is much botheration." This formulation is also found
in the traditional local rhyme, "Nigger is a nation, damn bodderation, always
in the station, stink of perspiration."

† **the proposed erection of a Negro-Industrial Institute in the West Indies:** As far as
we know, this institution is fictional, but it is clearly based on the ideas of
Booker T. Washington (see notes to pp. 58 and 103), whose famous Tuskegee
Normal and Industrial Institute, founded in 1881, emphasized agricultural
and industrial education and training for young African Americans. E.W.
Blyden's influence (see note to p. 59) may also be seen in the insistence that
the teachers should all be black and that the curriculum should highlight the
achievements of people of African descent, in order to inculcate self-confidence in the students.

† **Duke of Westminster:** Possibly Sir Hugh Richard Arthur Grosvenor, Second
Duke of Westminster (1879–1953), known now primarily for his extreme
right-wing tendencies during the 1930s. However, it is possible that Cobham
was thinking rather of his father Hugh Lupus Grosvenor (1825–99), First
Duke of Westminster, who was a patron of several progressive causes.

† **Baron de Rothschild:** Nathan Mayer Rothschild, First Baron Rothschild
(1840–1915), a wealthy banker and philanthropist.

† **Baroness Burdett-Coutts:** Baroness Angela Georgina Burdett-Coutts
(1814–1906), a wealthy philanthropist and administrator of charities whose
work was initially inspired by Charles Dickens, and the first woman to be
honoured with a baronage (in 1871) for public achievement.

Annotations

† **Mr. Cecil Rhodes:** Rhodes (1853–1902) was a famous and wealthy diamond magnate and imperialist. His exploits in Southern Africa in the years leading up to the Boer War make him a somewhat implausible donor to a "Negro-Industrial Institute", but Cobham may have been thinking more of Rhodes' public image after his death: the Rhodes scholarships established by his will in 1902 were designed to allow young men from English-speaking countries and colonies to attend Oxford University. (Women are now eligible as well.)

† **statue of Wilberforce:** See note to p. 102.

† **The Duke of Devonshire was in the chair. "Joe Chamberlain," with his William Pitt's face, represented the Colonial Office:** The Eighth Duke of Devonshire (1833–1908) was a prominent Liberal politician in Britain, and a Cabinet minister (1895–1903). He was a close colleague of W.E. Gladstone until they fell out over Irish Home Rule. Joseph Chamberlain (1836–1914) was also a prominent Liberal politician, and served as an unusually assertive secretary of state for the colonies between 1895 and 1903. In Trinidad, he was notorious for abolishing the Unofficial majority in the Legislative Council in 1898 and for dissolving the elected Borough Council of Port of Spain in 1898–99; he was a strong opponent of representative institutions for colonies with mainly non-European populations. Chamberlain had a long face with a prominent nose, in this respect resembling William Pitt, prime minister of Britain (1783–1801 and 1804–6).

† **a black bishop from the West Coast:** We have not been able to identify this particular bishop, but he may be a fictitious figure inspired by the example of someone such as Samuel Ajai (Ajayi) Crowther (*c.*1807–91), the first African Anglican bishop. The long quotation from his speech is puzzling because in it the bishop seems to oppose the miscegenation that the novel has just resoundingly approved in the marriage of Rupert and Gwendoline. The speech may reflect black pride (and a thinly veiled criticism of the marriage), or it may have been tailored to its audience, with an eye to pleasing such conservative men as Chamberlain and the Duke of Devonshire, assuring them that Rupert and Gwendoline's case is exceptional, not the beginning of a trend towards mixed marriages.

p. 124

† **"I am black but comely, O ye daughter of Jerusalem. – As the tents of Kedar as the curtains of Solomon.":** A quotation from the Song of Solomon (1:5); see note to p. 78.

† **"the sun hath looked upon you, your own vineyard never shall you keep.":** Another borrowing from the Song of Solomon, but the sense diverges somewhat from the original: "Look not upon me, because I am black, because the sun hath looked upon me: my mother's children were angry with me; they made me the keeper of the vineyards, but mine own vineyard have I not kept" (1:6).

REFERENCES

Anon. 1853. *Adolphus, A Tale*. Repr. in *Adolphus, A Tale and The Slave Son*, ed. Lise Winer. Kingston: University of the West Indies Press, 2003.

Anthony, Michael. 1997. *Historical Dictionary of Trinidad and Tobago*. Lanham, MD: Scarecrow Press.

Baksh-Comeau, Yasmin. 1992. "Walter Elias Broadway: Botanist/Naturalist Extraordinaire". *Living World, Journal of the Trinidad and Tobago Field Naturalists Club* (Special Centenary Issue 1891–1991): 14–17.

Brathwaite, Kamau. 1973. *The Arrivants: A New World Trilogy*. London: Oxford University Press.

Brereton, Bridget. 1979. *Race Relations in Colonial Trinidad, 1870–1900*. Cambridge: Cambridge University Press.

———. 1981. *A History of Modern Trinidad, 1783–1962*. London: Heinemann.

Brontë, Charlotte. 1847. *Jane Eyre*. Repr., Oxford: Oxford University Press, 2002.

Brown, Wayne. 1975. *Edna Manley: The Private Years, 1900–1938*. London: André Deutsch.

Collens, J.H., ed. 1908. *Trinidad and Tobago Yearbook, 1908*. Port of Spain: Government Printing Office.

Cudjoe, Selwyn. 2003. *Beyond Boundaries: The Intellectual Tradition of Trinidad and Tobago in the Nineteenth Century*. Wellesley, MA: Calaloux Publications.

de Lisser, H.G. 1913. *Jane's Career*. Repr., London: Heinemann Educational Books, 1971.

de Verteuil, L.A.A. 1858. *Trinidad: Its Geography, Natural Resources, Administration, Present Condition and Prospects*. London: Ward and Lock. Revised edition, London: Cassell and Company, 1884.

Drayton, Richard. 2000. *Nature's Government: Science, Imperial Britain, and the "Improvement" of the World*. New Haven: Yale University Press.

Dreiser, Theodore. 1925. *An American Tragedy*. Repr., New York: Library of America, Penguin Putnam, 2003.

Fielding, Henry. 1749. *Tom Jones*. Repr., Oxford: Oxford University Press, 1998.

Froude, James Anthony. 1888. *The English in the West Indies, or The Bow of Ulysses*. London: Longmans, Green and Co.; New York: Charles Scribner's Sons.

Gonzalez, Anson. 1972. *Self-Discovery through Literature: Creative Writing in Trinidad and Tobago*. Trinidad: A. Gonzalez.

Grainger, James. 1764. *The Sugar-Cane*. London: R. and J. Dodsley.

References

Grand, Sarah. 1893. *The Heavenly Twins.* Repr., Ann Arbor: University of Michigan Press, 1993.

Hodge, Merle. 1970. *Crick Crack, Monkey.* London: André Deutsch.

———. 1972. "Peeping Tom in the Nigger Yard". *Tapia* 25 (2 April): 11–12.

Hooker, J.R. 1975. *Henry Sylvester Williams, Imperial Pan-Africanist.* London: Rex Collings.

Hoyos, F.A. 1974. *Grantley Adams and the Social Revolution.* London: Macmillan.

James, C.L.R. 1936. *Minty Alley.* London: Secker and Warburg. Repr., London: New Beacon Books, 1971.

Joseph, E.L. 1838. *Warner Arundell, the Adventures of a Creole.* London: James Moyes. Repr., ed. Lise Winer. Kingston: University of the West Indies Press, 2001.

Kaul, Mythili. 1997. "Background: Black or Tawny? Stage Representations of Othello from 1604 to the Present". In *Othello: New Essays by Black Writers,* edited by Mythili Kaul, 1–19. Washington: Howard University Press.

Kincaid, Jamaica. 1996. *The Autobiography of My Mother.* New York: Farrar, Straus and Giroux.

———. 1999. *My Garden (Book):.* New York: Farrar, Straus and Giroux.

Kingsley, Charles. 1871. *At Last, a Christmas in the West Indies.* London: Macmillan.

Magid, A. 1988. *Urban Nationalism: A Study of Political Development in Trinidad.* Gainesville: University of Florida Press.

Marshall, Paule. 1959. *Brown Girl, Brownstones.* London: W.H. Allen and Co. Repr., London: Virago Press, 1982.

Mathurin, Owen C. 1976. *Henry Sylvester Williams and the Origins of the Pan-African Movement, 1869–1911.* Westport, CT: Greenwood Press.

McKay, Claude. 1933. *Banana Bottom.* New York: Harper and Bros.

McWatt, Mark. *West Indian Literature and Its Social Context.* Cave Hill, Barbados: Department of English, University of the West Indies.

Mendes, Alfred. 1934. *Black Fauns.* London: Duckworth. Repr., London: New Beacon Books, 1984.

Naipaul, V.S. 1967. *The Mimic Men.* London: André Deutsch.

———. 1987. *The Enigma of Arrival.* Harmondsworth: Penguin.

Noel, Ronald. 2003. "Agnes Harriet Gertrude Sylvestre-Williams". Seminar paper, Department of History, University of the West Indies, St Augustine, Trinidad.

———. 2004. "The Legal Career of Henry Sylvestre-Williams". Seminar paper, Department of History, University of the West Indies, St Augustine, Trinidad.

Ramchand, Kenneth. 1983. *The West Indian Novel and Its Background.* Revised edition, London: Faber and Faber.

Reid, V.S. 1949. *New Day*. New York: A.A. Knopf.

Rhys, Jean. 1966. *Wide Sargasso Sea*. London: André Deutsch.

Samaroo, Brinsley. 1969. "Constitutional and Political Development of Trinidad, 1898–1925". PhD thesis, University of London.

———. 1971. "C.P. David: A Case Study in the Emergence of the Black Man in Trinidad Politics". *Journal of Caribbean History* 3 (November): 73–89.

Sander, Reinhard W. 1988. *The Trinidad Awakening: West Indian Literature of the Nineteen-Thirties*. New York: Greenwood Press.

Sayers, Dorothy L. 1937. *Busman's Honeymoon*. Repr. New York: HarperPaperbacks, 1995.

Schreiner, Olive. 1883. *The Story of an African Farm*. Repr., Peterborough, ON: Broadview Press, 2003.

Selvon, Samuel. 1952. *A Brighter Sun*. London: Alan Wingate. Repr., London: Longman, 1971.

Shephard, Ben. 2003. *Kitty and the Prince*. Johannesburg: Jonathan Ball.

Smith, William. 2000. "Advocates for Change Within the Imperium: Urban Coloured and Black Upper-Middle Class Reform Activists in Trinidad, 1880–1925". PhD thesis, University of the West Indies, St Augustine.

Thomas, J.J. 1869. *The Theory and Practice of Creole Grammar*. Port of Spain: Chronicle Publishing Office. Repr., London: New Beacon Books, 1969.

———. 1889. *Froudacity*. London: T. Fisher Unwin. Repr., London: New Beacon Books, 1969.

Walcott, Derek. 1990. *Omeros*. New York: Farrar, Straus and Giroux.

Wilkins, Mrs William Noy. 1854. *The Slave Son*. Repr. in *Adolphus, A Tale and The Slave Son*, ed. Lise Winer. Kingston: University of the West Indies Press, 2003.

Will, H.A. 1970. *Constitutional Change in the British West Indies 1880–1903*. Oxford: Clarendon Press.

www.ingramcontent.com/pod-product-compliance
Lightning Source LLC
Chambersburg PA
CBHW051920110726
47902CB00002B/356